Memoirs

of the

Red Seven/Columbia Showband Arklow

Joe Weadick

Published in 2011 by

Joe Weadick
44 Fernhill
Arklow
Co. Wicklow
Ireland

e-mail: joeweadick@eircom.net

Isbn: 978-0-9568782-0-5

Printed by Naas Printing Ltd.
19 South Main Street, Naas, Co. Kildare
Tel: (045) 872092
email: naasprinting@gmail.com

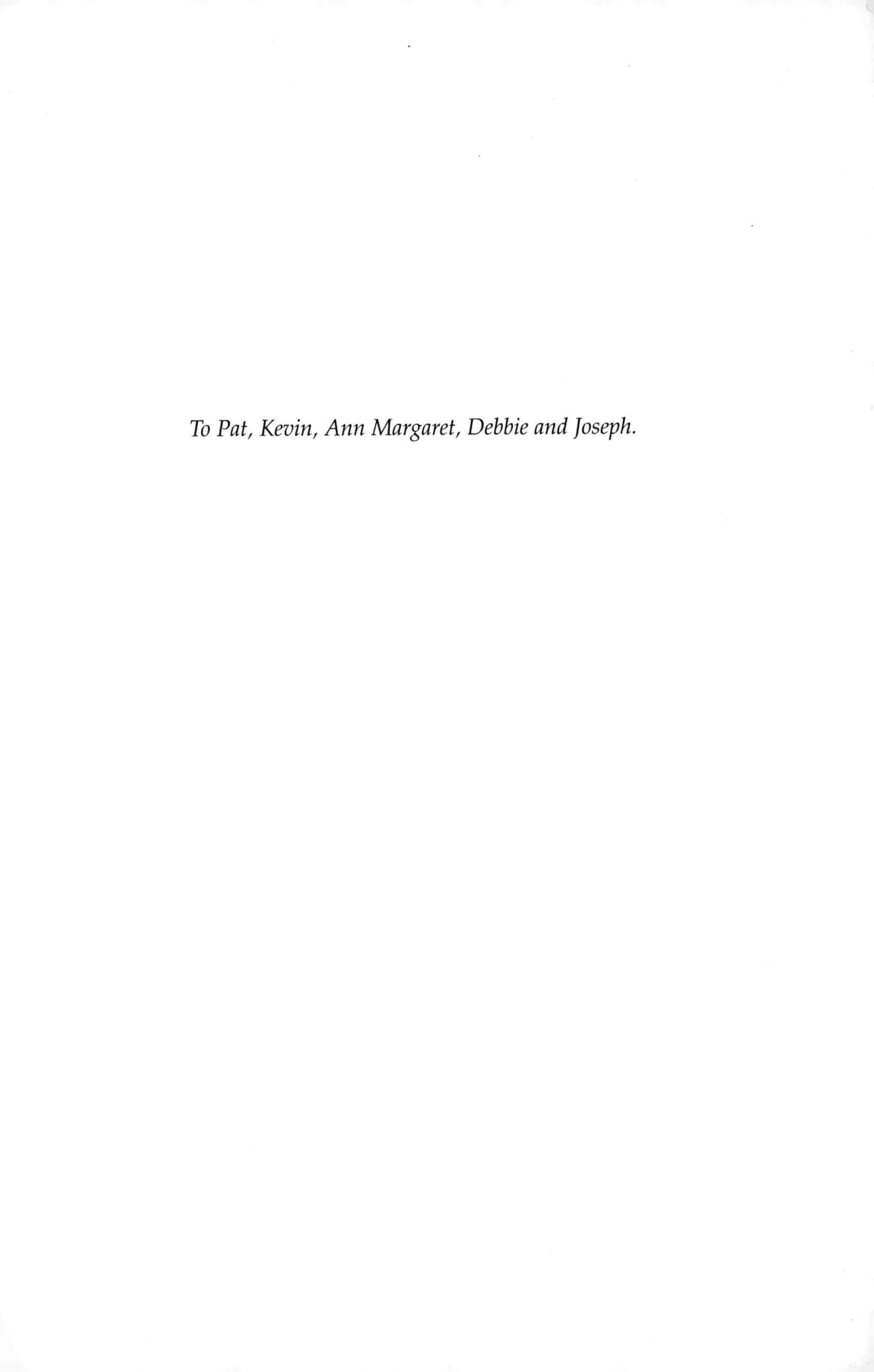

To Pat, Kevin, Ann Margaret, Debbie and Joseph.

CONTENTS

ACKNOWLEDGEMENTS

Without the contributions and help of so many people for which I am truly grateful, this book could not have been written.

For their stories, photos and other material, many thanks to Pete Coburn, Des Mulhall, Larry Kenny, Paud O'Brien, Pat Tyrrell, Freddy Cutland, George Byrne, Leo McHugh, Paddy Merrigan, Jimmy McManus, Eddie McElheron, James Kenny, Michael Tyrrell, Liam O'Reilly, Pat McCarthy, Oliver Merrigan, Timmy Weadick, Michael Gilmore, Dan Bolger, Vincent McElheron, Ritchie Hall and Billy Lee.

To Freddy Cutland for sowing the seed in my mind ten years ago to write the book and for his continued technical help and encouragement since.

To Peg Bonner, Liam Garrett, John Kenny, Robert Kavanagh, Tommy Dunne, Mary Quirke, Linda Tyrrell and Maureen Willoughby for loaning photos.

To my daughter Debbie and her friend Siobhan Manley for the art work and layout of the book cover.

I am indebted to historian Jim Rees for his generous time, expert advice, editing and layout of the book.

Finally a very special thanks to my wife Pat for her patience and help throughout the years as I struggled to keep the project on course.

INTRODUCTION

Music is one of the most profound and beautiful gifts in life. Throughout the centuries mankind of all cultures and creeds have used lyrics and melodies to express their innermost thoughts and emotions, both joyous and sad.

Not everyone is fortunate enough to have the opportunity of learning, or possess the capability of playing music, or is blessed with a singing voice. But most, if not all, get immense pleasure and solace from listening to music of some genre, particularly that with harmoniously pleasing sounds.

There is a school of thought that people who go through life without the opportunity or ability to make music of some kind or other, secretly regret missing out on something divinely pleasurable and self satisfying. I subscribe to that philosophy.

Musicians and singers who perform their talents in any format or forum for the enjoyment and pleasure of others make an invaluable contribution to their listeners' happiness and well-being. The poet Shelley once said *"Music, when soft voices die, vibrates in the memory"*.

History teaches us that each generation is marked by some change in musical culture. In the late nineteenth century popular dance music consisted of waltzes, polkas, quadrilles and ballads. Followed in the early twentieth century by the charlton, jitterbug, jive, jazz, swing and bop.

In America in the early fifties a new music and dance craze called rock-'n'roll started and spread like wildfire throughout the western world. The man most credited with its inception was none other than Bill Haley and his band The Comets. Following his success with 'Rock Around The Clock' and 'Shake Rattle and Roll' he became known as the 'Father of Rock'.

Haley's music quickly caught on in Ireland and it was not long before orchestras and dance bands were playing rock'n'roll in ballrooms throughout the country. It made the more progressive bands change their style. Instead of sitting and playing their orchestrations in a strict tempo fashion they started standing and moving to the beat, effectively putting on a show while playing and singing. The new beat movement of rock and other popular music emerging at the time electrified the dancers and they responded with massive energy and so the showband and rock'n'roll era was born.

The Clipper Carlton from Derry quickly embraced this new phenomenon and were widely credited with being the first Irish 'Showband'. They were immediately followed in the late fifties by the Royal Showband from Waterford. The initial trickle in the early sixties turned into a flood of new showbands over the next ten years.

Their love of making music and entertaining in dance bands, as expressed above, encouraged seven young Arklow men to throw away the chairs too and start the Red Seven Showband. This was in January 1960 and three years later the name was changed, for marketing reasons, to the Columbia Showband.

These memoirs give an appreciation of the 'Sixties Showband Life and the Dancing Culture of that Era' through the stories of the original seven members of the Red Seven/Columbia Showband as well as the individual stories of thirteen other musicians who played with the band at various times during its ten years existence. It also includes the experiences of five other people associated in some way with the band over that time.

Many interesting, hilarious and gripping stories are told throughout the book and the many photos included will put context and realism to those stories.

This is essentially a book of memories and memories, as you know, can be selective.

Sit down, relax and imagine yourself back in the misty past of the Swinging Sixties through these pages.

Enjoy the journey.

Red Seven Showband
January 1960

Paud O'Brien, Joe Weadick, Des Mulhall, Pat Tyrrell, Larry Kenny.
Sitting: Pete Coburn and the late Eamon Lee

Chapter 1

Joe Weadick

My parents had little or no opportunity to read and play music. As a result, it was their desire to have those of us children who were interested learn some instrument even though they could hardly afford the cost of lessons. They bought an old violin for my eldest brother Peter and arranged tuition with the late Miss Furlong of Coolgreaney Road – she lived beside the Tennis Club. Peter wasn't long with her when he changed to another violin teacher, a Dublin man called Paddy Kearns – he was the owner and leader of the orchestra that was resident for the summer season in the Marquee - as it was then called - later known as the Ormonde Ballroom. In those years, 1941 and 1942, they played for three months seven nights a week from 8.30p.m. to 11.30p.m. Dancing was the main social activity and Arklow was one of the prime holiday resorts for Dublin people. Peter recalls that Paddy Kearns used to ride a bicycle to our house at 53 Lr. Main Street from his lodgings to give the lessons.

My sisters Bridget and Mary had piano lessons for a while. Their teacher was Miss Tyrrell, aunt of the three brothers Jim, Pat and Michael who I was to become very involved with in the Red Seven/Columbia Showband many years later. Unfortunately my sisters and brother Peter gave up music lessons when they started working. Incidently they used to practise on our next door neighbour's piano – the late Mrs McMullen – mother of Mrs Sheila Bentley (McMullens clothes shop). It was very generous of her as we did not have a piano until much later. My brother Tim was a member of the Marian Arts Society where he took part in variety shows and my brother James (r.i.p.) was a very good singer but shy, until he loosened up with a few drinks, at which time he always gave a beautiful rendition of 'Stranger in Paradise'.

I, too, was interested in music from a very early age. I listened a lot to the radio, and loved two songs in particular - 'Buttons and Bows' and 'Mockingbird Hill'. Isn't it funny how specific tunes stick out in your mind. Even now when I hear those songs, they bring back wonderful memories of my free and happy youth playing cheerfully all day long on Saturdays or during holidays with my pals in the natural open spaces like South Green (before any houses were built there) with the open stream flowing from the Togher to the Avoca river where we often fished for and caught eels; like The Warrens at the golf links, where birds seemed to never stop singing; like the sound of the wild life in the rushes around the lake at north beach; and the sight of the stingos we used to try to catch in the little stream along by the old Kynochs factory road.

My interest in music started seriously after our family moved house to Hungry Hill - I mean St. Peter's Place, in 1952. A friend of my late mother, Tom Kelly (r.i.p.), who lived across the road from us, decided to emigrate with his family to America in 1953 and he was selling his old piano. I encouraged my mother to buy it, which she did for £5.0.0.

Two school pals, Larry Tallon and Frank Byrne, were learning the piano from the late musical genius Seán Bonner. He was a young teacher at the time, not long in Arklow and called once a week to Frank's home at 68 St. Peter's Place to give them both their weekly lessons. My mother arranged for him to give me lessons too in our house. His fee was a half crown then (just over twelve cents in today's money). I recall that when he was preparing me for my first examination, with the Trinity College of Music, London, he decided that I was not quite up to the required standard when the date was notified and told my mother he would enter me for the following sitting. Needless to say, I was extremely disappointed and cried my eyes out. When I finally sat the examination in November 1953, at the age of eleven, I passed with honours.

After the exam, Seán told my mother that our piano was not really good enough, it was very old and would not tune well, which made her go and buy a new one from Pigott's Music Store in Dublin on hire purchase. She could hardly afford it at the time but went without other things for my advancement. You know, I never really appreciated the sacrifice my mother made then as I'm sure even today children don't - too many things are taken for granted.

At such an early stage in his career Seán Bonner was very forward thinking. He taught me to play his own arrangement of Glenn Miller's 'In The Mood' on the piano, a great number then which subsequently became a classic. Seán's name crops up in almost everyone's story in this book and has rightly received many accolades from them. He was sadly missed by everyone in the musical life of Arklow when he died in 1987 at the age of 58 with motor nuerone disease. I will always remember him saying to me one night in the Royal Hotel, while having a drink, that one of his fingers was giving him trouble and it was affecting his piano playing. I realised some time later that it was the start of his MND.

When we were practising to form our own showband in the autumn of 1959 Seán Bonner was an immense help. He arranged tunes/songs and encouraged us every possible way. Many a night we practised in his sitting room. I often wondered how Peg's patience managed to hold out. Among other things, he arranged for us the version of the national anthem which we used throughout our showband years.

Before I move on, I must refer again to Tom Kelly from whom my mother bought our first piano. Tom, a brother of the late Vincent, Shay & Bob and uncle of Josephine Birthistle among others, became very involved in the Ancient Order of Hibernians in Bethel, Connecticut where he, Esther and family settled in America. For a number of years in the eighties, he was instrumental in bringing the Avoca Céile Band, which at the time included Eddie McElheron and Matt Sharpe, to perform in the Irish Clubs there. He, along with his wife Ethel, arranged for their transport and accommodation and made sure they were well looked after in every respect.

Army School of Music

One day in May of 1956, towards the end of my first year attending the Commercial Course in Arklow Technical School, the late Paddy Murray, Principal, (father of Stafford Murray who played trombone in the Blue Notes), knew I was interested in music and told me that there was an advertisement in the national press looking for recruits for the Army School of Music. He encouraged me to apply which I did and was successful in getting a place. The minimum age was 14 years and I had just turned fourteen on April 16th.

I started in June in Cathal Brugha Barracks, Rathmines, Dublin, where the Army School of Music was and still is located, as is the Army No.1 Band. The Army No.2 Band was in the Cork Barracks, the No.3 Band in the Curragh and the No.4 Band in Athlone.

I had to sign up for twelve years - a very big decision at the age of fourteen! However, release could be achieved within the first two years on compassionate grounds, but after that one had to buy oneself out. The training period was three to four years, depending on musical ability. The training also included the continuation of secondary school education. All with a starting salary at the time of one £1.6.0. including full board. Not too bad for a young teenager! After the training period, and subject to reaching the required standard of playing, one would be placed in one of the Army Bands.

I was given my choice of instrument. I chose the slide trombone which I knuckled down to learning. We had a minimum of three hours music tuition every day including theory. A really good foundation for any young fellow interested in music. The rest of the day was taken up with the usual school subjects, P.E. and army marching/drills.

I progressed very well on the instrument and also started taking lessons again on the piano from Lieutenant Fred O'Callaghan, our conductor at the time, who was to become conductor of the No.1 Army Band and eventually Director of the Army School of Music from 1981 to 1987. Fred is a brother of the late Jim O'Callaghan who was an engineer and tragically killed in an accident in NET in 1978. Jim was an excellent exponent of the clarinet and saxophone and played with a number of local bands in the seventies including the Coolgreaney Jazz Band.

I thoroughly enjoyed the tuition and the knowledge gained in the Army School of Music. However, as the months rolled by, I gradually became disenchanted with the army culture. Also, most of the band boys were older than I and perhaps more streetwise - quite a few were from the cities of Dublin, Cork, Galway and Limerick. On a few occasions I was being bullied and had to physically defend myself. Being a small town boy with little experience of the big outside world made me a bit nervous and I longed to be back in Arklow. After nine months I finally requested to leave and fortunately was allowed out. Had I stuck it out perhaps I would have ended up in the Army No.1 Band and played with orchestras/showbands in Dublin at night which a lot of the army bandsmen did in those days, and I'm sure still do. It was not unusual for lads to desert the army bands and head for Great Britian rather than pay the substantial fee to buy themselves out.

I remember well, when touring Britian with the Columbia Showband seven years after I left the Army School of Music, the resident band in the 32 Club in Harlesden in London, where we played one night was almost entirely made up of deserters from the Irish Army Bands. One of them was a class mate of mine - also a trombone player. I remember that night for another reason too. I won the jackpot on one of the slot machines in the club - money all over the floor - sixpenny pieces! about £5 in all - quite a good little haul in those days.

My first experience in a Dance Band

When I got settled back home after the ASM I continued practising the piano and in 1958 got involved with two neighbours the late Noel Maguire and the late Jimmy Hogan both of whom were excellent piano accordian players. They had a large repertoire of *"Ballroom of Romance"* music - quicksteps, foxtrots, slow foxtrots, oldtime waltzes, slow waltzes, tangoes, rhumbas and sambas.

We practised in my house once a week and sometimes Des Mulhall would join us on the drums. The late Joe Keogh, who was a friend of Noel's, decided to buy a saxophone and he, too, joined us. We were hoping to start a band, but it did not materialise. Noel Maguire did eventually get his wish when he started the Harbour Lights Showband in 1961 with great local success. Noel and Jimmy were tremendous characters to play with – a crack a minute – cigarette smoke everywhere. Incidently, Jimmy's son John was part of the very successful local group Boru and is still singing and playing today.

My first dance band engagement was with the late Kevin Harper's band. He was missing a piano player for a dance in Newtownmountkennedy on Sunday, May 11th, 1958 and asked me to fill in. I jumped at the chance and got on very well with them. All the practice I had with Noel, Jimmy and Des was put to good use. I had just turned 16 at the time. They were of real *"Ballroom of Romance"* vintage and Kevin was very popular with the dancers. The late Jimmy Smullen, a lovely man, played the double bass. The price of the dance was three shillings and I got paid £1. Not bad considering my wages in Brennans at the time was £2 per week.

I bought a secondhand multimonica (double keyboard) and did some

As a trainee in the Army School of Music

solo gigs during the summer of 1958, playing background music in the Royal Hotel lounge. I also played the piano on occasion in the Jolly Roger, which was the upstairs lounge in the Golf Bar. The Golf Bar was owned by Brennans, whose bakery and confectionery shop/restaurant was next door, and which burned down in April 1960. I was cashier at the time in the office and discovered the fire at 6.30 in the evening. The Golf Bar was subsequently sold and renamed the Westwood, now the Gin Mill. After the fire, Brennans built a new bakery on Wexford Road, where Pettits is now.

After the summer season of 1958, I sold my multimonica (always sorry I did, because it was a unique instrument) to finance buying a trombone, encouraged by Des Mulhall who was very anxious to start a showband. He was fascinated by the new phenomenon, spearheaded by the Clipper Carlton in the mid- fifties, followed in 1957 by the Royal Showband. I began practising the trombone again seriously and soon got my lip firmed up and was rearing to go if and when the opportunity arose. I didn't have too long to wait.

Another friend and workmate of Des was Larry Kenny and he, along with Pete Coburn, were two important members of the well known Avoca Dance Band of Mark Canavan. They invited me to join and shortly after Des was asked to play the drums in it, when their drummer left. The other members at the time were Paud O'Brien, Eamon Lee and Pat Tyrrell – all Arklow men - and one Wicklow man, the late Gerry Heaslip - a brilliant piano accordian player and true gentleman. Mark had not been playing for some months due to illness and, unfortunately because of that, I never had the pleasure of playing with him personally.

Incidentally, as history would have it, I did play with one of his five talented sons, Dave, from 1997 to 2002 in the All Stars Showband which John Joe Brauders and I formed specifically to perform at a fund raising dance for the Inbhear Mór Marching Band and it continued for no less than six years. That, for me, was a very nostalgic time, as it was for most of the other members of the All Stars, for most were, like myself, veterans of the sixties. They included the above mentioned Pete Coburn, Larry Kenny, Pat Tyrrell and Liam O'Reilly (all ex-Red Seven Showband) and John Joe Brauders of the Spotlights Showband of the sixties. Other younger musicians involved were, Pat Byrne, Yvonne Kenny, Geraldine and Eamon Delaney, Tony Linton, Gerry McDonald, Bobby Byrne and Reveonna Byrne.

Towards the end of October 1959, the enhanced line up of Mark Canavan's band - now all from Arklow except Gerry Heaslip - was beginning to show a real spark of energy in terms of material being played and the response we were receiving, especially from the younger dancers.

Taking a lead from the Clipper Carlton and the Royal Showband, who were leading the way, we too decided to throw away the chairs and started standing while performing and moving about energetically in unison - in 'a swinging way', as they might say today. This extra buzz we were experiencing was uplifting and made us determined to start our own showband.

The Red Seven Showband

We Arklow lads had a serious chat among ourselves and decided we were destined to follow this new phenomenon ... the 'Showband Craze'. So in January 1960 we, very reluctantly, informed Mark that we were leaving to start a showband. Mark was none too pleased but he had to accept that times and the music business were rapidly changing and wished us well in our new venture.

Gerry Heaslip remained with Mark, who resumed playing in his own inimitable style and continued to be extremely popular for sometime. But eventually he too succumbed to the inevitable and started a showband, The Avonaires – they say if you can't beat 'em join 'em. Ironically Paud O'Brien, Eamon Lee, Larry Kenny and Jimmy McManus ended up in that band when they left our new showband, The Red Seven.

Yes, The Red Seven Showband - the name we chose after much deliberation. At the time we were seven in number and we agreed on the colour Red because, in our minds, the word evoked a sense of fire, in terms of radicalism, energy and a determination to succeed. We decided it would be run on a co-operative basis (equal shares after expenses) and that Pete, who had experience in dealing with ballroom proprietors, clubs, bookings, etc., would be the manager ... at no extra cost of course!

We now badly needed somewhere to practice. I happened to be great friends with the late John Byrne, a popular bread salesman in Brennans Bakery, and I persuaded him to allow us practice in a section of the old defunct Johnson's Garage, beside the Memorial Hospital, now the Arklow Bay Hotel. John and his good wife, Maureen (nee Johnson) lived in the house beside the garage. There was no rent involved due to his generosity and his desire to help us.

Within a few months of our starting practice there, the late John Sweeney

Presenting :

Phone: 70

THE RED 7 SHOWBAND

R ELIABLE
E NTERTAINING
D EPENDABLE
7

ARKLOW

ENQUIRIES :
MANAGER,
18, ST. BRIGID'S TCE.,
ARKLOW

We Play to Return!

May I take this opportunity of introducing to you the above Showband——————Comprising :-

R	TRUMPET	:	(DOUBLING VOCALS)	S H
	TENOR SAX	:	" "	
E	ALTO SAX	:	" "	O
	TROMBONE	:	(DOUBLING PIANO)	W
D	SINGING GUITARIST	:		B
	DRUMS	:		
	COMPERE VOCALIST	:	(DOUBLING BASS)	A N
7	★ ★ *Featuring The Harmony Four* ★ ★			D

It is a young and versatile combination playing a varied, entertaining and up-to-the-minute programme,—specializing in—"Modern with a Beat"—and whose primary aim is to satisfy the paying customer.

This Combination has appeared with particular success in most of the Leading Ballrooms in Leinster and has proved its popularity by securing return bookings in all cases.

To our various successes we added the—"1960 Summer Season Residency"—in the Tara Ballroom, Courtown, which incidently is the Leading Ballroom on the East Coast.

If you can see your way to booking the Band then we can guarantee a First-class Performance.

TERMS ARE MODERATE AND ENQUIRIES WILL RECEIVE PROMPT ATTENTION.

BOOK NOW! AND

bought the premises and we thought we would be thrown out but John, being the generous man that he was, allowed us to continue. The only difference being that we had to share the building with the empty coffins John stored there, as he was Arklow's main funeral undertaker. Being squeezed between empty coffins on one side and the hospital morgue close by on the other, felt very scary and creepy at times, particularly on cold and dark winter nights when the rain was beating off the windows and the wind was howling. More about this aspect of our practice venue later on.

Pete took his responsibility very seriously and immediately got down to the business of promoting the new showband. The first thing he did was put the following notice in the February 6th, 1960 edition of the *Wicklow People* in the entertainment section announcing our entry into the showband business.

ATTENTION!

ALL DANCE PROMOTERS, BALLROOM MANAGERS, SOCIETIES, CLUBS, AND THE DANCING PUBLIC,

THE PERSONNEL OF THE MARK CANAVAN BAND, UP TO THE PRESENT TIME, HAVE FORMED THEIR OWN BAND, WHICH WILL BE KNOWN IN THE FUTURE AS

"THE RED SEVEN."

THIS BAND IS NOW AVAILABLE FOR BOOKING. ALL ENQUIRIES TO THE MANAGER, No. 18, ST. BRIGID'S TERRACE, ARKLOW.

Shortly after, Pete formulated the excellent promotional leaflet detailing the line-up of the band and distributed it to all ballroom managers, club secretaries and dance promoters throughout counties Wicklow and Wexford.

We were successful in winning the summer residency in the Tara Ballroom, Courtown in 1960, due to the hard work of Pete and Des negotiating with the proprietor, the late Peter Redmond. It was a great coup, because it gave us a great platform to get our name known in Dublin and throughout Leinster. You see, in those days, Courtown Harbour was one of the premier holiday resorts along the east coast. Every summer the hotels and caravan parks in this popular tourist location were packed with holiday makers, particularly from Dublin. Holidays abroad were almost unheard of for the average person - so expensive only the really well-heeled could afford them.

Peter Redmond was a very genteel and generous man. I do believe he took a particular liking to us as individuals and always made sure we were well looked after. Proof of this for me was when he gave us, on top of our weeky fee, a lucrative Benefit Night on the last Saturday of the two month season in 1960 and we had a brilliant crowd ... testament to the esteem we were held in by our fans. This lovely gesture is not to say that Peter was not a shrewd businessman, he generally drove a hard bargain ... as some examples in this book will attest to.

During our residency days in the Tara Ballroom we got very valuable mention, with photographs, in the entertainment sections in the *Evening Herald* and the *Evening Press*. Here is an example of one such photo and write-up in the 'Strict Tempo' column of the *Evening Herald* in May or June of 1960.

The write-up accompanying the above photo read: "We were dancing out of town and met the most promising newcomers that have yet crossed our

Four of the Red Seven—the new Arklow dance band. Des Mulhal Joe Weadick Pete [illegible] (bossman) and Larry Kenny

path. It was at the Tara Ballroom in Courtown where seven, tall dark, very dark, young men with good musical sense took the bandstand. They know a lot about strict tempo and good music both danceable and listen-able. Maybe that is the reason why they call themselves 'The Red Seven Showband'. But they are fresh – fresh as the quayside fish of their native Arklow. I am going to mention them to Christy at the Ierne and George out at Clondalkin because I believe that they have something. And by the look of the bushy beard of Des the Drummer it is something worth bringing out. They started only four months ago and already they have a season engagement at the Tara. They have a good bass and know how to handle the brass".

These positive comments helped us get bookings throughout Leinster, and we were received very well everywhere we went. We continued practising hard and continued to improve our performance. Like the other early arrivers on the showband scene, our policy was to keep updating our repertoire in line with the top twenty tunes of the day, as well as classics by the top performers, usually American and British.

They included songs by Elvis Presley (e.g. 'Jail House Rock', 'Hound Dog', 'It's Now or Never', 'Return To Sender', 'Old Shep'), Cliff Richard ('Living Doll', 'Devil Woman', 'Travelling Light', 'Here Comes Summer', 'Congratulations'), Roy Orbison ('Only the Lonely', 'In Dreams', 'Dream Baby', 'Lonesome Me', 'Pretty Woman'). Jim Reeves' song 'He'll Have To Go' was also very popular. Of course, I can't leave out Bill Haley and the Comets 'Rock Around The Clock', the man who was credited more than any other artist in popularising rock'n'roll throughout the world in the fifties.

The above selection of very powerful songs, mostly sung by our lead vocalist Pete who had a distinctly melodious voice, a wide vocal range with falsetto being his specialty, comparable if not better than most frontmen in any of the top showbands then or after. On top of all that he was an excellent compere, which I always regarded as very important to connect with the patrons. Eamon sang some of the rock numbers and Pat's bass voice was just right for Jim Reeves' numbers.

Dixieland music was also very popular in the early sixties. Artists like Kenny Ball ('Midnight in Moscow', 'Alexander's Rag Time Band', 'Hello Dolly', 'So Do I') and Acker Bilk ('Stranger On The Shore', 'Memphsis Blues', 'My Blue Heaven') were also featuring in the hit parade. We were pretty apt at playing all those numbers and this section featured prominantly during '61/'62 when Leo McHugh was with us.

Leo McHugh, a great dixieland player, joined in the spring of 1961 when Paud O'Brien decided to leave. Paud married in September 1960 and did not wish to hold the band back. Freddy Cutland was recruited in June 1961 as lead guitar player and improved the sound of the band immensely. His addition brought the band number up to eight. It gave us tremendous latitude in playing all the popular guitar solos arriving in the top twenty, as well as guitar solos in some of the popular songs. Freddy became invaluable to the band right to the end.

Our growing success in 1961 made us focus seriously on going professional, which I will have to admit was very tempting. But the debate went on far too long for Des Mulhall, who was a man in a hurry, and he left to join Jack Ruane's Orchestra, in Ballina in July 1961. We were very sad to see him leave as he was primarily responsible (along with Pete) for starting the band, an excellent drummer and a fine colleague - we wished him well in his new venture.

Des did ensure that we were not let down as he recommended his prodigy, George Byrne, who took over as drummer – the youngest and smallest drummer in Ireland at the time in the showband business. A record that has never been broken thoughout the years to my knowledge. George proved very quickly to be an excellent replacement for Des and, indeed in a certain way, raised the popularity of the band higher because of his uniqueness. Few people know that George was a very ill boy just prior to joining the band. He had a heart condition which had to be rectified and he spent a long time in hospital. I remember we, the band that is, once visiting him in the Mater Hospital when passing through Dublin to play at some venue. He relates this stressful period of his life in his own story and it is further expounded by Des.

Our next big shock was when Pete decided to leave in September of 1961 - only two months after Des. He did not wish to go professional for a number of personal reasons and did not want to hold the band back in pursuing its goal. The continuing talk of going full time finally made up his mind. I know that the rest of the lads were taken aback but I will have to admit I was devastated. I could not envisage us getting anyone to replace him that would come near to his singing ability. Deep down I felt that going professional without Pete would not be the success that it could be.

Not only did we have the problem of looking for a new singer but managing the band was another issue. We had a very serious chat one night in the practice room about whether we should call it a day or continue. Nobody wanted to take the responsibility of doing the bookings/books, etc. To avoid meltdown, I offered to take on the responsibility - all agreed and we ploughed ahead.

With new vigour we picked ourselves up and started looking around for some suitable local singer to replace Pete. Leo McHugh recommended talking to Paddy Merrigan of Kilahurler, who he worked with in the Avoca Mines and was aware that he had a good voice. We asked Paddy if he would be interested in joining and he was keen. We auditioned him and he agreed to give it a go, singing and playing rhythm guitar. But he only stayed a few months, as he had started studying that October in University College Dublin. He enjoyed his time with the band, particularly performing in the Entertainment Centre and Courtown. Paddy was a very good singer. One of his popular renditions was the song 'Poetry In Motion'.

So on we went again looking for a lead singer. Larry Kenny suggested that Jimmy McManus, though a bit young (17) had a pretty good voice. I suggested Joe Donnelly, who I heard singing regularly during his work shifts in Brennans Confectionery Department. I thought he had a brilliant voice then and still has today, but unfortunately he had no experience in playing in bands. Others mentioned and auditioned at the time were Eamon McDonald and Larry Mythen (r.i.p.). Jimmy McManus won out on that occasion as he had some experience playing in the Harbour Lights Showband which was obvious during the audition. He started with the band towards the end of 1961 on a three months trial.

Meanwhile Jim Tyrrell, Pat's brother, who was working in Dublin at the time, was very interested in the band's progress and getting involved with it. When Leo McHugh announced that he may be leaving to go work in Dublin, Jim was brought in to replace him on trumpet. This helped to fill the void left by Pete as Jim also played guitar and was a strong singer. At the time Chubby Checker numbers were among his favourites.

Jim was also extremely proficient on piano and in doing arrangements, which was very valuable to the band. In fact his addition put the band on a very sound footing for the future and before long we asked him to take on the band leadership. He also agreed to take over the management of bookings for the band because of his connections in Dublin and a notice was put in the *Wicklow People* to that effect in January 1962.

In March 1962, Eddie McElheron was approached and agreed to take the lead singer slot in the band to strengthen the ballad and country & western section. Jimmy McManus had completed his trial period and, while he did well, it was decided that Eddie was that bit older, more mature and better suited the band's needs. I got the unenviable task of breaking the bad news to Jimmy, who was very disappointed but was glad to have had the experience. In fact, he went on to other bands where he had great success and eventually headed up the Kynochs group for a long number of years. This is documented well in his own story in this book.

Meanwhile, Eddie's first gig with the band was on Whit Sunday night of 1962, and he immediately took to the job with great enthusiasm, moulding himself into the ballads and country & western slot. The favourable response from the crowds gave us band members renewed hope for a successful future.

But all was still not well in the camp. Within a couple of months, Eamon decided to leave because he, too, was not interested in going professional. Larry Kenny's brother Jimmy was brought in for a while to replace Eamon, but he also left shortly after and was replaced by Michael Tyrrell (Pat & Jim's younger brother) who had expressed an interest in the same job. Michael proved over time to be an excellent bass player and a good rock singer, as well as contributing to harmony numbers. After leaving the band, Jimmy Kenny joined Arklow's Echos Showband, where he had a very successful and happy time.

Jim did well during the summer of 1962 in securing for us our third residency in the Tara Ballroom, Courtown for one month and it was again very successful. We continued to get an increasing number of bookings throughout Leinster and further afield. But just when the band was settling down, Larry decided to leave because he was not interested in pursuing professionalism. This brought the band number back to seven. Larry's leaving was another bitter blow, because he was one of the stalwarts in the band, who could be relied on to keep the show going during any crisis on stage. If that wasn't enough, there was a new worry in that Eddie might have to leave to take up a new day job away from Arklow, as he had finished in Avoca Mines. We had to prepare for this possibility and looked around for another vocalist.

On that occasion we auditioned Tom Craine, who had a pleasant voice, and Liam O'Reilly, who was a good all round singer and played rhythm guitar with the Echos Showband. Liam won out and it brought the membership of the band to eight. Eventually Eddie decided to stay with the band, but we kept Liam on as his contribution was proving effective. It gave us an even wider repertoire, consolidating our position in the showband business. Liam relates his own experience with the band in this book.

My wife Pat – the X Factor

Writing about this period in the band brings to mind how concerned I personally was with all the changes, particularly in what I regarded as the most important section - that of the lead vocalist. If we were to be successful as professionals we needed someone special, particularly if we were to lose Eddie. When we were considering who we should ask, I, unknown to the others, asked my girlfriend and future wife, Pat Shiel, if she would consider auditioning as I believed she had, in today's parlance, the X factor. Pat, of course, laughed at me and thought I was joking, but I was very serious. By the way, we met in 1961 at a dance during our summer season in Courtown.

Pat had, and still has, a wonderful voice with an exceptionally wide vocal range and I was convinced that, had she been interested, she would have proved extremely popular. I had no doubt that the band would have greatly benefitted. At that time, Eileen Reid and the Cadets had just come on the scene and Eileen, with the exception of Maisie McDaniels, was the only female vocalist in a showband and she was very successful. But it was not to be, as Pat, who often sang at family occasions and weddings, was too shy to take to the stage and told me to forget it. Two of her favourite party pieces were 'Summertime' and 'Ava Maria'.

We got married on December 29th, 1962 during one of the worst winters we experienced for many years. It was even a problem getting to Gorey for

Pat and me in the Gresham Hotel Dublin for the Royal Showband celebration dance in 1961 when they won the British 'Carl Alan Award'. Joe Loss and his Orchestra played at it.

the wedding, due to the snow and ice on the roads that morning. Would you believe we were the first couple to be married at 10 a.m? Before that, marriages in Gorey Catholic Church were at 8 a.m! That's why, I believe, the term 'Wedding Breakfast' was used - because of pre-communion fast. Times have indeed changed since then. Three nights before, St. Stephens Night, we played in the Mayfair Ballroom in Kilkenny and we thought we would never get home because it snowed continuously. And the bad weather continued well into January. We had only two days honeymoon in Dublin and I drove through a blizzard of snow to get there. Were we happy to get to the warmth of the bed that night! I had to be back to play with the band for Brennans Staff Dance in the Royal Hotel on New Year's Eve. See photo below - playing at the staff dance. L to R – Pat, me, Jim, George, Eddie, Michael, Liam and Freddy.

We were now into January 1963 and I, because of my new marital obligations, announced at a crucial meeting regarding the future of the band that I was relinquishing control of the finances, which I had managed since Pete left. Jim, who was already band leader and booking manager and who was anxious to upgrade the band equipment, gladly took full responsibility for the entire operation.

Preparing for full time

The band was forging ahead and we were dead set on going fulltime as soon as possible. All were very happy with our musical competence on the brass, with the guitar section headed by Freddy, Eddie as lead vocalist, complemented by the variety of singing talents of Jim, Pat, Michael and Liam, Georgie's drumming skills and Jim's music arrangements meant we were ready for anything. We certainly were not afraid of any competition from the showband fraternity.

We had also overcome the one major problem that was keeping us from getting bookings in Dublin city. We all did our musical ability examination with the Irish Federation of Musicians (if I remember correctly the late Jack Flahive, Orchestra supremo, was the examiner), passed with flying colours and were accepted as members. I suppose you could say it was like a union. An orchestra, dance band or showband was not allowed play in Dublin in those days unless it was a member of the Federation. That does not apply nowadays. The Fed fee was two shillings and sixpence per week. I still have and treasure my contribution card.

The Hucklebuck

The 'Twist' dance was all the rage around that time. Chubby Checker's 'Lets Twist Again' and 'Twist and Shout' had been in the hit parade and were extremely popular. We made a point of doing the twist on stage where possible when Jim sang them and really got the crowd going. Another number that Jim got off Eddie's Chubby Checker LP was 'The Hucklebuck' which was not in the hit parade but we liked it and Jim did an excellent band arrangement and performed it. The dancers went mad about it and it became one of our top showpieces – nearly always finishing up with it due to popular demand. To my knowledge we were the only Irish showband to perform it until the Royal Showband took it up. And it became so popular with them that Brendan Bowyer recorded it in 1965 and it immediately went to the top of the Hit Parade in Ireland and became a classic, renowned to this day and synonymous with the showband era.

I remember well one night in the Entertainment Centre, when we were playing warm-up to the Royal, we concluded our performance with 'The

Hucklebuck' and they took great interest in it. They enquired about it with some of our lads after the dance. That particular event is well documented elsewhere in the book.

Brendan Bowyer did a marvellous job on it. Of course he was, and is in my view, the best vocalist from the showband era and a nicer guy you could not meet. Our only regret was that we did not record 'The Hucklebuck' when we popularised it, but in 1963 Irish showbands making records was only in its infancy – 'Come Down the Mountain Katy Daly', sung by the late Tom Dunphy of the Royal was the first Irish showband record made and that was in 1962. We did not make our first record until early 1965 (Eddie with 'Before This Day Ends/In Your Arms').

Brendan Bowyer and me in Arklow Bay Hotel August 2010

According to information I gathered from the internet 'The Hucklebuck' was first recorded in 1949 in America as a Charlie Parker jazz tune called 'De-Natural Blues' by Lucky Millinder and his Orchestra. Later that year words were added to it by Andy Gibson and it was recorded as a rock 'n' roll number titled 'The Hucklebuck' by Paul Williams and the Hucklebuckers and it became an instant hit. Over the years since then, many top singers and musicians have recorded it, including Frank Sinatra (1949), Louis Armstrong (1954), Chubby Checker (1960), Bill Haley (1961) and Brendan Bowyer (1965).

The Columbia

Our crucial meeting of January 1963 also discussed another matter that we regarded as vital to further heighten our profile. It was the need to change the band name to something more catchy and up-market in this ever-growing showband arena, which at its peak numbered about 800 - quite a major national business. After much deliberation over what the new name should be, we hit on Columbia because it was easy to say, sounded well with an American flavour, (e.g. Columbia Pictures, Columbia Records) universally known and easy to remember. I do believe the decision to adopt it proved very beneficial.

The following notice was put in the local and national papers in January 1963 to announce the change of name.

THE

Columbia

SHOWBAND, ARKLOW.

The members of the RED SEVEN SHOWBAND, ARKLOW, wish to thank all Dance Hall Proprietors, Committees, Promoters, etc., for past favours.

The Band, having now registered with the Irish Federation of Musicians, will, in future, be known as THE COLUMBIA SHOWBAND. The personnel remains the same, and are looking forward to your continued support in the future.

Enquiries to THE MANAGER,
54, LOWER MAIN STREET, ARKLOW,
or
8, St. Alban's Road, South Circular Road,
DUBLIN, 8.

As Jim worked in C.I.E., Dublin he found it very difficult playing with the band and driving to work daily, so he was the first to give up his good job to go full time with the band. It was felt that devoting all his time seeking bookings and getting to know the ballroom managers, promoters etc., would lead to more engagements.

New Contract Manager

Jim's efforts were proving reasonably successful, but we felt that with the ever increasing competition - with more and more showbands exploding onto the scene - we needed extra help to break into the network of hall propietors, managers, promoters, who were, one might say, controlling the bulk of the business nationally. We were really new to the game in this bigger arena. We quickly learned it was not just quality that mattered, it was also about money. And the band, no matter how good it might be, did not always get its just reward. The real money mostly went elsewhere.

One night during the summer of 1963 while playing in the Palm Beach Ballroom, Portmarnock the opportunity came our way to penetrate the circle expounded above. An Arklow friend of ours, Dan Bolger, came along to the dance to listen to our performance, was very impressed and had a chat with Jim afterwards. He asked if we would be interested in doing a deal with him to take over as band manager. He explained that, as an engineering student in University College Dublin, he was on the fundraising committee that ran student dances in the city on a weekly basis. Because of this, he had made many contacts with dance promoters and showband managers in the business and suggested that his influence would be very valuable for the band's success into the big time. And Dan, showing his good faith, arranged a booking for us in the Four Provinces Ballroom in Harcourt Street for September 1st, 1963.

In August, Liam O'Reilly decided that he did not want to give up his good day job in the Arklow Pottery and resigned wishing us all the very best for the future. It reduced the band membership back to seven again and we decided to hold it at that.

We discussed Dan's proposal at our next practice session and were a bit sceptical but in the end went for it with great expectations. The deal was that

CONCESSION ELEKTRONS

Great First Dance

Columbia Showband

and BOB ORMSBY ALL STARS

in the Four Provinces

SUNDAY, 1st SEPTEMBER, 1963

DANCING 8-1 **SPOTS**

(5/- Payable at door on production of this ticket)

we would each get an agreed minimum weekly wage of £12, irrespective of whether we played or not, and it would be reviewed periodically, depending on how the band progressed financially into the future. Also to ensure that our instruments and sound equipment were up to reasonable standards Dan financed the purchase of whatever each member needed (on an individual loan pay back basis) and a number of us availed of the offer. I traded in my trombone for a better model.

The deal was signed in the autumn of 1963 and, in the months after, those of us who still held down day jobs gave them up including myself. Needless to say, being married only a short time and with our first child on the way, I realised I was taking a hell of a chance. However, I calculated that if the showband business went into decline or the Columbia's popularity waned I could always look for a job in the new fertilizer factory, N.E.T., that was under construction at the time.

Our association with Dan started off brilliantly. He worked flat-out to showcase the band throughout the country and beyond and had great success. He arranged a promotional write-up in a national paper announcing our entry into the professional showband arena which had very positive results (see overleaf).

★ THE COLUMBIA ★

The **COLUMBIA SHOWBAND** are from Arklow, formed to play at local hops by seven boys who enjoyed their talent for music, talent which has brought them to heights they had never expected. Now, as a fully professional Showband, as well as playing all over Ireland, the boys look forward to further English tours and Continental appearances, and an attractive recording contract—a well deserved bouquet to their musical ability.

JIM TYRRELL is the leader. He sings, plays trumpet, piano, rhythm or bass guitar as occasion arises, and does all the band arrangements. Jim likes swimming, tennis, traditional and modern jazz.

PAT TYRRELL is Jim's elder brother. Pat plays sax, clarinet, rhythm or bass guitar. His voice ranges from a deep bass to a raucous shriek on comedy numbers. Pat's main interests are reading and films. He likes Chinese food.

MIKE TYRRELL, bass guitarist and the boy with the big voice in the band is baby brother of Jim and Pat and stands six feet something in his socks. Mike collects records in his spare time and is a great Beatle fan.

EDDIE McELHERON is on rhythm guitar, is lead vocalist and sings Country and Western style mainly, with a leaning towards the Clancy Brothers at the moment. He is also the man for the slow sentimental ballads which he can render with deep feeling in his own inimitable manner. Eddie likes to go fishing, sailing or do anything relaxing.

JOE WEADICK plays trombone and can put a great sound into the brass. He is an accomplished pianist — an ability featured mostly in Country and Western numbers. Joe's hobbies are reading and records. He likes golf and chess.

FREDDIE CUTLAND is lead guitarist and joins in the harmony vocals. His ability influences greatly the Columbia's style and is a vital factor in their successful combination. Freddie's main interests are photography and fishing. He likes to go sailing occasionally.

GEORGE BYRNE is drummer and the big noise in the band. He is responsible for the beat the dancers really enjoy. The bulwark of the outfit, George is five feet tall — Ireland's smallest professional drummer — a showman par excellence whose drum solos never fail to amaze his appreciative audiences everywhere. His interests are cars, racing and sailing.

Enquiries :—
Manager,
"Bayview,"
Arklow,
Co. Wicklow,
Ireland.

Phone Arklow 302.

Photos taken by Joe Murray at Arklow Entertainment Centre 1963

When our first born son Kevin came into the world on Saturday, February 15th, 1964 the band was playing in Dungiven, Northern Ireland. I had brought Pat to Gorey Hospital on the Friday night - I was not allowed stay as in those day fathers were banned from the delivery room! The boys left without me for the gig early on Saturday afternoon as nothing was happening with Pat, but I had to leave with our manager Dan in his car later that evening. I was lucky to make the dance at all, as due to our lateness, Dan only hit the road in spots. It was the most frightening 250-mile journey of my life - remember there were no motorways then. In the end, we were a half-hour late for the dance and, needless to say, I felt very bad about being there at all under the circumstances. But each member was required for the band to give a quality performance and as new professionals trying to make our mark it was vital. I guess you've heard of the maxim "The Show Must Go On".

Mobile phones were light years away at the time. Even landline phones were hard to come by. After the dance that night, we drove into Derry on the way home in search of a phone box and eventually found one. I rang Gorey Hospital at 1 a.m. and was told a son was born to Pat at 8 p.m. and both were doing fine. I shouted out to the lads waiting in the minibus "Its a Boy" and the cheers erupted. We drove to the nearest chipper and I treated all and sundry to fish and chips. Kevin was christened at a quiet and simple ceremony at 2 p.m. in Gorey church the next day, Sunday – Pat was of course still in the hospital. That was the norm then … no such thing as waiting a few months to arrange big party celebrations.

Throughout 1964, Dan secured many bookings around the country, mostly in the top ballrooms and did deals with promoters who were bringing British and American artists on tour in Ireland. We were booked as the accompanying showband with them. I remember one particular American artist, Big Dee Erwin, who had a hit with 'Swinging On A Star' in 1963. We played with him three nights in a row, taking in the Arcadia in Cork, the Astor in Belfast and the Royal, Castlebar. A hell of a lot of travelling and playing involved in three days but, like most young musicians then, we revelled in it. Attendances in each venue were between fifteen hundred and three thousand people depending on the size of the ballroom.

Another very popular act we played on the same bill with was The Brook Brothers - a British duo who you see here performing with us in the Ritz, Carlow in 1964. They had a hit in the early sixties with 'War Paint'/'Sometime'. They also recorded 'Welcome Home Baby'/'So Long' and a cover version of 'Please Help Me I'm Falling'.

Other band members have included a comprehensive list of artists played with during the lifetime of the band, so I won't go through them here except to say that those events I was involved in were all very enjoyable experi-

THEY BACKED BIG DEE

COLUMBIA SHOWBAND

Backing "Swinging On A Star" man Big Dee Irwin during his recent Irish tour were Arklow's Columbia Showband—and the general opinion appeared to be that they all but stole the limelight from the American star.

Big Dee thought they were terrific and so did dancers in venues where the Columbia had not appeared before, such as Cork City.

The Columbia are in fact one of the fastest rising of the new Showbands. They've only been on the road for a year but already they're a star attraction on the East Coast and in other parts of the country, they've just completed a highly successful English tour and two further tours are lined up for this year.

Also on the books are a German and Swedish tour and they've just signed a very attractive recording contract.

The line up is Jim, Pat and Mike Tyrrell (brothers), Eddie McElheron, Joe Weadick, Freddie Cutland and George Byrne. At 4' 9" George is probably Ireland's smallest drummer, also one of the best

ences and broadened my knowledge of the entertainment world of that era and I'm sure the same applied to the rest of the boys.

Touring Britian

Our first experience of playing in Britian was a short tour of Irish ballrooms in London during Lent 1964, organised by the late Joe New of Abbeyville who worked there at the time and had good connections with the Irish com-

Columbia backing 'The Brook Brothers' in 1964

munity. On that occasion we flew with Aer Lingus to London and hired a minibus from Johnson Bros. of North Islington, where we also stayed. They specialised in looking after Irish bands. The accommodation with them was very basic but homely.

The highlight of that tour for me was playing in the Gresham, Holloway Road, where we had between three and four thousand people attending and they included many of the Arklow diaspora working in London (e.g. my brother Peter and his then girlfriend and future wife Mary Timmons (r.i.p.). It was the first time we performed on a revolving stage (unique at the time). The resident orchestra played off as the bandstand turned and we played on with 'Deep in the Heart of Texas', which was a hit by Duane Eddy in 1962. We were received enthusiastically making it an exciting and unforgetable experience for us.

Dan organised the second and extensive tour to England in April 1964 when we spent three weeks taking in Irish Ballrooms in London,

Birmingham, Coventry and Manchester. And this time I brought Pat with me (thanks to the boys who welcomed her along). It was a marvellous experience for us all. In Manchester we played in the Árd Rí Ballroom. My brother Paddy and sister Mary lived there at the time, as well as my aunt Bridie, who insisted on having the whole band around for supper after the dance at 1 o' clock in the morning – she recently died at the age of 87.

Columbia Flying to London on Tour 1964

'Arklow Notes' in *Wicklow People* on 11th April 1964

Columbia Showband's Tour — The Columbia Showband have left Arklow for a tour of the principal cities of England, including London, Birmingham, Liverpool, Manchester, Coventry, Leeds, and many others. This is the Band's second tour in 1964 their last visit to England being a great success. They played to packed houses everywhere. The present tour is for a period of three weeks. The leader of the band is Jim Tyrell, who plays trumpet, and is also a polished vocalist. His brother, Pat, plays the saxophone and is also a vocalist. Pat helps on rhythm guitar when needed. Lead guitarist is Freddie Cutland and he lends a hand with the harmony vocals. Lead vocalist is Eddie McElheron who plays rhythm guitar. George Byrne, Ireland's smallest professional drummer is a big hit with the fans everywhere. Bass guitarist and youngest of the Tyrrell brothers is Michael Tyrrell. Michael is also an accomplished vocalist. Joe Weadick plays trombone, piano, and lends a hand with the harmony vocals also. The boys return to Arklow at the end of April, when they will be making appearances locally, and in various parts of the country. They are now fully professional, and all are belonging to Arklow. Travelling with them on the tour is their permanent minibus driver, Jimmy Cullen.

'Arklow Notes' in *Wicklow People* on 2nd May 1964

Saturday Night Dancing—Patrons of Arklow Entertainment Centre eagerly look forward to the dance on this Saturday night which is in the nature of a big welcome home for the Columbia Showband This band has recently had a most successful English tour and were selected to back singing star Big D. Irwin on his Irish tour. That was, indeed, a great tribute to this group of local boys who have recently gone professional. — The management and patrons of the Centre look forward to giving then a big welcome on their native soil on Saturday night, and judging by the popularity of this band not only in the Arklow area but throughout the Co. Wicklow generally and also Co. Wexford, it seems as if the "house full" notice will be displayed at an early hour on Saturday night. As usual there will be no admission to the ballroom after 11.30 p.m. See advt.

Towards the end of 1964, concern was emerging that Dan was finding it difficult to secure the level of bookings into 1965 necessary to maintain the band profile at a high level, and it was starting to affect us financially. There was no apparent deterioration in our performances and we were still getting good responses from the dancers. As a result we were starting to doubt Dan's abilitiy to push us effectively. I suppose at the time it was natural for us to wonder, with his commitment to his studies in UCD, was he able to give it his all. But looking back on it now – hindsight is a great thing – he was still paying us a minimum weekly salary, which meant that he had to be working his best as he too was beginning to lose out financially. However, we were preparing to release our first record at the time so we hoped for better things to come.

THE WICKLOW PEOPLE—Saturday, May 2, 1964.

The Centre, Arklow

Where All the Big Bands Play!

THIS SATURDAY NIGHT, 2nd MAY—Big Welcome Home DANCE to

★ **THE COLUMBIA SHOWBAND** ★

(NOW FULLY PROFESSIONAL). DIRECT FROM FABULOUS ENGLISH TOUR!

DANCING: NINE—ONE-THIRTY. ADMISSION 6/-

In January 1965 we finally cut our first record, which was a great achievement and milestone for the band. Eddie singing 'Before this Day Ends' and 'In Your Arms'. They included some brilliant harmony and guitar acccompaniment by the boys and Pat did an excellent sax solo in the middle of 'In Your Arms'. I played keyboards. We were very happy with the record and it was well received by our fans, but it did not get anywhere in the charts, which was a bit of a disappointment.

Even after the boost with the record, bookings under Dan were not improving so, at a meeting in February 1965, it was reluctantly decided to break from him. It was felt that Jim could do as well, or better, with new bookings and it was agreed there was nothing to lose by going that road. Inwardly I was not so sure and was very concerned for my financial future with the responsibilities of a wife and family.

Breaking with Dan was not just a matter of saying goodbye. We had a contract with him which had to be honoured so, although the parting was amicable enough, because there was money involved we had to get our solicitor, the late Billy Fallon, to draw up the termination agreement. We each signed it and shook hands with Dan. It was a very stressful time for all of us because we had great respect for him, and his brother Paddy who helped out a lot when Dan was unavailable.

We embarked on another (two week) tour of the Irish Clubs in London in Lent 1965. But this time we were once again back to relying on the actual money coming in to pay all our expenses and salaries. I cannot remember how this tour was organised, but I do remember that there were quite a lot of blank dates and when we arrived home after the two weeks I had the sum total of £10.0.0 to hand over to Pat for the housekeeping – and the bookings still continued to be slow coming in.

Thinking of the above reminds me of another money worry I experienced a few months previously. We had travelled north for a weekend of bookings and passed the time away on the journey playing poker. We stayed over in Strabane on the first night and carried on playing in the hotel after the dance. Because there was a lot of money at stake, we continued playing poker again the following night on the way home after our gig in Belfast. It got out of hand (forgive the pun) and by the time we got to Dundalk I was down £13.0.0 - my week's salary. Some of the lads were getting pretty tired and wanted to sleep, but I wouldn't let them because I wanted a chance to recoup my losses. We decided to switch to pontoon and I was lucky to get 'banker'. By the time we hit Arklow I had won all my money back. Needless to say, I sweated a lot on that journey home and swore I would stick to playing forty-five for a shilling a time in future!

My Decision to Leave

After the poor return from the London tour I sat down at home one night and considered the potential of the band to earn enough to maintain all seven of us with a reasonable standard of living into the future. I came to the conclusion that it was not a viable option. We were good, but in terms of crowd drawing capacity we were slipping down the ladder. I felt that, while all our vocalists were very professional and excellent in their own spheres, there was no one person with that exceptional voice and charisma that the crowds would flock to see – particularly the girls! No one to compete with the likes of Brendan Bowyer, Dickie Rock or Joe Dolan. Apart from that, the ever increasing number of new showbands coming on stream were saturating the market, and ballroom proprietors, managers, promoters, clubs, etc. could play one against the other to keep the fees down. The net result was that most bands, in my opinion, were making very little.

On top of all that, the explosion onto the scene in 1964 of the Beatles and the Rolling Stones completely changed the live band entertainment scene. The young people were being drawn away from the ballrooms to concerts and lounges/cabarets. A new pop music culture was rapidly growing. My gut feeling was that the showband/ballroom dancing era was slowly receding.

Taking everything into account, with a heavy heart I made up my mind to leave the band, provided I could find someone suitable to take my place, as I did not want to leave the boys with a gap to fill in the line-up at this crucial time. I knew that Pat McCarthy, a member of the Echos Showband at the time, was an excellent piano accordian player, could sing well and play the trombone. I was satisfied that if Pat was interested he would be an ideal replacement as I could not sing and he would add that valuable new element to the band.

I asked Pat to drop down to my house and we discussed it confidentially. I could see he was open to the idea, but said he would have to think it over and talk with his parents as he had just got a job with NET and it would mean leaving it. A few days later he told me he would give it a go if Jim and the boys accepted him. I then broke the news to the lads that I was leaving, cited financial reasons and they accepted my decision with regret. Of course, they were very happy that Pat was agreeable to take my place, which meant they still had a full crew, and with brighter prospects for the future.

My last performance wth the Columbia was on St. Patrick's night, March 17th, 1965 in the Entertainment Centre, Arklow, and I started working in NET two months later on May 17th. My last night with the band was a very sad occasion for me as I had really loved the showband scene and the buzz of the entertainment life surrounding it. There was nothing more satisfying than playing to packed ballrooms and watching dancers letting their hair down and enjoying our performances with exuberance.

I was proud of the achievements everyone involved in the band had made over the previous six years and I was really going to miss their company. You can appreciate that being part of a showband meant that, as a group, we spent a hell of a lot of time together; almost like a close-knit family. For example, practising long hours, travelling long distances to and from venues in a minibus with very limited space, and of course performing at events for four, five or even six hours.

Musically we bonded very well together and it helped tremendously our stage performances, which was vital. There was the odd argument which could result in tension when having to get on with the job. No matter what problems there were behind the scene, the show had to go on. It was particularly difficult for anyone not feeling well. Each person was an important cog in the wheel and was depended upon to perform, irrespective of any personal problems one may have had at any given time. One other very important point to make is that we never had any problems with alcohol. Sobriety was a strict rule before and during performances when we went professional. And to my knowledge, drugs were not part of the Irish showband entertainment scene in the sixties.

Even in our spare time we were there for each other when called upon to help out in any situation. I distinctly remember Eddie, Freddy and some of the other boys helping me paint and wallpaper my new house (built by my brother Tim at 30 Lr. Main Street in 1963) before we moved in with our new born. It was something I appreciated very much.

My Musical After Life

When I finished in the Columbia in 1965, I gave up playing music until 1975 when I got the bug again. I was invited to join the Gorey Brass Band by my father-in-law, the late Paddy Sheil, who had many of his family involved in it during his fifty years as a member and my brother-in-law Michael Fitzpatrick (drummer) who is the renowned Gorey historian. I greatly enjoyed playing with them for fifteen years. During that time I also played six years with the Arklow Silver Band.

In 1979, I joined with Liam Garrett in a new big band he started called Black Velvet. It was special, playing for the bigger local events, but it only lasted one year. The other members included two of my friends of Red Seven/Columbia Showband fame, Pat Tyrrell and Freddy Cutland, the other members were Bobby and John Byrne, Seán and Jackie Olohan, Ann Kenny (Nichols), Ian Byrne and Richard Gill.

From 1980 to 1984 I played in another new band called Vintage - again started by Liam. The other members of that band were my old colleagues Jim Tyrrell, Bobby Byrne, Michael Tyrrell, Pat McCarthy and George Byrne. That was followed in the late eighties by the Elite with Liam, Bobby Byrne, and another two of my old pals from the Red Seven days, Larry Kenny and Pete Coburn.

Earlier in my story I mentioned the Allstars Showband which ran successfully from 1997 to 2002. And finally, from 2003 to 2008, I was involved with a country & western group called The Nashville Experience. Its members included John Joe Brauders, Pat Byrne, Eamonn and Geraldine Delaney, Reveonna Byrne, John Mahon, Paddy Delaney, Ritchie Hall, Paul Russell, Matt Sharpe and Red Seven /Columbia pal Freddy Cutland.

A new chapter in the band's history, Spring 1965

With my departure, Pat Tyrrell was now the only original member left in the band. With their new colleague Pat McCarthy on board the Columbia reinvented themselves and for the next two years they had their greatest successes, appearing on RTE's *Showband Show* and other programmes. They produced another single 'Way Out of Reach'/'Spinning Wheel' in 1965, which went to number six in the Irish hit parade, mentioned here in this *Evening Herald* write-up. It also publicised our new outside manager, by the name of Hugh Hardy (now deceased). The arrangement with Hugh included percentages of fees, but the band did not profit to any great extent.

Then, in 1967, a new bombshell befell the band. Pat McCarthy was headhunted by the Miami Showband with an offer he could not refuse and said goodbye to the boys. Naturally, they were very disappointed, but with him going to one of the top five showbands in the country, they could only be pleased for him. However, that move by Pat proved to be not so successful

EVENING HERALD Entertainment Guide

The Colombia's new manager

HUGH HARDY has taken over as manager of Arklow's Columbia Showband. The Columbia musicians have been together for some time. Most of them went to school together and they have been a professional outfit for the past 12 months.

Their one disc, "Before This Day Ends" did not make the charts but greater names than they have fallen by the wayside in this respect in the past year.

The band will cut another record soon labelled Out Of Reach." It was penned specially for them by George and Audrey Meredith who composed "I Stand Still," the number which took runner-up honours in the Eurovision Song Contest and which was later recorded by Butch Moore.

In the future the lead singer Eddie McIleron will be known as Eddie Mack.

There are six singers in the band, the line-up of which is as follows: Jim Tyrell (leader and trumpet); George Byrne (drums—one of the youngest and smallest in the country); Freddie Cutland (lead guitar); Michael Tyrell (bass guitar); Pat McCarthy (organ and trombone); Eddie Tyrell (lead vocalist and rhythm guitar) and Pat Tyrell (tenor sax).

The Columbia Showband, Arklow.

for other reasons and before long he was on the move again – as things turned out it was a blessing for him. His own story in this book will explain why.

Even though the band had recorded four more records in 1967/68 ('Back to the Hills'/'Song of the Sea', 'She Thinks I Still Care'/'Thats My Pa', 'Someday you'll call my Name'/'Devoted to You' and 'Baby come Back'/'Born to Lose') the loss of Pat in 1967, I do believe, was the turning point of the band's success. Manager Hugh Hardy also left the scene around the same time and Mick Nolan came on board.

They were once again fortunate to recruit another excellent local singer in the name of Oliver Merrigan - brother of Paddy Merrigan who was our lead singer for a few months in 1961. Unlike Pat McCarthy, Oliver did not play a trombone and had to learn it over time. But he had a powerful voice excelling in the big songs like 'Boolavogue', 'Danny Boy', 'The Swallow' and 'Young Girl'. Unfortunately, just when he was establishing himself with the fans, Oliver decided to leave the band - in 1968 - much to the disappointment of the boys. His reasons are outlined in his own story.

All these changes in personnel had to be very unsettling for the continued success of the band. It seemed like one headache after another. However, they were again lucky to find yet another great singer and sound Arklow man, and may I say a relation of mine, Timmy Weadick. Timmy was an all round singer with a big voice favouring songs by Tom Jones, the Beach Boys and the Beatles. And he too went down very well with the patrons and justified the lads' faith in him. Like Oliver, Timmy did not play a trombone and had the difficult job of learning to play one.

Mick Nolan moved on from the band and they were taken over by the late Jim Hand, who also tried his best to promote them, but without any great success. The showband era was coming to an end and the writing was on the wall for the Columbia Showband. The boys finally succumbed to the inevitable and called it a day in August 1969. Jim, George, Michael and Timmy got involved with a new country & western band being formed by Jim Hand called the Ranchers, and on the side Jim, George and Michael started the Jim Tyrrell Trio. The Ranchers were launched with a big publicity campaign, but they never hit the big time and gave up in 1973. However, the Jim Tyrrell Trio had instant success in the new era of small groups in the seventies - entertaining in lounges, hotels, cabarets and weddings. They were to continue professionally for eighteen years, giving up in 1986.

Eddie, Freddy and Pat started up the Family group with the addition of Pat's wife Breda and Matt Sharpe, and they too had great success for over ten years, playing more or less the same circuit as the Jim Tyrrell Trio. It's interesting to note that, when talking of the financial side of the business, it was generally accepted that more money was made in the Trio and Family groups than was ever made in the latter years of the Columbia Showband.

Summary

I have attempted to give an insight into my music life before, as a founding member of, and my happy and sometimes not-so-happy journey throughout the six years with the Red Seven/Columbia Showband, winding up with my musical afterlife.

I have also tried to give an account of the Columbia's progress after I left in 1965 up to September 1969 when the boys said goodbye to the showband era. Those who stayed to the end, as well as all the other lads who played with the band for a time throughout it's history, tell their own detailed and interesting stories in the following chapters. As well as the band members, other colleagues and friends, who were involved in one way or another with the band, give their own accounts and fond memories.

Read on and enjoy

Columbia going on tour to London 1964

Black Velvet Band 1980 at the Meetings of the Waters.
L to R:- Bobby Byrne, Joe Weadick, Richard Gill, Ian Byrne, Jackie Olohan, Liam Garrett, Freddy Cutland, Seán Olohan, John Byrne, Pat Tyrrell.
(not in photo - Ann Kenny)

All Stars Showband 1997
L to R:- Joe Weadick, Tony Linton, Dave Canavan, Larry Kenny,John Joe Brauders, Reveonna Byrne, Pete Coburn, Eamon O'Reilly,Pat Tyrrell and Liam O'Reilly.

All Stars Showband 2000
L to R: Joe Weadick, Bobby Byrne, Larry Kenny, John Joe Brauders, Pete Coburn, Dave Canavan, Geraldine Delaney, Eamon Delaney, Pat Byrne.
Others who were members for a period but not in photos were: Gerry McDonald, Yvonne Kenny, Tony Fox, Kieran Furlong, Trevor O'Sullivan and Niall Kavanagh (r.i.p.)

Nashville Experience 2003
Back Row:- John Mahon, Richie Hall, Eamon Delaney, Freddy Cutland, Pat Byrne, John Joe Brauders, Joe Weadick.
Front Row:- Paddy Delaney, Geraldine Delaney, Reveonna Byrne, Paul Russell.

Chapter 2

Pete Coburn

During my early school years music was very much part of my family's culture - in an informal way. Nearly all my brothers and sisters were good singers, in particular my late brother Ben, and he also played the mandolin. My eldest brother Harry (r.i.p.) played the violin (or fiddle as we used to call it then). This interest in music probably came from my father who was very musically inclined. He could knock a good tune out of a button accordion and was a decent singer.

As a young school goer I, too, was recognised as having a good singing voice and was encouraged to join the Marian Arts Society, which was the main social outlet in the town at the time for teenage boys and girls. I was only 15 when I joined and I'm not sure if I was more interested in the girls in the organisation or performing on stage. I guess it had to be both. However, I quickly came to love every minute of it and took part in all shows, singing and acting as well as many other activities. I sang solo as Boy Soprano in many concerts.

Looking back on it now, I realise how fortunate my generation was in having such a valuable organisation in the town. Even today there is nothing really to compare to it. Not only did it put on musicals and pantomimes but also dramas, variety concerts, boxing displays, Irish dancing and many other activities besides. At a time when there was very little money or work, it was an invaluable asset in introducing young people to the arts and other worthwhile activities. I can honestly say it shaped the lives of many for the good. A great debt is due to two founder members, the late Fr. Brian M Byrne C.C., and the late Michael Gunson who started it in 1941. Like everything in life, situations change in time and the Marian Arts Society folded in the early sixties, primarily due to the need for a replacement venue as the old McGowan's Hall on the South Quay was no longer viable.

I was about 23 years of age and still very active in the Marian Arts Society before I got involved in singing in dance bands. It happened one day in 1957 when the well known dance band leader from Avoca, Mark Canavan, came to my door and asked if I would be interested in joining his band. He had heard me singing in the Marian Arts concerts and said he was very impressed. Naturally, I was delighted and did not hesitate. I figured it was going to broaden my experience and, of course, there were the extra few shillings (long before decimalisation) which would come in handy.

I was determined to perform well in the band and started learning suitable songs and compiling my own repertoire. I will never forget the night I went to see the famous Slim Whitman in the Ormonde Ballroom and stood listening to him (almost under his nose) singing 'China Doll' and other songs for an hour and a half to get familiar with his songs and singing technique, and must say I learned a lot that night. I used the knowledge to improve my performance.

I remember very well one of the first gigs I did with Mark was a Hunt Ball in County Wexford, which was held in the mansion of the famous hurler Nicky Rackard. It wasn't long before I got the hang of the dance tunes and got to love the singing. The interaction with the dancers was brilliant, particularly the girls, and of course the crack with the band lads was mighty. Mark Canavan's orchestra was very popular all over County Wicklow and Wexford so we were very busy. For some months toward the end of 1959, Mark was unable to play due to a bout of illness and he asked me to run the band. Most of the members at the time were from Arklow. They included Larry Kenny, Paud O'Brien, Pat Tyrrell, Eamon Lee and, after Mark got sick, Joe Weadick and Des Mulhall came on board.

As the showband phenomenon was taking off rapidly in Ireland in 1959, with the Clipper Carlton and the Royal Showband leading the way, we, the Arklow lads, were very interested in this new craze and had a serious chat about what way we should go. We decided, reluctantly, to part with Mark to start our own "Showband", even though we were all very grateful to him for the time and experience he had given us. It seemed the obvious thing to do, as the seven of us were from Arklow and would find it much more convenient for practice, travelling etc. But the main reason was that we were smitten with the new and fresh type of shows the Clipper and Royal were putting on and felt we had the talent and ability to go that route.

Mark's band was the more traditional sit down orchestra and the main philosophy of a showband was to have all personnel (except the drummer) standing at all times and they specialised in various movements to the rhythm of the music. Some showbands also put on suitable short musical comedy shows during their performance to capture the full attention of the dancers and, hopefully, create a memorable impact.

Breaking from Mark Canavan's orchestra to be a founder member of a new showband was a big decision, especially for me as I was particularly conscious of leaving his band stripped of the vast majority of its members, which was going to be hard on him for a while. He was such a gentleman to play with and had been very fair to me during the three years I was with him. But, as I said before, life moves on and we had our dream to follow, such as it was at the time.

Starting our own showband was not as simple as it seemed. It meant buying our own microphones and amplification equipment and arranging a permanent practice room in Arklow. It meant arranging suitable transport at reasonable cost as none of us, except Des, had a car or any form of transport. But most importantly, it meant using all our efforts and contacts to get bookings, because no matter how good you might think you are, hall owners/managers and clubs/organisations running dances are always very careful to book a group which they believe is going to be enjoyed by the dancers and also profitable. They know they are taking a certain risk with a new band.

The decision to go our own way was taken about October of 1959 and from then on, while continuing to play in Mark's band, we started organising ourselves - practising suitable showband material for our eventual launch. We were fortunate to obtain a very suitable practice room at the back of the old Johnson's Garage at 1 Park Terrace (beside the Arklow Bay Hotel). For those who do not know, it was the building eventually bought by the late John Sweeney, who used it for some time for his funeral undertaking business, and is now run by his son Pat Sweeney as a windscreen, tyre and exhaust service business.

While our new showband was to be a co-operative set-up where all members were equal in every sense (including an equal split of the takings after all expenses), the boys asked me to manage it because I was already managing Mark's band and had plenty of experience dealing with bookings. It put an extra responsibility on me but I always liked a challenge and agreed to take it on. Fortunately, I was successful in getting bookings in most of the venues that we had played in with Mark. Of course, we were all convinced that once we were heard performing in the new set-up, the dance hall proprietors, managers and patrons alike would want us back and, of course, this belief in ourselves did prove right.

During our practice sessions leading up to the launch, we discussed what we should call the new band. All sorts of names were put forward and finally we came up with the name The Red Seven Showband - 'Seven' because we numbered seven in the band, and 'Red' because we felt it represented energy and brightness. Of course, in the excitement and eagerness of our new venture, we never worried too much what slagging we would get if the number in the band increased or decreased. Although one of our group, the late Eamon Lee (God rest him), always with an eye on the money, worried that we might have a problem in getting full payment if anyone was ever sick and we ended up playing with six!

We officially finished playing in Mark Canavan's band in January 1960. We launched the Red Seven Showband with a special notice in the entertainment page of the *Wicklow People* on February 6th, 1960 announcing (a) our severance from Mark, (b) the name of our new band and (c) the installation of myself as manager. My management fee was not disclosed - only joking - remember we were all equal in the new venture! Our philosophy was the old adage: "All for one and one for all". Looking back on it now, I'm delighted to say that, even though Mark's band was almost terminally depleted by our move, he was gracious about it and managed to keep going and rise again from the ashes, which was great testimony to his talent and popularity. From February 6th, 1960 onwards, I gave my full energy to promoting the band, making personal contact with most of the proprietors I had done business with in the past and, I have to say, I made very good progress. It was not long before we were playing as often as we wanted, having regard to the fact that everyone was holding down a day job. Even more important was the fact that we were starting to secure better fees, more prestigious bookings and in more venues.

Interestingly, our first engagement as the Red Seven Showband was in the Tara Ballroom, Courtown, one of the leading ballrooms on the east coast at the time and it so happened that it became synonymous with the success of our band. The dance was on Sunday 21st February from 9 to 2, admission price of six shillings. On the same night, the most popular band in the area at the time, the late Jay Byrne, who will be known to everyone reading this book old enough to have danced during the sixties in County Wicklow or County Wexford, played in the Glen Hotel Ashford from 9 till 2 with admission price of five shillings. As his band was our main local competition in the popularity stakes, we were naturally delighted to be on a par with him on our first night's performance.

Incidentally, Jay Byrne was also the main band, apart from the major visiting bands, that played in the Arklow Entertainment Centre every Saturday night. You might say his was the resident band there. The complex had only opened in 1958. As well as a ballroom, it included an outdoor swimming pool, tennis courts, paddle boating lake, crazy golf and pitch and putt. Being new, it was extremely popular and a great asset for locals and visitors alike. The Centre ballroom was next in popularity to the Tara Ballroom in the east Leinster region.

We were very anxious that our own town dancers would have an opportunity to hear us in the Arklow Entertainment Centre. The late Paddy Lynch was the manager there at the time and, he being a shrewd operator, was reluctant to give us a Saturday night because he was getting the crowds with Jay Byrne. He was not going to change a good thing - fair enough. However, out of the goodness of his heart, he did give us our first engagement on Easter Sunday afternoon, April 17th, 1960. Yes, afternoon dancing was popular then amongst young people on Bank Holidays and summer Sundays. We were very happy with the crowd we got that day. I would say it was partially out of curiosity to see what this new local showband was like.

We also went down very well with the dancers in Courtown on our first night there, and it eventually led to us getting the 1960 summer season residency. It is an understatement to say that this was a very prestigious booking as it meant six nights a week playing in the months of July and August (a total of eight weeks). It was so important to us because it gave us excellent exposure, being the premier ballroom on the east coast outside Dublin. Apart from featuring us as the resident band, twice a week (Sundays and Wednesdays) it had two visiting top showbands that attracted crowds from as far away as Waterford, Wexford, Kilkenny, Carlow and dancers from all over County Wicklow. So you can imagine that by the end of the season we were exceptionally well known and extremely popular right across Leinster Remember also that Courtown was, and still is, one of the most popular seaside resorts in the country. But alas the Tara Ballroom is no more – just another block of apartments – a sign of the changing times. It was thronged every year with people, particularly Dublin people. In those days, there were very few ordinary working class people going abroad to the sun on holidays as it was so expensive and the choices were not as they are today. Most people were very happy to get to a good Irish seaside resort, where there was regular entertainment and, hopefully, decent weather. Funny enough, there was nearly always good summer weather in Courtown (you know the famous saying 'the sunny southeast'). Winning the summer season residency in Courtown did not happen without great effort on our part, convincing the owner, Peter Redmond, of our talent and trustworthiness. Peter, who we came to know and respect greatly over the following few years, was a very astute businessman. While he was impressed with our band and, more importantly, knew his patrons were very keen on us, he was worried that such a new outfit may not be capable of staying the pace for two months at six nights a week. I suppose if you were in his shoes you, too, would have certain reservations. If we did not continue to perform well, or if the crowd got fed up with us, he would have a major problem on his hands in that his ballroom's reputation would be at stake.

While I was making good progress with Peter Redmond in negotiations for the residency, he was hedging. We decided to reinforce our request by asking a good friend of Des Mulhall, who worked as a manager with him in Arklow Pottery at the time, Paddy Lafferty, to go separately as a representative of the band, to have a chat with Peter and further convince him that we were well worth booking. Our combined pressure tactic worked and Peter took the chance and booked us. He did not regret it.

Testament to our popularity was an article that appeared in the prestigious "Dancing with Paul Jones" page of the *Evening Press*, at the beginning of the season with a photograph of the band and mentioning ourselves as "the versatile resident orchestra from Arklow who have already proved themselves with County Wexford Dancers". In the same article, Paul Jones went through the list of top bands appearing during the summer months in Courtown and other leading ballrooms around Ireland, such as Victor

Silvester, Vince Eager, Chick Smith, Royal Showband, Clipper Carlton, Dunny and Singleton. He also mentioned that Humphrey Lyttleton was due to appear in the Top Hat Ballroom, Dun Laoghaire - another beautiful ballroom that has bit the dust to modern times. We were mentioned in the dance column in a rival evening national newspaper during the season, along with a photo of four of the band and a few appropriate words: "Red Seven Showband fresh as the fish from the sea in Arklow".

The season was one of the best Peter Redmond ever had and, because we were new to the business, he got us for a very reasonable price. I personally believe we would have secured more if we had held out, but that is now history. So much did Peter like us, and perhaps because he did so exceptionally well out of us financially, he agreed to give us a benefit night on our last Saturday dance of the season. We had a brilliant crowd, a great financial success and a most memorable event, thanks to all the regulars and fans we had built up over the season and that includes those of you reading this who danced to us then.

We all had a good two weeks rest at the end of the residency as we were really exhausted after playing six nights a week for two months, especially when two of those dances each week went on until two a.m., resulting in us getting home at about three in the morning, if we were lucky. I say 'lucky', because more often than not one of us would get chatting to a pretty young girl, mainly after making eye contact and a nod and a wink during our performance. And, of course, being gentlemanly! would offer to walk her to her home ... or to her hotel, caravan site, beach! or wherever she might be staying. The rest of us had to sit and wait until our fellow Romeo arrived back. I must say we never left anyone behind even though our driver and minibus owner, the late Martin Byrne, would not be too happy.

Because we were so busy playing in the Tara Ballroom during the season, we had no time to spend any of our hard earned cash so we agreed not to touch it until we finished the residency. I remember well the meeting we held early in September, upstairs in the then "56 Bar", Arklow (now Egan's) to celebrate our success and divvy out our earnings. It was quite a significant lump sum at the time. We all felt rich and, needless to say, the comments and crack were rich too. Each of us had our own priorities for spending it. Paud O'Brien was planning to get married, so it came in very handy for him. Even now, when I think back on that night, I can't help dwelling on the nice gesture the lads made to me. While we were all equal with regard to the share out, the boys insisted that I take what was some odd few quid left over in the kitty in appreciation for all my extra work in managing the bookings and finances. The amount was not insignificant - it could have represented three weeks' wages then.

When we got back to business in September our diary looked good and the bookings were flowing in at a steady pace in counties Wicklow and Wexford. Being wise, I had taken out an advert in the *Wicklow People* in early August announcing that we would be available again for bookings from September 21st after our very successful residency in Tara Ballroom urging ballroom managers, promoters, clubs etc., to book early.

By Christmas 1960, we were well established and put a notice in the Wicklow and Wexford local papers wishing all our fans, ballroom proprietors, managers, and club committees a 'Very Happy Christmas and Prosperous New Year'. We played in the Tara Ballroom on St. Stephen's night to a crowd of about seventeen hundred people. For all of us it was a very special night ending our first and extremely successful year as the Red Seven Showband. Our performance was, I believe, electrifying and the crowd responded likewise.

Mentioning the late Martin Byrne earlier reminds me of how much of a character he was and how special he became to us. He was of the old school and had the most unique way of expressing himself, which was entertainingly priceless. I remember one night while waiting in Courtown after a dance for our guitar player, the late Eamon Lee, Martin said to me: "Well Co ... (short for Coburn) ... we are all here in the van and ready to go home except young Lee - where the hell is he this time of the night ... probably down there on the beach with some young one ... he does keep us a bit late de ye see ... is he goin' to stay *all* night ... we'll get no sleep at all de ye see".

Yes, Martin was very special to us. You could always depend on him for some entertaining comments or anecdotes during our travels together. Here are a few examples:-

On the Stephen's night dance in Courtown I referred to above, Martin came up to me at the bandstand and quipped, "God Co, be jasses there's a great crowd in her tonight. - I never heard anything like the click of the pennies in the shithouse … its un-natural down there".

"Haaay Co… when are we break'n for tea de ye see" – "Why, what's wrong Martin?" asks I … "well, when we are, make sure Tyrrell goes in last" … "Why Martin?"… "It's like this, de ye see Co, if I take a bun I am able to get three bites out of it before I finish it but if Tyrrell takes one … de ye see … he will put the whole bun in his mouth and pull the paper away in one go and there'll be nothing left for the rest of us if he goes in first".

One night when leaving town for a gig, Martin stopped outside A. O'Connor's drapery shop in the Main Street (where Dunne's stores is now) and ran across to the 56 bar (now Egan's) to have a quick one (whiskey) and when he came back to the minibus he muttered to himself as he took off rather rapidly: "How could anyone have a drink in comfort when you have seven hooligans wait'n outside".

One evening when he picked us up Martin asked: "Where are we going tonight?" When I said Adamstown in County Wexford he was delighted and said: "That's a great place, Co"… 'How is that, Martin?' … "Well, for the simple reason is that ye get a cup of tea when ye arrive, which is very nice, half way through the dance ye go in and get sandwiches and stuff, and when the dance is all over ye get a big salad and tea. That's a great spot … I hope we get more bookings there de ye see".

Martin had a terrible habit when driving of looking at me (I used to sit beside him as I always felt sick in the back seats) when talking instead of keeping his eyes on the road. Often times I was petrified in case he would crash. I remember in particular coming home over the Wicklow Gap about four o'clock one morning. There was a sheer drop on one side of the road. As usual I was sitting beside Martin and on the outside at the door was Pat Tyrrell. In his usual dry wit, Pat opened the sliding window beside himself and started saying in an authoritative priestly accent: "How many times … how long has it been … six Hail Marys …" and shut the window. Martin started laughing while looking at me instead of the road and nearly fell out of the van trying to drive. Needless to say, I wasn't the better of it. How Martin didn't crash I will never know.

"Haaay Co", Martin would say when he was looking to put up the fee. "Ye know the petrol is going up all the time, I think I am giving a good service, and we are getting home much later every night from Courtown than I anticipated, so I'll have te put up the fee from seven and six to ten shillings a night, de ye know". He would look at me sheepishly and wait for my reaction.

I could go on and on with funny stories all night about Martin. He seemed dour at times, but a lovable character behind his facade. And we all loved him. I do believe he treated us like we were his family.

Some of the tunes I loved singing, which were in the hit parade and extremely popular at the time were:

1 'China Doll' - Slim Whitman who recorded it was my idol.
2 'Only the Lonely' - Roy Orbison, we always got a standing ovation for it and it was nearly always requested a second time.
3 'Devil Woman' - I remember I always had some difficulty on the timing much to the annoyance of drummer Des. However, I'm pleased to say that after fifty years practice I've now got it right (I think).
4 'Doctor I'm in Trouble' - (sung by Peter Sellers and Sophia Loren in the film *The Millionairess*) one of our showpiece sketches which was always very entertaining and always drew a big crowd in around the stage. I dressed up in a dress and at the end of the tune I used to jump into Pat Tyrrell's arms. Pat being big and much stronger and heavier than I, meant I was never afraid that he would let me fall.

Pat Tyrrell had a deep voice and he was excellent at singing Jim Reeves songs.

Larry Kenny was popular singing 'Old Shep' and some dixieland numbers like 'Ice Cream'.

I'm sure it is hard for young people reading this book to visualise the numbers of people who danced in the early sixties - fifty years ago. It was a completely different world. Remember, dancing was the main social activity then. In most cases there was no alcohol drinks sold at the dances. The men would come in after pub closing time and the girls would be lined up along the hall waiting for them - few women went to the pubs.

It was not unusual for a hall to be filled well beyond its official capacity. To give an example I remember many a time looking down the dance halls from the stage and thinking that I could walk all the way to the back of the hall on the shoulders of the male dancers, such were the crowds attending. A little bit like Crocodile Dundee in the film.

Our second year – 1961 – and my last year with the band, started on a high with plenty of prestigious bookings. I was in touch early with Peter Redmond in Courtown about the upcoming Summer season and did a very lucrative deal…much better financially than 1960 - £120.0.0 per week compared to £80.0.0 - a fifty per cent increase. However, we were only booked for the month of July, due to a policy change by the ballroom management. They decided to have a different band for the month of August. Perhaps we were costing too much and Peter booked us for the first month to get the crowds fired up and create the holiday atmosphere.

With the upsurge of new showbands all over the country and the assumption that big money was being made by everyone involved, the taxmen must have been rubbing their hands. It was not long before I, as manager, got the usual official letter from revenue asking for the names of all the members in the band and their earnings for the first year of operation. Needless to say, it was a headache for me to come up with credible accounts as we, like, I suppose, many bandsmen, were not too concerned about keeping detailed

Red Seven Showband in Ormonde Ballroom, Arklow 1960

financial accounts - we were more concerned with keeping time playing the music! However, I did my best to submit as near as damnit an accurate income and expenditure account and a cheque for something like £120.0.0., which at the time was a fair few bob for a bunch of amateur musicians in our first year. The revenue must have been happy with my accounts because they were accepted without question. The following are the accounts submitted – it gives an interesting picture of the cost of running a part-time band in those times.

Income and Expenditure Account of Red Seven Showband for Year 1960.

Income		
Booking fees for the year		1423.0.0
Expenditure		
Transport for band for year M Byrne –	228.0.0	
Rent for Practice room – J Sweeney –	52.0.0	
Purchase 7 Band Blazers – T Cannon –	36.15.0	
Purchases of 7 Band suits – G O'Toole –	40.5.0	
Purchase of Amplification equipment –	25.0.0	
Purchase of music sheets etc. –	25.10.0	
Music Stands –	12.0.0	
Hire of Amplification equipment-year –	62.0.0	
Commission - promoter for bookings –	40.0.0	
Occasional Office rent –	15.0.0	
Postage, Telegrams, phone –	10.0.0	
Stationery, Circulars, Envelopes, Printing –	20.0.0	
Advertising in Irish Press –	8.0.0	
Photographer Plunket Rathdrum, Photos –	7.0.0	
Purchase tape Recorder Fitzgerald Elect –	28.0.0	
	609.10.0	
Band members income for the year	813.10.0	
	1423.0.0	1423.0.0
	========	=======

Income Tax assessed and paid on members' income = £120.0.0

It was not unusual for fans to leave stout or beer (never minerals - even though some of us were teetotallers) up on the bandstand for us during our performance. At any one time there could be five or six pints stretched out like soldiers across the front of it. This meant that, when I had to make my way hurriedly in the middle of a set from my double bass at the back of the bandstand to the front to do my number, I had to be very careful not to knock over any of these drinks. And what would I hear from Des - "careful there Co - mind where you put those feet"... from Pat - "for Christ's sake don't spill those drinks"... from Eamon - "now Co, thread carefully and leave the scoop (Eamon's favourite word for the Guinness) upright"... from Larry - "go easy Pete that stuff is precious". As for Joe and Paud they abstained from comment, then, of course, they were not on the drinks panel.

I recall that on an occasion when we got a very prestigious booking from the Mayfair Ballroom in Kilkenny I was unfortunate to contract German Measles a couple of days before that Saturday night's gig. My face was like a tomato with spots when Des called to make sure I was fit to travel. Well, you couldn't say I was fit. I was fit to die. I felt so bad and here was Des sitting in a chair in front of me telling me I was fine. To this day he still doesn't wear glasses (joke). I missed that gig and was very sorry about it, but like troopers the boys travelled, performed and had a very successful night.

Another little episode crossed my mind. I recall a nice booking we got in the very popular Arcadia Ballroom, Bray - now long gone – it burned down years later. We were booked as the main attraction. The resident orchestra there on the night, I think, was Amelio Macari, a strict tempo dance orchestra. The seven of us were walking together up the centre of the dance floor to go on stage for our performance. Amelio had left the stage and was walking towards us. I noticed as we got closer that he had a horse load of sheet music pressed to his chest. Well, what do you know - he swept by without a single word. He passed us as like you would pass a dog or dogs in the street. I could almost hear his thoughts... 'Showbands Ye ... What do they know!' So much for friendly welcomes. Of course, it wasn't like that all the time, we were welcomed, wined and dined almost everywhere we played.

You know things weren't always peaches and cream for me personally. I had my disappointments too. Although now they seem so trivial and even funny looking back. Yes, strange to say it concerns the bould Eamon. I am aware I have talked a bit about him, but nevertheless I have to tell you this episode. First of all at 18/19 years of age he was a very handsome fellow. So much so, he was likened to that great actor of that period, Tony Curtis. Anyway, to get to the point ... here I am, the lead singer, after doing a song and looking down at a young crowd on the floor in Courtown, when two or three pretty girls approach me at the bandstand. I await with keen anticipation ... I am waiting for the smiles, the praise and the pleasant small talk. Alas ... what's the first thing they say? ... "Who is the guy on the guitar? What's his name? ... tell him we think he's fab and we will talk to him later". Well how do you think I felt? Words fail me. However, one had to do the right thing, so I told them through clenched teeth all about the bould Eamon. May I add that I told Eamon afterwards to put his name in large letters on that guitar and from that moment on he could do his own answering and explaining to his admirers. So much for the odd spot of jealousy and envy - it was great!

Oh yeah... another fond memory, Eamon'd always say to me wherever we were setting up, "Hey Co ... any scoop on the job tonight?" - he liked a glass of Guinness. I'm sure he is laughing down at me now as I reveal that.

As I said at the beginning of this chapter, I enjoyed my time greatly with Mark Canavan and owe him a lot for introducing me to the dance band world and for the experience I gained with him. But being part of the Red Seven Showband was, of course, a very special and most rewarding time. It was without doubt the most memorable two years of my musical life. My Red Seven Showband colleagues, Des, Paud, Larry, Pat, Joe and never-to-be-forgotten Eamon were the best friends you could have. We are still very close today, fifty years on.

I left the band in September 1961 after a lot of soul searching. The boys were intent on going professional and I decided I could not make the move because I had a good secure job that I liked and, at the time, led a very active life in sports when I was not involved with the band. And there were other important family reasons for my decision.

Finally, I want to say that after fifty-two years performing on and off in dance bands and, if I may say so myself, still singing a good song at seventy-five years ... and still loving the buzz. In the seventies I sang with Liam

Garrett in a duo called Just 2 which I enjoyed very much, in the nineties I sang with the Allstars Showband, and for the last five years in a duo called Easy Listening and, believe it or not, my partner, a brilliant keyboard player, Dave Canavan ... is a son of the famous Mark Canavan whose band I started with in 1957. I don't know what you call that - but I call it Fate.

Postscript: I'm just thinking what a hell of a job Joe has given himself writing this book on the Red Seven, the Columbia and the showband era in general. All I can say is the best of luck, Joe, in your endeavours. I know you

Mark Canavan's Band, Avoca, taken about 1958
Standing: Mark Canavan, Pat Tyrrell, Larry Kenny, Abie Jacob, Owen Canavan.
Sitting: Pete Coburn, Sylvester Green, Christie O'Toole.

The Red Seven Showband

"The Red Seven", the band that started it all in Arklow in 1958, reunited recently for a wonderful night of nostalgia.

It was the first time in 40 years the boys were all together - the original seven and founder members.

It was a night of going back in time to gigs they once played and reliving stories of the Showband era.

The Band played all over Ireland and were most popular with County Wexford dancers, where they played in practically every Ballroom in the county.

Most important of all were the two summer seasons they played in the Great Tara Ballroom in Courtown, entertaining dancers from far and wide six nights a week. Some stories there, I can tell you!

There are plenty of over fifties out there who remember the boys and the two summers in Courtown, especially in Gorey, Fems and Enniscorthy.

What a great outfit they were. Mary Coburn was the perfect hostess on the night, and many nights went on until the early hours.

I hear a video was made of the party, I'm looking forward to seeing that. Congratulations lads, and thanks for the memories of a wonderful musical era.

THE RED SEVEN SHOWBAND, ARKLOW (1958)
Back Row (l. to r.) - Paud O'Brien (Clarinet/Saxophone), Joe Weadick (Trombone), Des Mulhall (Drums), Pat Tyrrell (Piano/Bass/Vocals), Larry Kenny (Trumpet/Clarinet/Saxophone).
Seated in front: Pete Coburn (Lead Vocalist), Eamonn Lee (Guitar/Vocalist)

Members of the original Red Seven Showband pictured at a reunion recently

The Elite in 1984
Left to Right:
Liam Garrett,
Pete Coburn,
Joe Weadick,
Larry Kenny,
Bobby Byrne.

Chapter 3

Des Mulhall

Coming from a farming background I often wondered down the years how I ended up playing in bands. When I was travelling to a gig I used to say to myself I should be bringing in the cows for milking or making hay. However, music won the day. My mother played the piano (not many people knew that). Whether she played by music or by ear I never knew, and my sister Rosaleen played piano too.

But me! I was only interested in drumming as far back as I can remember. My father knew this and one evening we drove out to visit a friend of his, Mr. Jim O'Neill of Muchlagh. Now Jim had been a drummer with the Tinahely Brass and Reed Band and he had an old side-drum. The skin was burst but the snare and the rest was intact. He graciously gave it to me and wished me luck. I was a proud little boy on the journey home. Look out everyone... I was on the way! I had already made myself a pair of sticks (rough) but somehow I managed to get a proper pair, I think from a member of the Pipe Band. Thank you, if you are still out there.

The first tune I played to was called 'The Bluebell Polka', recorded on an old 78 by the great Jimmy Shand Band from Scotland. Little did I realise then that, later on in years, I would be playing with the man himself on a St. Patrick's Night in Northhampton. What an honour. Can you imagine me playing with a big recording star like that?

Word had got around that I was interested in the drums and I'm sure my neighbours knew too well! Then I discovered you could play drums by music, OH BOY!, what was all this about. I later found out.

I never joined the Pipe Band but occasionally I'd hang about on their practice night. Their headquarters, at that time, was on the South Quay, in a building near the former McGowan's Hall, now the site of the Brookview apartments. I'd listen to long rolls, short rolls and paradiddles. I'd practice these when I'd go home as well as my 'Bluebell Polka'. At least I had something to carry on with. The late Charlie Gaul was the pipe band's top drummer at the time.

Then I started working in the Arklow Pottery (as you do).... I was a wages clerk in the Clay-End. It was just as well I was tops at maths in school or I wouldn't have lasted a week. Not alone did I make up the wages but I had to count every piece of ware that left the Department for about 180 piece workers and maybe 50 different items and all at different prices. Looking back on it now I must have been a "Human Walking Computer" (if there is such a thing, I was it).

However to get back to the music, Rosaleen Bolger, a world class ballroom dancer in her day, came to me in work one day, and showed me a page of the *Evening Herald* advertising a drumming school starting in Dublin teaching drumming by music. I thanked her and I enrolled straight away. Jon Murray, a professional drummer, ran the school.

Every Tuesday night I travelled to the classes in Dublin, either by getting a lift with someone I knew, by thumbing or by bus. The bus back after night classes only went as far as Wicklow and many a time I had to arrange for someone to come from Arklow to collect me or, indeed on occasion, I had to thumb home and that was some job late on a winter's night. There weren't many cars on the roads then, but funny enough people were more inclined to give you a lift even though they may not know you. Crime was not really a problem. On one occasion, I had to walk all the way to Barndarrig before I got a lift.

This was before the showband scene. The top Irish orchestras at the time were Maurice Mulcahy and Mick Delahunty. Not to mention the top visiting orchestras from Britain like Joe Loss and Ken Mackintosh. They, along with many well known Irish bands, came to play in the Ormonde and Mayfair ballrooms. For those of you who may not remember or were not even born then, Arklow was one of the premier seaside resorts of the period. Every summer, the town was packed with holiday makers. And the weather appeared to be sunnier, warmer and drier for longer than nowadays.

There was nothing I liked better than to go up to the Ormonde Ballroom early and watch the bands setting up, especially the drummer. The best band to play Arklow, in my opinion, was The Johnny Quigley All Stars from the north (Derry maybe). What a band. Tommy McMenamin, the drummer, was a great reader.

Then low and behold a miracle – a dance marquee came to South Green (near where I live). I helped the drummer carry in his gear and watched him set them up. He asked me would I like a bang which I did ... brilliant ... He packed away his sticks and went for some refreshments. As soon as he had gone, I ran home and got my own sticks and had a little session all on my own before he came back.

In the meantime I had decided to buy my first set of drums. I got in contact with Ireland's largest mail order store, Cott's of Kilcock, filled in the necessary forms, paid them the deposit and promised to pay by monthly instalment. I came home from work one evening and there they were, packed in boxes in the front room. My set of "Olympic Drums" had arrived. My mother nearly had a heart attack that day - what was going on at all? The excitement was electric while unpacking the boxes and, with great difficulty, erecting the set. It looked beautiful, I thought. I lost no time in getting down to practise with them. One night, I'd be playing with Pat Boone - he was No.1 in the charts at the time - other nights with Fats Domino. These records were the old 78's. I played them on my record player, which I had bought in Joe New's shop on Main Street. He was the first to stock records in Arklow.

My big chance to play in a dance band came at last in 1959 when Larry Kenny, a friend of mine in the music business and fellow worker in Arklow Pottery, told me that Mark Canavan, the leader of the popular Avoca band he was playing trumpet in, was stuck for a drummer to play the following Sunday night in Dunlavin, west Wicklow. After questioning Larry on the set-up, and pondering whether I was competent to come up to scratch, I decided, with Larry's encouragement, to jump in at the deep end.

The dance turned out to be a big test in that we played six hours, from 9 p.m. to 3 a.m., which was normal in some dance halls on a Sunday night. I, of course, was hooked after that. Not only because my playing ability was proved o.k. but because the crack among the lads in the band was great. The one downside was that we did not get back to Arklow until 7 a.m. and I had to be in work in the Pottery at 8 a.m. I said to myself; "This is the life".

By this time the showband scene had blasted off in Ireland. The Clipper Carlton had started it all. They threw away the chairs, all hands stood up playing and they copied the artists from the hit parade. All that was called a "Showband".

It so happened that my addition to Mark Canavan's band meant that there were now seven Arklow men in his band, namely Pete Coburn, Larry Kenny, Paud O'Brien, Pat Tyrrell, the late Eamon Lee, Joe Weadick and now myself. So, we made a decision to start a band of our own, after having several meetings on the pros and cons.

We practised every Monday night in a room in the old Johnson's Garage beside the Memorial Hospital (now the Arklow Bay Hotel). The late John Sweeney bought it shortly after we started practising there. John, as most Arklow people know, was an undertaker and he used the rooms at the back of the shop to make coffins. We were lucky that John let us stay in one of the rooms. I can't for the life of me remember what the rent cost us or did we pay any? – maybe £1 a week. I think John was proud of the fact that the band was from Arklow, so was helping us to get on the road.

We also practised and arranged music in Seán Bonner's house. Seán (a musical genius) helped us a lot. The name, the Red Seven, was decided in his house.

The first night we played as the Red Seven Showband was in the Tara Ballroom in Courtown on Sunday, February 21st, 1960. It was a big test for us, but we needn't have worried, because we were very well received.

Eamon Lee had made music stands, but we couldn't get them painted. However, we were rescued by the late Liam O'Connor, who was an artist from Meadows Lane. Liam stepped in and painted them on the same Sunday we were playing. We had to be careful the dancers didn't touch up against them. Also we decided to appoint Pete Coburn to look after the bookings. I don't think we could have got a better man to look after our money than Pete. We hired Mr. Martin Byrne as our regular driver. Martin owned a Volkswagen mini-bus. He stayed at Mrs. Going's guesthouse at No. 5 Lower Main Street. One of my abiding memories of Martin was one night, when playing in Bunclody, he, who had no real concept of the delicacy of musical instruments, came up to talk to me and accidentally knocked over and broke my high hat and cymbals, which I had to replace.

By the way, Martin loved his food during a dance. He would suss out what kind of refreshments were available for the band and, if they were on the scarce side, he would come up to the stage and tell us to 'get there fast before young Tyrrell eats the lot'. Pat also liked his grub. When we stopped for a break on the road to buy chocolate or a drink, Pat would sometimes buy a Spanish onion and eat it like an apple —- OH GOD. On the way home, we would stop the wagon and open all the doors to let the air in !!!....PHEW.

Me with my new set of Pearl Drums in our Practice Room 1960

Me with my new Premier Drums

Any of us who took a drink would make our way to the 56 Bar (now Egan's) or the Royal Hotel (now Sally O'Brien's) and wait for Martin to pick us up. The band was playing great stuff then and we were popular all over. That old Arklow gentleman, Mr. Laurence O'Toole, was very proud of us and told me so on many occasions. Mr. McNamara, manager of the Bank of Ireland, often joined us in the 56 Bar and he would want to know where we were playing that night and the night before and where at the weekend - a lovely man. I always thought it was grand to see folk of that era interested in us ... a crowd of young lads out for a night's playing. It made me feel good.

Looking back on it now, those few jars we used to have while waiting for Martin to collect us produced some great stories in themselves. I remember one evening, while waiting in the Royal Hotel with Eamon and Michael Gilmore, who used to come and play with us on occasion, a man and his entourage came in for a break and a drink. We quickly discovered it was Roy Orbison, who was on the way to perform in Waterford. When we introduced ourselves as bandsmen, he proceeded to buy us all a drink and was quite cordial. If he had been looking for a drummer, I was gone.

Johnny McEvoy, who was only starting out on the road at that time, often asked us to let him get up and do a spot, but the answer was always "No". Anyway he made the big-time without our help - fair play.

Val Doonican, a young lad from Waterford, performed a few songs in the Tara Ballroom in Courtown during the summer. Before he arrived, we learned that he stayed in the hotel for free, provided he helped out in the kitchen and they paid him £5 a week.

As I mentioned earlier, the showband phenomenon was just starting in the late fifties. Bill Haley, Fats Domino and Elvis Presley were leading the way internationally. Their style of music /dance was not yet being fully welcomed by the established ballroom managements/owners. A lot of proprietors were afraid they would corrupt the young dancers, so only the brave owners, or perhaps the ones who saw the lucrative aspect, stepped out in front and took a chance on booking the new showbands.

Peter Redmond of the Tara Ballroom was one person who embraced the new culture, but with a certain amount of caution. He was the person who really gave us the break that put us on the road to success. After booking us on chance a few times, thanks to Pete Coburn's hard work, he liked us and offered the residency for the summer season in 1960. This meant playing six nights a week Tuesdays to Sundays. Monday was the Irish night in the ballroom with a traditional group.

In winning the residency, credit must also go to a most unlikely person to be associated with the band, and I'm sure unknown to a lot of people. This was my good friend and work colleague in the Arklow Pottery at the time, Paddy Lafferty, who was manager of the Clay-End. When we started the Red Seven, I used to bore Paddy in work every day about how it was doing and speculated how we could get more bookings and recognition. He listened with interest and, when I posed the question of how we might convince Peter Redmond that we would stick the pace in the residency slot for the whole summer season in the Tara Ballroom, he offered to help. He went to see Peter Redmond and discussed the possibility. After many visits and coaxing by Paddy, much to our surprise, Peter took us on for the months of July and August for £80 a week. That was Paddy's only involvement with the band and he was very happy to do it, particularly when we went on to be so successful. All the band members were indebted to him at the time.

Because the Tara Ballroom was one of the premier dance halls on the east coast outside Dublin we got great exposure. In the summer time, literally thousands of people stayed in Courtown and surrounding areas like Tara Hill, Riverchapel, Ballymoney, Gorey, Ardamine, Ballygarrett and as far down the coast as Kilmuckridge.

It was not long before the ballroom and entertainment writers in the national papers were commenting on the new fresh showband from Arklow. So popular were we as the resident showband in the Tara Ballroom that one night, when the Clipper Carlton were playing there the leader, Hugo Quinn, came into the bar after we had finished playing and asked us to go back on for a while as the crowd were asking for us. We naturally agreed and I got up on stage slightly inebriated to start playing again ... and as I sat down I swayed forward and fell over the drums with a crash and bang of the cymbals. You can imagine my embarrassment ... Mick Hanlon, the drummer, was less than pleased!

I remember that the biggest crowd we ever played to, when I was in the band, was in Courtown on St. Stephen's night in 1960, when we played to seventeen hundred and fifty people. There was no standing room in the hall. There was an alcohol drinks extension in the bar until one a.m., and there was not one bit of trouble, either inside or outside the hall.

We were the first band in Ireland to play a residency standing on stage. Playing the summer season was brilliant. I had no drums to haul about night after night, and the band could leave the gear rigged up as well. The line-up was Larry Kenny (trumpet), Joe Weadick (trombone), Paud O'Brien (sax/clarinet), Pat Tyrrell (piano/vocals), Eamon Lee (guitar), Des Mulhall (drums), Pete Coburn (lead vocalist). What a band. The big mistake we made was, we didn't realise how good we were. I'd say we were in the top three in Ireland at the time. We got numerous offers to go professional, but the boys declined on every occasion. If we had gone down that road, where would we be today?

Pete, I believe, was one of the best singers in the country and his rendering of Roy Orbison's 'Only the Lonely' was a big hit with the crowd. We would be requested to play it two or three times in a night. Courtown was really buzzing then, with a real holiday atmosphere and the girls were lovely. It was my favourite gig. Peter Redmond was a bit worried about the transition from ballroom orchestra to showband so he insisted on a pianist. We had no problem with that as Pat played piano. But then Peter thought a double bass would look good to remind the dancers of the old days. Peter was such a gentleman, how could we refuse him? So, Pete bought one. It cost £29.10.0. Pete Coburn plucked it and spun it and spun it again. I'm sure Pete would agree he got great enjoyment out of that double bass. I wonder how much you would pay for it today. Pete called it his little baby.

Then there was Michael Gilmore, one of our seafaring friends from Arklow. Michael was an outstanding guitar player and was a great fan of the band. He loved to travel with us to Courtown when he was home in Arklow on holiday. During the break he would get up and entertain the crowd with the No.1 hits made famous by the Shadows, the Avengers and Bert Weedon. Duane Eddy's 'Forty Miles of Bad Road' was the most popular hit with the crowd. Well done, Mick.

Michael formed his own group in Arklow - The Swinging Sailors. They entertained in the Centre on Sunday afternoons and other gigs. They also played aboard ship when away at sea. George Kinch (a great pal of mine) played drums. Michael's twin brother Colin (r.i.p.) played rhythm guitar, Michael, of course, was on lead guitar and Eamon Lee helped out on bass. They were good.

Now that we were on the road, we had to dress properly. We bought our first set of seven tailor-made blazers from Tony Cannon, who owned a drapery shop in Main Street at the time ... do you remember? They worked out at £5.5.0 each - that came to £36.15.0. Hope you understand this currency. We then replaced the blazers with seven red suits we bought from George O'Toole at £5.15.0. each, which came to a total of £40.5.0.

Our next suits were a very professional job. Louis Copeland had only just opened a shop in Capel Street in Dublin with show people in mind. We got measured and fitted with him. The suits were wine coloured with a silver lapel and dickie-bows. I really looked snazy. Louis' shop became famous after, as most of the showbands went to him for gear. Today, Louis still runs the shop and has a national reputation for men's style-wear and contributes regularly on related programmes in the media particularly radio.

As you might already have gathered that Peter Redmond, while a true gentleman, was also a true businessman. One very famous funny story about Peter was related by himself when he told us that the parish priest of Riverchapel asked him to refrain from having any dances during the mission. Peter took out a piece of paper and wrote down the amount he would take in on the dances and eventually came up with a figure of £1000. He handed the piece of paper to the priest and said there would be no problem in cancelling the dances during the mission provided he was reimbursed with the £1000 loss. Needless to say, Peter did not have to cancel any dance then and was never asked to cancel a dance again.

Another funny story, this time showing how honest our band members were, also involved Peter Redmond in Courtown. One night, when I was jokingly getting on to Pat Tyrrell for sitting on a torn stool at the piano, I put my hand in under the hole/tear on the seat and discovered, much to my astonishment, £36 hidden there wrapped up. It was a lot of money at that time. £8 would have been about the average industrial weekly wage. We decided to give the money to Peter Redmond who looked very surprised when told where it was found, but he swiftly took it and thanked us. We often wondered did he plant it there to test us, but we will never know now.

I doubt it, because I do believe he was genuine and trusted us. Peter gave us the door takings on our last night. Our farewell dance.

Mentioning Pat Tyrrell reminds me of the many funny incidents he was involved in with us - always game for a laugh. Like the night he got out of the wagon at Woodenbridge at 4 a.m. in the morning on the way home from a dance to let Leo McHugh out and he had his band suit on inside out!

Dancing with Paul Jones

THE SUMMER BAND MOVES HAVE STARTED

LEADER OF THE BAND

JACK FLAHIVE

OLYMPIC

"MY old man said 'follow the band'," So went an old music-hall favourite and so, indeed, went young Jack Flahive who, at the age of 12, started playing the clarinet under the watchful eye of his father and who has since graduated to the Olympic Ballroom in Pleasants Street, where he leads a 10-piece orchestra with two vocalists.

FOLLOWING the band was no hard task for Jack Flahive, because his father was the late John Flahive, conductor of the No. 2 Army Band. Starting with the clarinet, young Jack was soon making quite a name for himself. Having joined the Dublin Postal Brass and Reed Band at the age of 14, we find him winning a gold medal at the Feis Ceoil in 1931.

HE played his first gig on the sax at Christmas of the same year and the following year joined a small group called the Lyricals, the pianist being Charlie Nutty. Charlie formed his own band in 1934 and Jack Flahive was his lead alto until the urge to form a group of his own proved too strong for him.

IN December, 1942, he decided it was time to

THE Coming of the Swallow, they say, heralds the Summer. But the comings and goings of Dance Bands in the Summertime would put any swallow to shame. The boys continue to eat up the miles by combining work with holidays.

Coming—the Victor Sylvester TV and recording orchestra directed by Victor Sylvester, Junior, to do a series of one-night stands from July 6 to 17. They play in Oldcastle, Ballybunion, Cork, Bray, Dundalk, Ruskey, Galway, Moate, Droichead Nua and Dublin.

Coming—top rock 'n' roll singer Vince Eager. Vince, 6 feet 4 inch 'teenage star, is flying here with his group from Blackpool for a special one-night stand at the Pavilion Ballroom, Blackrock, Dundalk. Rock 'n' roll fans need no reminding of this boy's appearances on such TV programmes as 6.5 Special, Wham and Drum Beat.

First tour

Going to Britain, the Melochords Showband on their first tour. This hard-working eight-man outfit has been climbing steadily to the top in little over a year. They play the North of England for the first week, with visits to Sheffield, Northampton, Manchester, Leeds, Birmingham and Liverpool, and London for the second week.

If this tour is attended with anything akin to the success of their Waterford visit of a few weeks ago, then they can really claim to have made it, and can look forward with confidence to a proposed American tour next year.

Lily Fitzpatrick—singing with the Paddy Kearns

sive renovations, to-night. The resident group here is the Red Seven Orchestra from Arklow, a versatile outfit, who have already proved themselves with Co. Wexford dancers.

The Red Seven—resident at Courtown.

Owner Peter Redmond plans to run six dances per week here, the exception being Monday. Peter, who has years of experience in the dance business, believes in giving his patrons value, hence his line-up (for two-band sessions) of the Royal Showband, the Clipper Carlton, Dunny and Singleton.

Jazzman

To the Top Hat, Dun Laoire, to-morrow night comes Humphrey Lyttleton. As a jazzman Lyttleton has few peers. As a commercial success, he is the first person to have edged a jazz record into the hit parade.

On record his music sells almost half a million copies every year. It should be a "real gone" night at the Top Hat.

The Saints All Stars play the Pavilion Ballroom, Westport, to-morrow. Playing in the Central Ballroom, Charlestown, Co. Mayo, to-morrow

night is the Dave Dixon U.T.V. Orchestra from Clones.

In town

TOP HAT, to-night, House Dance; to-morrow, Humphrey Lyttelton and his band; Wednesday, Fine Gael (Gearoid O'Sullivan Branch); Friday, Drumcondra F.C. Dance, a two-band show with Gay McIntyre and the resident orchestra.

THE CRYSTAL on Wednesday is the venue for another of those successful E.S.B. Swimming Club Dances.

MAYFAIR, Clondalkin: Earl Gill puts in an appearance here to-night.

KINGSWAY, to-night, two-band show, with Chick Smith and Charlie Nutty. Wednesday, a gay holiday dance.

OLYMPIC, to-night: Gay

IERNE, to-night, has Syd Shine, Athlone, paying a return visit; on Thursday as usual, the Altonaires.

FOUR PROVINCES, to-night: Gala Holiday Dance. To-morrow: Another Holiday Dance and Noel Coade presents the winners of the "Search for a Star" Contest—Miss Marie Kennedy and Owen Devine, both of whom won £100 last Sunday. Thursday: The Blue Clavons.

NATIONAL BALLROOM programme for the coming week: To-night and to-morrow, House Dances. Monday, Special Holidaymakers' Dance. Tuesday, the Galwegians. Wednesday, Westerns Social. Thursday, Caritas Social Club. Friday, Kerrymen's Association.

The sincerity and thoughtfulness - or otherwise - of some of the famous touring artists during our time on the road was always a talking point among bandsmen. One example of genuine warmth we experienced was one night in Knockananna when we performed there with the popular Maisie McDaniels who was touring Ireland at the time. Two men from the mountains arrived when the dance was over, because their car had broken down. They were extremely disappointed and when Maisie, who was getting ready to leave, heard this she sat on the stage and sang to them for half an hour. That's true show business.

Another great episode in the band was the tax man. He was after us, but Pete kept him at bay for months and months. I always said Pete handled it admirably but, in the end, we all ended up paying a small amount. Account settled.I was sure we would turn professional, but any time I mentioned it I only got a so-so response. Wouldn't it have been great on the road full-time. We were good, but we could have been great ... aaahhh ... it wasn't to be.

Every town, village and hamlet had a dance hall (or a hall they ran dances in) in those days. Some were named ballrooms and others they just called 'the hall'. I'd like to mention a few we played in. Adamstown, Ferns, Kilmuckridge, Glen-O-The-Downs, Glenealy, Bunclody, Bagenalstown, Dunlavin, Rathnure, Tara Ballroom (Courtown), Curracloe, Kilanerin, Mayfair (Kilkenny), Rathangan, Arcadia (Bray), Johnstown, Inch, Pallas, Knockananna, Carlton (Kilkenny), Screen, Marlborough Hall, Ormonde, The Entertainment Centre, Avoca, Wicklow, Ashford. Some great nights in that lot, I can tell you.

I was determined to go further. One day in June 1961, I decided to give in my notice in the Pottery. They said they were sorry to see me go - of course they were. It took three to replace me. The right opportunity came along soon afterwards. I got a job with the Jack Ruane Showband from Ballina. Jack had been a professional musician, on the road all his life. I was on the road again ... my ambition fulfilled. I really enjoyed the years with the Red Seven. We had plenty of laughs and the girls were beautiful. After fifty years, we still talk about it as if it was yesterday. Remember, it's not the miles that you travel in life – it's the stops that you make along the way.

Here I am still swinging … this time with the Swing Kings (2008)

The Avonsiders 1970
Left to Right: Des Mulhall, Jimmy McManus, Paddy Delaney, Dermot O'Connor, Paddy Coleman (r.i.p.)

Des at his surprise 70th birthday party 2009 with Pete Coburn, Joe Weadick and Dermot Greene (son of Sylvester Greene, sax player extraordinaire of the fifties).

Chapter 4 *Larry Kenny*

Music was a passion of mine from a very early age, even though there was no strong musical tradition in my family background. However, my mother was very good at playing the mouth organ in her young days, a popular instrument at the time, so I have always believed her love of music inspired me, and indeed two of my brothers who also got involved in playing music. I remember when I was about ten years old, I used to love singing the popular songs of the day, not that I thought I was a good singer, but I suppose it was the way the love of music manifested itself in me. My favourite song at the time was 'Danny Boy'. That was in the late forties when the majority of the community, including my parents, were finding it hard to make ends meet, so even if I wanted to play some sort of instrument there wasn't the money to buy one. Remember, World War II only finished in 1945 and most European countries were still in financial straits. Food was in very short supply – butter and tea were still being rationed in Ireland.

My first opportunity to learn to play a musical instrument was at the age of fourteen, when I was lucky enough to be accepted as a member of the Arklow Pipe Band. I had been following the band for some time and listening to them practise in the old band hall on the South Quay. The late John O'Brien and Jimmy Fortune were the band's principal tutors from whom I quickly learned to play the pipes. I remember well the first time I was allowed to march out with the band. It was 'An Tostal' celebrations in 1952 – and I was as proud as punch.

Playing in the Arklow Pipe Band, while very enjoyable, was soon not enough for me. This I realised one night when I was invited to the 21st birthday party of my late friend Sandie Pierce. It happened that Joe Horan, who was the trumpet player in the recently formed Arklow jazz group, The Blue Notes, was invited to play at it. Joe played 'Blueberry Hill' and I was so impressed that I went home that night determined that I was going to get a trumpet somehow and learn it – yes, it was the instrument for me.

Remembering that party night, I must tell you an unrelated very funny musical incident that occurred at it which still makes me smile to this day when I think of it. Those of you who knew the legendary violin player, the late Mick Cullen of Liam Mellows Avenue (father of the very popular Mick Cullen, leader of the Céile Band), will appreciate his quick wit. He arrived at the party, after the pubs closed, to play a few tunes on his violin. Joe Horan decided to join in the session with Mick and blew a note on the trumpet to check if they were in tune. Joe said to Mick "bring her down a bit". Mick loosened the relevant string on the violin a little and played it. Joe said "down another bit" which Mick did obediently - all the time checking the tuning. Still Joe was not happy and asked Mick to go down another bit. By this time, Mick had enough and got off his chair, sat down on the floor and said to Joe "is this low enough for ye". After a few more *'choice'* words, they called a truce and played great stuff together late into the night, to the joy of all those present.

That party night also awoke in me the love of modern dance music and, from then on, I took every opportunity to listen to the dance bands playing in the Ormonde Ballroom - outside the main door as I did not have the money to pay in. The late Billy Cullen, who was the ballroom manager, got used to seeing me there and took pity on me as he knew I was interested in playing music. He let me in every dance night to sit and listen for the whole performance at the back of the hall.

It was the era of orchestras and Arklow was one of the foremost towns on the east coast for ballroom dancing. There was at least one dance every week in the Ormonde and also one in the Mayfair Ballroom, just across the road from the Ormonde. In the summertime, there were dances almost every night, as Arklow would be thronged with holidaymakers. Remember, foreign holidays were practically non-existent for the ordinary man or woman at the time and places like Bray, Arklow, Courtown, Wexford and Tramore were very popular with Dublin people for summer holidays, and ballroom dancing was the main pastime.

So anxious was I to get a trumpet that I could not wait to save up the full price. I decided to get one on the "Never Never" (that is through hire purchase for those of you ex-Celtic Tigers who might not understand). I bought it from the then only Irish mail order company that I knew - Cott's of Kilcock. I had to pay something like a half crown per week (equivalent to about sixteen cents for those of you too young to know), for about three years. The day it arrived in the post I was so excited that I couldn't put it down. My father, God rest him (who's patience almost ran out listening to the weird sounds I was making with the trumpet), asked an ex-member of the old Arklow Brass Band, the late Martin Walsh, to give me a few lessons. Thanks to Martin I progressed very well.

In 1954-55, I got my first opportunity to play with a dance band. It was Jimmy Jordan's band from Rathdrum. He was looking for a trumpet player and a friend of my family, Peter Lee, told him about me, so I got the job. Much to my surprise, he handed me a lovely Besson trumpet. It was far superior to mine and I was always grateful to him for it. At the time, the famous Eddie Calvert played a Besson - he had a big international hit with "Oh Mien Papa".

In 1956, I got an opportunity to play with the renowned Jay Byrne dance band from Glenealy. Jay, who died in the eighties, was very popular throughout the county. I gained great experience during the short time I was with him. In 1957, I joined Mark Canavan's band from Avoca, by which time I was fairly competent on the trumpet. Mark was also well known and respected in dance halls throughout Wicklow and Wexford. With him, I was fortunate to play a wide variety of ballroom music, which has stood to me to this day.

By October 1959, most members of Mark's band were from Arklow including the lead singer Pete Coburn, who was in fact running the band as Mark was going through a bout of illness. At the time, there was a new phenomenon emerging throughout the country in the dance business. Rock'n' Roll was all the rage and Irish showbands were coming on the scene, following in the footsteps of bands like the Clipper Carlton showband from Derry, which was in the forefront of this new rage. Instead of the dance bands/orchestras culture whereby members sat down, played reading music in a very formal way, the new idea resulted in showbands abandoning their chairs, standing throughout their performance and moving rhythmically to the music. This brought a new feature to the entertainment of dancers and was quickly catching on throughout Ireland.

We, the Arklow lads (Pete Coburn, Paud O'Brien, Pat Tyrrell, the late Eamon Lee, Des Mulhall, Joe Weadick and myself), had a chat about this new fresh approach and decided that we should form our own showband and go with the times. This decision was no reflection on the culture of

Mark's band, which was still the norm in most places, and remained so for a few years after. So we started practising separately in the autumn of 1959, while still playing in Mark's band.

I remember we got invaluable help with arrangements for songs and instrumental pieces from the late Seán Bonner. Seán was a young teacher at the time in Arklow Boys National School, but in his spare time he was also very involved in everything musical in the town, including the Marian Arts Society. He was a brilliant pianist and had a sharp musical mind. He used to invite us up to his house on occasion to practise and, apart from what we learned musically from him, the general craic was mighty – he was a great wit and had yarns to beat the band – forgive the pun! He was a great mentor to us all. We all loved him and have many happy memories of him.

In January 1960, we considered we had enough of a repertoire to start our own new band, so we finally called it a day with Mark and commenced playing under our new name, The Red Seven Showband. I don't remember how we arrived at naming the band, but I do believe it was decided in Seán Bonner's house.

Our new showband was very well received and, with the hard work of Pete, who we voted to look after the bookings, we quickly got good and regular engagements. By May 1960, we had landed the residency for the summer season in the Tara Ballroom, Courtown, one of the most important dancing venues on the east coast outside Dublin.

It meant playing six nights a week during July and August. The dances went on from 9 till 2 a.m., on Wednesdays and Sundays and on these nights there was always top visiting showbands. We normally started the dance and they came on from about ten-thirty and had another break around midnight when we played again for a half hour. The visiting band would then come back on to finish the night. These showbands included the Clipper Carlton from Derry, the Royal from Waterford, the Capitol from Dublin, the Dixies from Cork and the Black Aces from Kilkenny. It's fair to say that we competed very well with all of them and generally got very positive reaction during our performances.

The season in Courtown really established us on the Wicklow/Wexford circuit. This trend continued in 1961 when we succeeded in getting half the summer season residency in Courtown (the month of July), and at a significantly higher fee, thanks to shrewd negotiating by Pete with the proprietor Peter Redmond. Because of our increasing popularity and professionalism, serious thought was given in 1961 to going full time. Paud O'Brien was not in favour of the idea and was the first person to leave the band. He had just got married and was not interested in leaving his permanent job - and he did not want to stand in the way of the success of the group. Pat Tyrrell, who had been playing piano up to that time, had also learned to play the saxophone, so he took over Paud's job.

As the guitar sound in showbands was getting ever more popular, we decided we needed someone to play lead guitar alongside Eamon, who was essentially a rhythm guitar player and vocalist. The name Freddy Cutland was mentioned as a person who was pretty handy on a guitar. Des and I were designated to talk to him. Freddy, who had played for a short time with Mark Canavan, was very interested and joined with us in June 1961. He proved to be an excellent player, a committed member and a great addition to the band. He was brilliant at playing the Shadows guitar solos that were big international hits. The Shadows were, of course, the backing group for Cliff Richard, who was becoming world famous at the time with hits like 'Living Doll'. Pete sang that song magnificently in the Red Seven when it came out and it was often requested two or three times in a night.

Des, who was very eager to go professional, got itchy feet in 1961. With no decision forthcoming from us, he got an opportunity to join Jack Ruane's Orchestra. He was the second original band member to leave, and he did so with our very best wishes. He played with that band for three years, before calling it a day in the business. Des, when leaving the Red Seven, was happy that his protégé, George Byrne, would be quite capable of taking his place in the band.

George had been taught to play the drums by Des and, when he joined the band, at the age of sixteen, he was the youngest showband drummer in Ireland. Because of his small stature, he looked even younger than his age. George stayed with the band to the end and is still playing professionally to the present day.

In 1961, I started having trouble with my teeth and was finding it difficult to maintain a good sound on the trumpet, so I decided that I would have to eventually change onto a saxophone and clarinet, if I wanted to continue playing music. I remember going to Walton's Musical Instrument Shop in Dublin to look at instruments with Des and, while trying out some of the saxophones, a young, now famous player, Paddy Cole, happened to be in the shop and got talking to us. After telling him the story, he advised me to learn the clarinet first and when I got used to it, moving onto the sax would not be a problem. He said that if I learned the sax first I would not automatically be able to play the clarinet. Needless to say, that on the day I hadn't a penny in my pocket to buy anything. However, taking Paddy's sound advice, I managed, eventually, to gather the money to purchase a clarinet and later a sax.

Finding someone to teach me the clarinet was a bit of a problem. As it happened, Des was dating the daughter of the late Garda Kane from Gorey, who in his spare time was the conductor in the Gorey Brass Band. He agreed to give me a few lessons on the clarinet. This was a great help and it was not long before I got the hang of it.

I was determined to continue to improve my playing and reading, so I decided to do a six-month course in the Royal Academy of Music, Westland Row, Dublin, even though I realised that getting to the classes was not going to be easy. Travelling to and from Dublin once a week was a major problem, as I did not have a car. In order to get to my lessons on time (7 p.m.) I had to go straight from work at the Arklow Pottery at five o'clock, without time to get a meal at home. I depended on lifts every week or use the bus. Sometimes my brother John would give me a lift on the back of his scooter and I can tell you that on a winter's night I was freezing by the time I got to Dublin. I did not have the right protective clothing for such a journey. Yes, it was an ordeal but, in the end, it was worth the sacrifice, because I became very proficient at reading music and playing both the clarinet and sax.

In the autumn of 1961, Pete Coburn decided to leave the band because he, too, was not interested in going professional. This was a big blow to us, as Pete was a popular and exceptional singer and was greatly missed by all of us - and our fans. His rendition of songs like 'Only the Lonely', 'Danny Boy' and 'Special Angel' were showstoppers and put us on a par with the best showbands in the country. Pete's decision was mainly due to work and family commitments. While we were all devastated by his decision, we understood and wished him every success for the future.

With Pete leaving, we needed a good replacement vocalist to maintain our popularity. This was not easy in a small town like Arklow, but after auditioning a few people we brought in Paddy Merrigan from Kilahurler, who had a good voice, but he only stayed with us for a very short time as he decided the showband business was not for him. After Paddy left, we tried out Jimmy McManus for a while, but he was a bit young. Eventually another talented singer, Eddie McElheron, was available and interested. Eddie had a softer voice and was excellent at country & western numbers and ballads. He proved to be a valuable addition to the band and progress continued. Progress also continued in my personal life in 1961 as I got married to the love of my life Lil, who unfortunately passed away in 2008, God rest her, after a long and happy life together.

I continued playing the trumpet but we were always on the lookout for another trumpet player who would eventually take over from me. We were very lucky to hear about a man called Leo McHugh, an engineer working in the Avoca Mines. Leo, a Sligo native and a gentleman, was very interested in playing jazz and was delighted to come on board. He only stayed with us from October 1961 to May 1962, as he left the mines to work in Dublin. So, for a period we had two trumpets in the band and could do some lovely trumpet solos and duets, which was a great boost to the band. He also made a great contribution in the jazz numbers. They always went down well. 'Hiawatha Rag' was one of his favourite showpieces.

Jim Tyrrell, Pat's brother, joined the band to replace Leo McHugh on trumpet and he also doubled on vocals. Shortly after Jim arrived, Eamon Lee decided to leave for personal reasons. My brother James was brought in on bass guitar (and vocals) but only stayed for a very short while and he was replaced by Pat and Jim's brother Michael on bass guitar/vocals.

Towards the end of 1962, I too decided to leave because the boys were still very strong on going professional, and I did not want to make a full time career of it. I must say, I had enjoyed the band immensely and knew when leaving that I would miss playing with the boys and the craic that went with it. I have many happy memories of the three years with the band – as well as a few unhappy ones – which I share with you here.

Playing in the Tara Ballroom was always a pleasure for me. There was such a holiday party atmosphere there and we were extremely popular with the dancers. However, I remember one of the owners, Mr. Lennon (Peter Redmond's brother-in-law), nearly always had a sour face on when he visited the ballroom on the big nights. His wife would be with him and she used to ring us up on the bandstand (a phone on the bandstand for giving messages to the band for announcements to the dancers was a facility I never saw anywhere else, even to this day) and complain about the music being too loud. Of course, we would agree to turn the sound down but we never did. Because her husband was such a dour individual, we christened him 'summer', and every time he came into the ballroom I used to start playing the tune 'Here Comes Summer'. Pete got very worried about this after a while, because he was concerned our contract might be terminated if Lennon realised what was happening, so reluctantly I decided to refrain.

I remember one night when we were playing before the Royal Showband came on in Courtown, Michael Coppinger was looking and listening to us playing 'Z Cars'. He spoke to me after the show and complimented the arrangement and our playing of it. He said he was interested in recording it for their use. I believe it was one of the tunes that Seán Bonner arranged for us.

Again in Courtown, I was unfortunate to have an accident on stage when one of the lads accidentally hit against me when I was playing, causing my trumpet to split my lip badly. The ballroom proprietor Peter Redmond brought me in to Dr. Nixon in Gorey to have it stitched. I was out of action for a week because of it.

I'm sure many bands would have plenty of stories about electrics in dance halls throughout the country. I was the one who would normally set up the amplification and when I asked the manager of a small country hall where we were preparing to play, "Where are the sockets?" he just pointed to two bare wires hanging down on the stage. Needless to say, I had to do a major job on them to make everything safe.

Our contract minibus driver, the late legendary Martin Byrne, was obsessed with money matters. His famous answer whenever we gave out about having to pay income tax was 'ye should be happy that ye are earning enough money to pay income tax, dee ye see?" That used to shut us up pretty quickly. We often had girls travelling with us to and from the dances. Either girlfriends of some of the boys or fans. Someone (who shall remain anonymous) decided to christen the minibus the 'Passion Wagon' - not that much went on in it to warrant such a title, but Martin being very reserved was none-too-happy. Writing about Martin and money reminds me that in 1962, because we were going so well, we decided we could afford to buy our own minibus. Much to Martin's disappointment, not just because he was going to lose the business, but I believe he really enjoyed the whole music road-show and our company.

Having our own transport was a great advantage in one way, but it had its risks too. Especially when we decided that we should take turns in driving, rather than pay a non-band member. We never did have an accident, thank God, but we did have a major scare. We were returning home after playing in Barry's Hotel in Rathdrum after a Sunday night dance in September 1962 (at 4 a.m.). I remember it was an All Ireland football or hurling final day, because Freddy and Eddie came to the dance direct from Dublin after attending the match and they were driving behind us on the way home.

Joe was driving the minibus. It was a wet night and the road was greasy. As we rounded the sharp bends before the descent to the Meetings of the Waters, the left front wheel caught the grass margin. The minibus went out of control and veered across the road, hitting the grass margin on the other side, at which time Joe somehow managed to get it under control again. He straightened it up and stopped. During the swerving of the bus, the offside front door opened and George, who was sitting at it, was being thrown out with the momentum, but I was quick enough to grab him and pull him in. I was sitting in the middle between Joe and George. Freddy and Eddie, coming behind, observed the back wheels of the minibus jumping off the ground. All the band gear, which was stored in the compartment behind the back seat came down on top of Michael and Pat who were sitting in the back. Needless to say, we were all pretty shaken. I offered to drive the rest of the way home, but Joe insisted he was fine and we got home safely.

It's interesting to note that the dance that night started at 10 p.m. and finished at 3.a.m. Five hours playing was regular in Rathdrum in those days. And that was on a Sunday night when people had to get up for work early the next day, and there was always a bar extension there. Nowadays, it's hard to get a band to play two hours.

I remember we got another big scare one night driving home from Cork, when we met a truck coming towards us on the wrong side of the road. The driver managed to get to his own side just in time. He didn't stop so we never did find out why he did it, we reckoned he must have been tired and started to doze off.

One of the most embarrassing moments I remember when playing was in the Arcadia in Bray, when we came on after the resident orchestra. We were using their amplification for handiness rather than take the time to set up our own. Because they had just finished playing we were happy that the mics were set up properly. However, when we started to play the sound was all over the place and it took us a while to get it right – you can imagine how we all felt as we obviously wanted to create a big impression with our first number. We learned a very dear lesson that night – never trust another band's equipment, use your own! We were satisfied that we were sabotaged by someone in the resident band. It was deeply embarrassing and did not do us any good with either the ballroom management or the dancers. Generally amongst bandsmen there was great camaraderie and, in our experience, the majority were most helpful, but unfortunately you will always get a few bad apples.

I know that there are many more interesting stories to tell of my time with the Red Seven, if I could think of them, but I hope you enjoyed the few I related.

Looking back fifty years to the era of the showbands and my involvement in the Red Seven, I have to say it was a most memorable and exciting time for me. I often wonder how things would have played out had I stayed and gone professional. But life goes on and I continued to play with many local bands and groups since then and, to this day, I still love every minute of it.

The bands I played over the years with since the Red Seven Showband included the Avonaires, Harbour Lights, Elite, Brass Tacks, East Coast Jazz Band, Rhythm and Blues, All Stars and the Larry Kenny Trio to name but a few.

Photo taken in Tara Ballroom, Courtown 1960 wearing our summer season residency red jackets and white slacks with No 7 in red on the pockets.

Brass Tacks 1988
Larry Kenny, Bobby Byrne, Liam Garrett

Larry with his late wife Lil at his surprise 'This Your Life' presentation in 2000.
Joe Weadick with the Red Book and Helen Plummer of the Echos
who attended to honour Larry, giving an eloquent speech for the occasion.

East Coast Jazz Band 2000
Standing: Peter Power, John Joe Brauders, Bobby Byrne.
Sitting: Larry Kenny, Gerry McDonald.

Larry moonlighting in Noblett's Pub, Wicklow Gap about 1970

Chapter 5

Paud O'Brien

I was born into a musical family where there was a tradition of violin playing and performance in local musicals, in particular the renowned Arklow Marian Arts Society.

For many young Arklow men and women, looking for a social outlet in the depressed late forties/early fifties, the Marian Arts Society was the organisation to be in. I, like my brothers Eamon, Dave, Thady and sisters Maureen, Elizabeth and Noreen joined. I mostly took part in the chorus line but, from time to time, had small parts to play.

Like my brothers and sisters, I had learned to play the violin to some degree and when a new Arklow group called the Blue Notes started rehearsing jazz type music in the early fifties, I got interested and joined them; playing my violin in the style of a banjo rather than the traditional way and doing some backing singing. The line up was Joe Horan on trumpet, the late Gerry Fennell on piano, Joe McDonald on drums, the late Colin Wolohan on double bass/vocals and Stafford Murray on trombone.

As the group was following the jazz scene rather than the "Ballroom of Romance" type music, they were very keen to have a clarinet player. I was so taken up with the set-up that I volunteered to buy a clarinet and learn it for the sake of the group. In other words, I got hooked on the music.

In those days, for the ordinary person to have a car, or even access to one, to travel to Dublin to peruse the musical instrument shops for a clarinet was almost out of the question on economic grounds, and it was also difficult to get the time and money to avail of the infrequent buses or trains. Not to mention the difficulty for one who was not used to traversing the city, even if one got to Dublin. Taking all this into account, I made a visit to Owens shop in the Main Street, Arklow, where I knew some instruments were on sale and reckoned I might get information about clarinets.

Mr. Owens was very helpful and, on his next visit to Dublin, he brought back information for me and asked if I wanted a Simple clarinet or a Bb clarinet. I, not knowing anything about clarinets, quickly said the Simple clarinet, as I assumed it would be the easiest to learn and bought one shortly after on the "never never". However, the Simple clarinet turned out to be the more difficult one to learn, but I persevered and learned to play it with great help from the late Tommy Costello of the Wexford Road, who had one time been in the Army Band and who was very knowledgeable about instruments.

The Blue Notes took off about 1955, but the band was not as successful as they might have been due to the fact that they did not play much of the traditional ballroom dance music. Their jazz beat did not go down too well with the locals. However I, having struggled to perfect the clarinet, went on to play with the popular Kevin Harper Avoca band. I became really confident and ambitious and then bought - and mastered - a saxophone, which was a very popular musical instrument in the "Ballrooms of Romance" at the time. In 1957, I joined three other Arklow men, Pete Coburn vocalist, Larry Kenny trumpeter and Eamon Lee guitarist, in the well known Mark Canavan band from Avoca. I continued to improve my playing and all went very well with Mark, a gentleman, and the band until the autumn of 1959. In the meantime, Pat Tyrrell had come into the band playing piano. Mark had been out sick for some months and was not expected back. Pete was running the band for him. Due to other changes and sickness problems in the band, Joe Weadick was brought in on trombone and Des Mulhall in on drums.

As all but the late Gerry Heaslip, piano accordian player, were from Arklow, we thought it more practical to break away from Mark and start our own band. Under the circumstances Gerry, a lovable and witty Wicklow man, and a brilliant piano accordian player, opted out. As the showband phenomenon had started in the country, we decided to go that road and eventually came up with the name The Red Seven Showband. I remember Eamon Lee, God rest him, worried that if we put a number on the name of the band we might be cut money if someone got sick and only six turned up to play the gig! The Red Seven Showband was an instant success, not only in the Arklow area but throughout counties Wexford, Carlow and Kilkenny. So much so that there was serious talk in 1961 of going professional. I had got married in September 1960 and was concerned about leaving my secure job in Brennan's Grocery. Regretfully, rather than stand in the way of the band's progress, I decided to let someone else take my place and left in the spring of 1961.

I say 'regretfully' because I really enjoyed the band and the success we had. It was, without doubt, the happiest time of my life and, even though it is fifty years ago, the many great memories still live on within me.

Among those memories were the many performances we gave to packed dance halls. With crowd-stopping songs like 'Boolavogue' and 'Danny Boy', particularly in Courtown, sung by Pete, who I believe was one of the best singers in Ireland at the time. Another crowd stopper was the performance by Pete and Pat Tyrrell of 'Doctor I'm in Trouble', apart from the singing, their mimicking and acting on stage was second to none and the dancers/audience always lapped it up. For those of you who may not know 'Doctor I'm in Trouble' it was sung and performed in the hit film *Millionairess* of the early sixties by Sophia Loren and Peter Sellers.

Anyone who is or was involved in dance bands will agree that there is nearly always great camaraderie amongst the members of the group. Part of the joy of being in a band is the experience and craic surrounding the business of practising and performing.

We did our practice in a room in John Sweeney's undertaking business on Ferrybank, beside where the Arklow Bay Hotel is now, which was a hospital at the time. To get to the practice room, we had to pass through the workroom, where the carpenter made the coffins and there was always a coffin on a stand being got ready for the next customer. One of the greatest pranks played in my band experience was when Des Mulhall got into the coffin and lay in wait for Pete Coburn to pass through the room on his way to practice. That room was always very dark and creepy looking anyway, particularly on a wintry night, which it was. Needless to say, when Pete arrived and was confronted with a rising, moaning body from the coffin as he passed through the dark room he almost had a heart attack. Never again did he go into that room alone.

One of the funniest events travelling to dances, looking back on it now, but not very funny at the time, was when we were late for a very important Fancy Dress Dance in Kilmore Quay, County Wexford, because we got two punctures on the way - the first not long after leaving Arklow. The second happened a mile from Wexford and, of course, we had no second spare tyre. This meant that a few of the lads had to walk some distance before reaching a garage that was good enough to mend it and bring it back. There weren't many cars on the road then, particularly on a winter's night, to stop and help. When we eventually arrived at the venue, we were met by crowds of people - mostly in fancy dress, walking away from the hall because the dance had been cancelled due to our non-arrival. You can imagine the scene with people dressed up in all sorts of outfits, deeply disappointed after all their trouble in preparing for the special dance and looking forward to hearing one of their favourite bands. On the one hand, we were met with cheers by the dancers who realised their special event was saved and, on the other hand, by a very angry committee who were just waiting to lash out at us for being late. You must remember, there were no mobile phones, or phones of any kind conveniently available to ring up and let the committee know what was happening.

In response to the members of the committee who were getting very vocal, and in some cases very abusive, our driver, the late Joe Kenny, who was a great character but a very emotional personality, got up on top of the Volkswagen van and started throwing the punctured tyre tubes down in the vicinity of the committee members. He got down and followed the chairman of the committee, who was not prepared to listen to any excuses, around the hall holding a burst tyre, which was in fact in ribbons, saying in a very high pitched animated voice ... 'IS THAT A PUNCTURE OR NOT - IS THAT A PUNCTURE OR NOT'? You can imagine the scene - at the same time the delighted dancers were pouring back into the hall past the ticket desk, grateful that their special night had been saved.

The epilogue to that story was, to the delight of the dancers, we played an extra hour and a half to make up for being late, and we gave the committee a free booking on an occasion of their choice.

I remember another very funny event for the band - and some dancers - which happened at a dance we played at in Knockananna, high up in the Wicklow hills. About half way through the dance, when things were really swinging, someone let go in the hall a live hare. You can imagine what happened - or can you? - the women screaming their heads off in fright and the men laughing their heads off. And we, the band, kept playing until one of the hall committee managed to direct the wild hare, which was literally going wild around the floor, out through the door.

The smallest hall I can remember playing in was in the townland of

Annagh near Ballyfad in County Wexford. We were hired for a community dance and they looked after us very well. The hall was full to capacity, with about one hundred people. When the dance was over we were very hungry as was usual, after playing for five hours (9-2), normal dance hours for Sunday nights, the main weekly dance night at the time. We were preparing our gear to go home and at the same time wondering what and where we were going to eat - particularly Pete! Next thing, the dance organiser tore down a curtain from the back of the stage and spread it out across the floor of the stage. He proceeded, with the help of some of the hall committee, to put out mugs and sandwiches on the curtain and called us all to dine. It was a sight to behold and an experience to cherish - the looks on our faces and the wisecracks uttered were hilarious. They must have been for me to remember them so vividly after fifty years. And I do remember that the sandwiches, cakes and tea were delicious, as was nearly always the case in country halls. You could not beat the women of the hall committees for feeding you.

The biggest and best laid out ballroom I remember playing in, when I was in the band, was the Mayfair or Carlton (I'm not sure which) in Kilkenny. The crowds were big and loved our music, and I particularly remember the girls were dressed immaculately. I believe there is still a Red Seven Dance poster in one of the lounges in Kilkenny after all these years. An Arklow person who saw it in recent years asked if he could buy it and was told categorically that it was not for sale.

One of my most embarrassing moments was when a valve stuck on my saxophone as I played the solo in 'Sail Along Silvery Moon'. It was a problem, I'm sure, that practically every sax, clarinet or trumpet player experienced some time in their career. All one could do was grin and bear it, and apologise at the end of the tune. Normally, the dancers understood but it did not stop some of the witty guys or girls shouting up with some funny or wisecrack remark like, "have you a screw loose" or "did the moon fall" ...

One of the most serious incidents I remember occurring during a performance was when the late Eamon Lee, in his enthusiasm, moving to the beat of the music on the stage, accidentally put one foot off it and was falling. I was next to him and was quick enough to grab and pull him back on, averting what would have been a catastrophe.

Finally, one of the most encouraging moments in my memory was on the second visit of the famous Clipper Carlton showband to Courtown in 1960, when we were the resident showband there. Speaking to us after the second occasion, they said that even though they thought we were good the first time they heard us only a few months previously, they agreed that on this occasion we were fantastic and really professional. At the time, these positive comments were a huge encouragement to us. And it showed how generous and genteel the Clippers were, a magnificent and extremely talented bunch of lads.

The Blue Notes - in the fifties
Left to Right: Paud O'Brien, Colin Gilmore, Stafford Murray, Gerry Fennell, Terry Horan and Joe McDonald.

The second of two original photos of the Red Seven Showband taken in Plunket's studio, Rathdrum in January 1960

Chapter 6 *Pat Tyrrell*

My introduction to music was primarily through my late Aunt Kathleen Tyrrell, who was an excellent pianist and a well-known piano teacher in Arklow in the fifties, sixties and seventies. She taught me the piano. She also taught my brothers Jim and Michael, who also eventually joined the band and who you will learn more about later in this book. We were very fortunate to have such a loving aunt and a great teacher. Our parents, God rest them, were very fortunate too in that my aunt would not take any money for the tuition for any of the five of us (sisters Margaret & Roisín) which was a great relief to them, because they would not have been able to afford it.

Perhaps my interest in music had also to do with the Arklow Marian Arts Society. My mother was very involved as a committee member and did some acting. Because of her interest in the society, it was only natural that I and most of my siblings also joined. I, too, did some acting in plays and pantomimes, and sang in the choruses.

The Marian Arts Society was a magnificent social outlet in the fifties, providing a platform for the talents of young people from the age of sixteen to the early twenties and beyond. At the time, there were very few other meaningful social activities in Arklow, particularly during the winter months. Great credit was due to the late Michael Gunson, who owned a shop beside the Bank of Ireland, for starting the society in 1941.

I started working in 1955, at the age of fifteen, as a trainee store man in the famous Arklow Pottery, now unfortunately long gone. While I continued playing the piano for pleasure at home, I did not get involved in any group or band until 1958. During that year, the renowned Avoca dance band owner Mark Canavan called to my house and asked me if I was interested in playing the piano in his band. Naturally, I was thrilled, because (a) the thought that someone of the calibre of Mark Canavan had heard about me as a piano player and wanted me to play with him was a great honour at my age, and (b) it meant making an extra few shillings a week, as they were then called.

Needless to say, I was very apprehensive because it was new to me and I did not know if I would be good enough; particularly when Mark explained that in some dance halls where he played there was no piano. Because of this, he wanted me to learn some tunes on his piano accordian (which he offered to lend me) so that I could play it if there was no piano available in the hall.

After considering the offer for a short time (a very short time!), I agreed to join. My fear of not being able for it was short lived as I had no difficulty playing the "Ballroom of Romance" type music of the era. And it did not take me too long to learn sufficient tunes on the piano accordian to justify my place in the band.

I remember vividly, one of the tunes I learned on the piano accordian was a popular quickstep at the time 'Whistling Rufus'. The first time I was stuck playing it on the piano accordian on stage was during an interval, when half the band went for a tea break and left the other half of us playing, as was the custom during dances at the time. Incidentally, in those days most dances went on for five hours and sometimes six.

I must have gone on playing the tune for about ten minutes because, not being used to playing solo for dancers and a bit nervous about making mistakes, I just did not know when to stop. I'm sure the good, fit dancers on the floor at the time were delighted - assuming they were also enjoying each other's company. But the not-so-fit couples, or maybe the not-so-good dancers - or maybe a poor guy who was giving a duty-dance to his mother-in-law or, worse still, his future mother-in-law, were probably furious and wondering when the hell I was going to stop. Did you ever get asked what tune do you hate most? I'd nearly bet there are still a few people alive today, fifty years on, who would say 'Whistling Rufus' on the basis of my performance that night! If there are, I hope they don't remember who was playing it.

By late 1959, Mark's band consisted of all Arklow musicians, namely Pete Coburn, lead vocalist who was running the band for Mark as he had not been playing for some months due to illness, Paud O'Brien clarinet & sax, Larry Kenny trumpet, Eamon Lee guitar, Joe Weadick trombone, Des Mulhall and myself on piano. As has already been mentioned in this book, we had a discussion on the feasibility of starting our own band and decided to break away from Mark, hence the start of the Red Seven Showband. At the time it seemed the right and sensible thing to do since the dance music scene was rapidly changing. Elvis Presley and Bill Haley were the whole rage in America and Cliff Richard was becoming big in Britain. The showband era was quickly taking hold in Ireland and it was our desire to follow that road rather than continue the 'sit down dance band tradition'.

Before continuing my story, I must put on record that I will always be indebted to Mark Canavan, a true gentleman, for giving me the start in what was, and still is after all those years, a wonderfully enjoyable and satisfying musical episode/period in my life.

As the Red Seven Showband we continued to play the usual halls we had previously played and, of course, sought out new venues. Due to the problem of the unavailability of pianos in some halls, coupled with the fact that pop music culture was requiring more and more the sounds of saxophones and clarinets, I decided to buy these instruments (on the never-never in Walton's) and learn them, so that I could augment the music played by Paud.

One of the venues we were fortunate to get a booking in was the Tara Ballroom, Courtown. Remember that Courtown was, along with Arklow (believe it or not), one of the foremost holiday destinations for Dublin people at the time. It was also popular with people as far away as Waterford, Kilkenny and Carlow. After a few minor bookings, the proprietor of the ballroom, the late Peter Redmond, liked our music and we were successful in getting the summer season there in 1960. We played six nights a week for the months of July and August. It was hard going for us as we were all holding down day jobs. The only night we had off was Monday when they had traditional Irish music sessions.

Even though we were only the resident band, we quickly became very popular with both the locals and visitors alike. We always played two hours warm-up time before the major visiting showbands came on and this would happen twice a week, on Wednesdays and Sundays. Our repertoire improved by the week as we used to go down a bit early on the slack nights and go over new tunes entering the hit parade. By the end of the eight-week season we almost rivalled some of the top bands in quality.

Our greatest asset was Pete who was, I believe, one of the best singers on the dance band scene at the time. I will never forget his rendering of 'Only the Lonely' in particular, and indeed any of Roy Orbison's hits at the time. They were always show-stoppers, even when we were playing before the visiting big bands like the Clipper Carlton, the Royal, the Capital or the

Dixies. Pete also did Slim Whitman songs and yodelled perfectly. They too were always show-stoppers, very often with two or three hundred people standing around the stage for the performances and well over fifteen hundred people in the hall at the time.

Taking a leaf out of the book of the Clipper Carlton Showband, who were renowned for their musical sketches and showpieces, we arranged a few of our own, which were extremely popular and always got a standing audience and ovation around the stage. They were 'Doctor I'm in Trouble' (Peter Sellers and Sophia Loren), 'There is a Hole in the Bucket' (Harry Belafonte and Odetta), 'Jake The Peg With My Extra Leg' (Rolf Harris) and 'I'm Walking the Floor Over You' (Ernest Tubb). Young people reading this would be forgiven for wondering what these songs/sketches were all about, or what place they had in a dance hall, but I can assure you they were four comedy tunes in the hit parade at the time and very entertaining to look at and listen to when done well. Without blowing my own saxophone, I do believe we did the sketches very well and they went down like a bomb! ... I mean a treat.

Among my most memorable and satisfying events in Courtown was one Sunday afternoon when we were asked to play for a group of disabled people who were on a summer outing. They were mesmerized by our performance and songs. I will never forget their eyes transfixed on each member of the band for the whole period, in awe. It is times like that that one feels humble and thankful to be healthy and able to give some little joy to even a small number of less fortunate people.

In the early days of the Red Seven, we were occasionally joined by the Swinging Sailors. A local group and colleagues of ours, already mentioned by Des Mulhall. They were Michael and the late Colin Gilmore, guitarists/soloists, and drummer George Kinch. Their signature tune was 'The Sailors Hornpipe'. Michael was a brilliant lead guitarist. He was the first person I ever saw playing the guitar on his knees. The Gilmores moved to England and George Kinch married and settled in New Zealand.

One lovely piece of equipment, which would be very expensive to buy today, was Pete's double bass fiddle. It was a magnificent instrument, standing about five feet high, and Pete was slowly getting the hang of it when it had an accident. If my memory serves me right, it fell one night and the bridge broke on it. Pete had someone, who was not too familiar with instruments, make up a new bridge from steel conduit. Before long it collapsed. That was the end of Pete playing the double bass. However, his golden voice more than compensated.

Towards the end of 1960, we were getting more and more prestigious bookings and travelling greater distances. This prompted a discussion to start about the success of the band and the effect it was beginning to have on our day jobs. The possibility of working towards professionalism was mooted. The first person to decide that going full time would not be for him was Paud. He was not long married and had no desire to leave his permanent day job, even though he was enjoying every minute of the band life. He reluctantly decided to leave. He knew, of course, that I was progressing well in learning the sax, so the band would not suffer. In 1962, we decided to buy our own minibus, because we worked out that it would be no more expensive than paying for hire, particularly since we were getting more bookings and the band members could take turns driving. Also, it would give us more flexibility with loading/unloading gear, etc. We bought a second-hand Volkswagen minibus in Glenbrook Motors, Bray. It served us well for a year, but then started to give a lot of trouble. I will never forget one episode with it. When we were driving home one night after playing in Johnston parish hall, the half shaft broke. Because one door lock was not working myself and Freddy agreed to stay and sleep in it until the next day to mind the equipment. It was in the winter and was one long, cold night.

That old Volkswagen minibus was nearly the death of me. The heating in it only warmed the front of the bus. I remember one very cold night coming home from a gig. To keep warm on the long journey, I resorted to putting on, under my slacks, a woolly jumper … using the arms as legs!

We decided in 1963, having changed the name of the band to the Columbia Showband, to change the Volkswagen minibus to a more upmarket vehicle to reflect our steady progress in the business. We bought a NEW Ford Commer powder blue minibus in Buckley Motors, New Street, Dublin. It looked the real deal - and we all gloried in the perceived elevated status this new bus bestowed. The registration number was FNI 524.

Apart from a near miss we had one night coming from Rathdrum, when Joe was driving (and which is related by Larry Kenny), we only ever had one actual crash throughout the nine years we were together, which was a great tribute to all the drivers we hired, not forgetting our own band members who drove hundreds of miles, mostly through the night, in all weathers. The accident in question happened on our way home from playing in Carlow. It was a very foggy night and the late Jimmy Cullen was driving. We approached one on those zig-zag cross roads and Jimmy kept going straight through a fence and half way into a field before he managed to stop. Fortunately, the fence was only wooden stakes and wire.

The minibus was full. We had two girls, friends of some of the boys, with us and, while they and all the band members were very shook up, nobody was injured. All got out and we made attempts to push the bus back onto the road, but to no avail. In the end, two of the lads volunteered to walk to the nearest farm and knock them up for help. This was about four o'clock in the morning - there were no mobile phones then! The farmer was not too pleased as he roused himself, but eventually took pity on us, got dressed, brought his tractor to the scene and pulled the bus out onto the road. We were ever so grateful to him and gave him a few bob for his trouble. In due course, we also paid the owner of the field for repairs to the broken fence.

On the day the new Commer minibus was delivered, I got the job of keeping the Volkswagen running because the battery was so low that, if I switched off the engine, it would not start again. After all our effort to keep the battery charged, it broke down on the unfortunate delivery man in Rathnew on his way back to Dublin with it!

Mentioning batteries reminds me of playing in the Johnstown parish hall one Christmas night. We had to use car batteries to power our amplifiers and mics as there was no electricity ... they even used gas lights to illuminate the hall! I remember we had terrible trouble trying to stop the speakers from emitting cracking and shrieking sounds all night, because the vibration of the stage, caused by the movement of the dancers, affected the battery connections. To ease the situation, we had to get someone to hold the batteries up off the stage when we were playing. As they say, the show must go on!

Playing in the Imperial Hotel in Tuam, County Galway one night, our fee was £40. On the long journey from Arklow we stopped for a meal which cost £35, and the petrol for the trip cost £10. How we survived for nine years in the business I'll never know!

On the other side of the coin (so to speak), we did get the odd unexpected freebee. I remember when the late Eamon Andrews opened his new recording studio in the Television Club, Harcourt Street, Dublin, he invited, among others, any showband recording discs at the time, and we were on the list of guests. As we arrived, Eamon was there, larger than life, welcoming all and sundry. As he shook hands, the only words he spoke to everyone were; "help yourself to a drink at the bar". He didn't have to ask us twice. Seriously, he was a lovely and generous man.

We were generally a very well behaved band of young lads, but boys will be boys and will play games sometimes; and accidents will happen. One such occasion occurred in the Mayfair Ballroom, Kilkenny. We arrived early to set up our gear and test the equipment before the dance. Some of the boys started kicking a ball around the dance floor to amuse themselves and, of course, the inevitable happened. One of the boys (I forget who) thought he was George Best and hit the ball for home - but it went too high and broke one of the big ornamental lights in the ceiling! We quickly cleaned up the mess before any of the hall staff came in and it was never copped - at least we were never contacted about it afterwards. That was the end of us playing ball in ballrooms.

The cardinal rule when playing anywhere in Northern Ireland was to enquire which, if any, national anthem was to be played at the end of the night. We were wise to the situation, but we were told by the manager of St. Mary's Hall in Newry, when we arrived to play there one night, that the famous 'Joe Loss and his Orchestra' had played there a few weeks previously. Not knowing the rule about the anthem, Joe finished up the night with 'God Save The Queen'. St Mary's Hall, being mostly frequented by Catholic and/or Republican dancers, this unfortunate mistake resulted in some rioting outside the ballroom after the dance.

Northern Ireland reminds me of fireworks at Holloween and, of course, coming up to Guy Fawkes Night on November 5th. Fireworks were, and are still, banned here but not so then in the North. Every time we travelled there during October, we all came back with various types of fireworks. While we were always checked at the Customs going up, they were not too strict coming back. I can't remember anything ever being taken from us.

When we went on tour to London, we sometimes stayed in a well known bed and breakfast house in Islington, owned by an Irish family called Johnson. Because we would get in late from dances, we naturally would get up late. Our being in bed did not stop the cleaning lady coming into the room and hoovering every morning while we were still asleep; and being nice young Irish lads, we accepted this as the norm and never complained! But Michael had a brainwave one day and bought a fake dog poo in a trick shop and put it in the middle of his bedroom floor. When the cleaning lady came in the next morning, he watched her out of the corner of his eye and noticed she hoovered all around it, but did not touch it.

On another occasion, a crying child came into the room after the cleaning woman had hoovered and Jim, half asleep, got out of his bed and gently lifted the child and carried him out to the corridor and shut the room door. AAAhhh ... it was a long way from a luxury hotel. I'm sure many Irish showbands had similar experiences while on tour in Britain.

As the only founder member of the Red Seven/Columbia Showband to stay the full ten years - from 1960 to 1969, I will have to say that I enjoyed every single minute of it. I loved the continuous challenge of getting our music right in practice and experiencing the adrenalin on stage in response to the positive reaction of the dancers. I really loved the many musical and funny sketches I took part in. To me, they proved what the word 'SHOWBAND' was all about. Most of all, I was proud of the six records we made and our appearance on RTÉ's *Showband Show*. While we did not make a fiscal fortune, I finished up rich in memories which have stayed with me throughout the years. I would not have changed it for anything.

When my dear wife Breda once asked me in the early years of the band, if I had to make a decision between her and the band, who would win? Without hesitation, I said the band of course! Many times over the years she has reminded me of that - but Breda and I were so sure of each other's love that we had no problem in telling it as it was. We met while involved in music and drama in the Marian Arts Society in the fifties, fell in love and got married in June 1963, just before the band went professional.

After the showband ended, Breda and I sang together again for many more years in the highly successful Family group with Eddie Mac, Freddy Cutland and Matt Sharp. In the eighties, I joined the very popular Kynochs group and played with them for many more years. In the nineties, I played for a while with the Arklow All Stars Showband, which included my old colleagues Joe Weadick, Larry Kenny, Pete Coburn and Liam O'Reilly. Recently I played guitar with a newly formed local orchestra called the Swing Kings, along with Larry Kenny and Des Mulhall. I cannot wind up my story without mentioning my late brother Jim and my young brother Michael, who were both dedicated to the showband from the time they joined in 1961/2.

Jim to me was a true musical wizard on the piano, great vocalist and all round entertainer. He gave up a good pensionable job (as they said in those days) in CIE in 1963, to devote his full time managing the band and was instrumental in bringing it to a high degree of professionalism. Even though we had no less than four outside managers in the band's history, Jim guided it through thick and thin. When the end of the showband era was in sight in 1969, he called a 'spade a spade' and prepared us for the after life, so to speak. Jim, Michael, George and Timmy went on to start the Ranchers country & western band, and Jim, Michael and George formed the Jim Tyrrell Trio and The Coolgreaney Jazz Band. Eddie, Freddy and myself started the Family group with my wife Breda and Matt Sharpe.

Jim died too young - at the age of 69, in 2007. If there is a heaven or paradise in the hereafter, I have no doubt that Jim is there sitting at a piano, playing and singing the song he wrote (after the Columbia), recorded and loved - 'The Well Runs Dry'. God Bless You, Jim.

My young brother Michael was a brilliant bass guitar player and an excellent rock singer. He knew how to attract the younger punters and fans around the stage with his outgoing character, and he was always solidly dependable during performances. So popular was he with the girls that he gave us a lot of grief waiting for him after dances while he wowed some young lady. We waited so long for him one night that we taught him a valuable lesson - we left without him. I'm still not sure when or how he got home!

Unfortunately, Michael suffered a serious stroke in 1987 and has not been able to play music since. But he still enjoys listening to all the songs of the Red Seven/Columbia Showband era, bringing back the many beautiful memories of those heady days and, of course, those further famous years of the Jim Tyrrell Trio and the Coolgreaney Jazz Band. For my dear brother Michael, as for all of us musicians ... MUSIC IS THE FOOD OF LIFE.

Columbia
Photo taken at Arklow Entertainment Centre Swimming Pool in 1963

'The Family' – early seventies
L to R: Matt Sharpe, Pat Tyrrell, Breda Tyrrell, Eddie McElheron, Freddy Cutland.

Chapter 7

Eamon Lee (written by Joe Weadick)

Eamon was born at No. 1 Ferrybank, Arklow on March 4th, 1939. He attended Templerainey National School - even though his mother Ann, known as Bean Ní Laoi, was a teacher in the old Infant Boys School on Harbour Road (in fact, she was my first teacher - in the baby class). I don't think it was well known but Mrs Lee was a very fine pianist. Through his mother's love of music, as well as encouragment from his siblings, Kitty, Jack (r.i.p.) and Mary(r.i.p.), Eamon developed a liking for music too. Rewarding this interest, his mother and father bought him a small button accordian he was keen on learning. Through sheer determination and lots of practice he taught himself to play it. He loved, in particular, playing Irish jigs and reels.

In his late teens, when he was earning a few bob as a carpenter, following in the trade of his father Ned, Eamon bought himself a guitar and learned to play it well. He got an opportunity to join Mark Canavan's Band in 1959 playing rhythm guitar, which gave him great experience in the dance band world. He left Mark's band along with the rest of us Arklow members, in January 1960 to form the Red Seven Showband.

Many funny stories are told in this book about Eamon during his period with the Red Seven. He was a handsome looking fellow (a bit like Frank Sinatra, I thought) and a decent singer. He was very popular with the ladies. You'd very often hear Martin Byrne, our minibus driver, when we were ready to go home after a dance (particularly in Courtown during the summer season), shouting "where the hell is Shamba [Eamon's nickname] - he's not off with another woman is he!" When Eamon would eventually return, smiling from ear to ear, he would say to Martin, "take her up to 7000 feet Mr Byrne and level off"!

Three of Eamon's best friends were Michael and the late Colin Gilmore and George Kinch, all of whom were sailors. During the summer of 1960, when they took time off from sea, they formed the group The Swinging Sailors. Michael played lead guitar, Colin played rhythm, and George played drums. Eamon used to play bass guitar with them when the Red

Seven was free. They got gigs in the Arklow Entertainment Centre on Sunday afternoons and became very popular among the teenagers. We also got them to play support to us on occasion.

Like some others before him, Eamon decided to leave the showband in 1962, when there was serious talk about going professional. It was not for him. However, he went on to enjoy playing for some time after with the Avonaires Showband and other groups.

After a long period of poor health Eamon passed away ... too soon for his sorrowing family and friends, on February 25th, 2006. There was a large attendance at his funeral. We, the Red Seven/Columbia members, formed a guard of honour and Larry Kenny played 'Stranger on the Shore' as Eamon was laid to rest.

Red Seven Showband in their summer outfits in the Tara Ballroom Courtown 1960 with Eamon taking centre stage

I'm sure Eamon and Jim Tyrrell get together often on the other side and exchange stories about the showband days of the sixties - they might even have started another band there to re-live that wonderful and happy time!

Chapter 8 *Freddy Cutland*

When Joe Weadick first contacted me with the news that he was going to put the story of the Red Seven and Columbia Showband into print, my first thought was that he had 'a mountain to climb'. My mind wandered back through the years, picturing the changes that took place in the personnel, from the start of the changes when I joined on 1st June 1961, to the final performance in September, 1969. I wondered how Joe was going to get in touch with as many of these as possible but, as I write, I believe he has had a great response and I dearly look forward to reading each member's contribution. While congratulating Joe, in advance, on his great work with this literary project, I would like to mention two of our friends who have passed on to that great showband in the sky, Eamon Lee and Jim Tyrrell. Unfortunately, I didn't have much time on stage with Eamon, as he left the band shortly after I joined. A lovely country & western voice - I remember his renditions of 'Honky Tonk Angels' and 'Happy Birthday To Me'.

When thinking of Jim, the first thing that jumps to mind was his insistence that the music MUST be right. Jim had a great influence on my music, particularly in pointing out that there was always that 'extra' chord in a piece of music that took it from being 'near enough' to musically correct. I believe Jim, as a musician, had immense capabilities that may not have always been recognised.

Now - to the business at hand

In the beginning, 'St Aidan's', Ferrybank, Arklow, was where it all started for me. This was the residence of the Orr family. The family had moved to Arklow from County Louth. Among the family were David and Valerie. Both attended the national school in my "Primary Cert" year. David became one of my best friends. Around this time, I became involved with the Arklow Badminton Club. A local drama group, The Marlborough Players, also used this badminton hall for rehearsals and shows. In preparation for one of their variety shows, they decided that a skiffle group would be nice for the interval. Rhona Crammond, who was David's girlfriend, said that it would be no problem for us to fill this gap. Rhona sang and played guitar,

David was interested in drumming and another of our friends, David Purcell, had an electric guitar.

I had owned a guitar for a year previously but could not make head nor tail of it. Rhona told me that she would teach me to play it in two months - in time for the first night of the show. This she did! David's sister, Valerie, was brought in as an extra singer, as was Rhona's sister Nora and another friend, Betty Sherwood. We also brought in a friend of mine, Roy Keegan, to play the 'Tea Chest'. Our slot in the show was a reasonable success. When the show had finished its run, the two Davids and myself decided to form a group, with occasional appearances by Dick Power, on clarinet and George Byrne on drums. We rehearsed in the basement of Orrs' house most Saturday nights.

Skiffle Group in Marlborough Hall Show 1960
Left to Right: Roy Keegan, Rhona Crammond, Betty Sherwood, David Orr, Nora Crammond, Valerie Orr, Freddy Cutland.

Around that time, I got an opportunity to play with Mark Canavan's band from Avoca. This was following the departure of the members who left the band to form the original Red Seven. After a short time with these musicians, I once again got involved with the original group, and practice sessions started back in David Orr's house.

My Big Break

It was Saturday 13th May, 1961 when Des Mulhall and Larry Kenny, two members of the Red Seven Showband, called in to our practice session and asked me if I would be interested in coming to one of their rehearsals with the possibility of joining the band. Needless to say, I jumped at the chance, because they were regarded in the area as the up and coming band. I went to a session with them in Sweeney's garage on Ferrybank. I was asked back for another session on the following Thursday night and they said they would let me know.

On Tuesday 30th May, I was given an invitation to join the band and I grabbed it with both hands. The following Thursday, 1st June, I played with the guys for the first time. The venue was the Entertainment Centre, Arklow. A short while after I joined the band, they bought new suits - which were blue. With my addition we now numbered eight, we wore blue suits and were called the Red Seven. That was in June of 1961.

When I joined the Red Seven I found that we were booked as the resident band in the Tara Ballroom, Courtown, for the month of July, playing six nights a week. This was the band's second year playing resident there - they had been re-engaged because of their great success in 1960. It was a very prestigious booking, as the Tara Ballroom was one of the best dancing venues on the east coast outside Dublin. Thousands of people spent their summer holidays there every year.

This concentrated bout of playing gave me a good grounding in music. Any mistakes I made 'on the night' had to be corrected immediately as I was going to have to play it again the next night. Also, every Wednesday and Sunday night during the summer season, top showbands such as the Royal, Capitol, Clipper Carlton etc., were booked as the big attractions - we would do the warm-up for them, which meant that we would play the first two or two and a half hours. I learned a lot from looking at and listening to these guys. Interestingly, many years later - approximately twenty - I played two and a half month residencies with the group Kynochs in the Holiday Inn, just next door to this ballroom.

I was just one month with the Red Seven when I realised that some members, because of the continuing success of the band, had been seriously considering going professional. This had made all the lads think very deeply about their future and, as a result, many changes in personnel took place during the following years.

The Band Goes Professional

In terms of the showband scene the word professional meant that the person just gave up the day job to concentrate on the music. Five of the original seven left over a period. They were Paud O' Brien, Des Mulhall, Pete Coburn, Eamon Lee and Larry Kenny. Replacement members, who eventually went professional in 1964 with Joe Weadick (trombone), Pat Tyrrell (sax/vocals) and myself (lead guitar) were: George Byrne (drummer), Eddie McElheron (lead singer and rhythm guitar), Jim Tyrrell (trumpet and vocals), and Michael Tyrrell (bass guitar and vocals).

Among other bandsmen who joined and left during the following period were Leo McHugh (trumpet), Paddy Merrigan (vocals/rhythm guitar), James Kenny (vocals/bass-guitar), Jimmy McManus (vocals/guitar) and Liam O'Reilly (vocals/rhythm guitar).

A Travelling Band

Playing with the Red Seven/Columbia was most enjoyable for me, not just from the musical aspect but also because of the funny – and the not-so-funny incidents - we experienced. They were numerous and perhaps some would be better not recorded here! but I will give you a sample of the tellable ones - firstly those associated with travelling. Prior to starting these stories I must explain our travelling arrangements. Before we could afford to buy our own transport, we travelled to the gigs in a Volkswagen minibus, hired from the late Martin Byrne and mostly driven by him, but sometimes driven by the late Joe Kenny.

In 1962, we were earning enough to buy our own wagon. It also was a Volkswagen minibus, but second hand. We took turns in driving it ourselves. In 1963, as the success of the band continued, we progressed to a new, streamlined light blue Commer minibus - we were definitely on the up! As time went on and we got many more bookings and had to travel longer distances, sometimes to the U.K., we often hired drivers. The most frequent drivers we used were two brothers, now sadly passed away, Jimmy and

Larry Cullen. They were both very witty characters, great drivers and a pleasure to have with us.

The Good, The Bad And The Others

When I mention the good and the bad, I refer to interactions we had with other showbands through the years. I remember in our early days, we were playing interval for a well known Cork showband in the Entertainment Centre in Arklow. They did their sound check and asked us would we use their P.A. equipment. We were delighted with this as we were just starting out and our gear would have left something to be desired. We then went down to the cafe for a coffee and, at the appointed time, went on stage for our big experience. Much to our disappointment, the P.A. sound was unbelievably bad. When Jim attempted to adjust the controls there didn't appear to be any knobs on the amp. We had to soldier on - sounding terrible. At last, it was time for the main attraction to come on stage. As they did, one of the guys took several 'knobs' from his pocket and fitted them to the P.A., cranked up the tone controls and they sounded a million dollars - compared to us having a sound that seemed like it was coming from the bottom of a barrel.

Another experience was when we were considering going professional. We were playing warm-up for the Royal Showband. After the dance, one of our lads mentioned to the late Tom Dunphy that we were considering giving up our day jobs and going full time. Tom advised us not to bother, but said; "If you do, and the whole thing falls down around your shoulders, as it surely will, don't forget Tom Dunphy told you not to do it". It was probably at this dance that I noticed something unusual. We were finishing our set as the Royal members approached the stage. Our second last number was an instrumental version of 'Eileen Óg' that I had arranged for guitar. Our final number was 'The Hucklebuck', that Jim had found on an old LP. Jim's delivery of the 'Hucklebuck' was a great hit with the dancers, so much so that we would get several requests to repeat it. I noticed the guys from the Royal paying great interest to our performance, and later I was chuffed to see that Jim Conlon, the Royal's guitar player, used this same 'Eileen Óg', having changed the name to the 'One Nighters', and used it as the theme music for their film of the same name. They then recorded the Hucklebuck, which went on to be THE song that is synonymous with showbands to this day.

On the other hand, during a chat I was having with Jim Conlon I mentioned that we were due to cut a record. He advised me that I should invest in a Fender guitar as you need the best for the studio. He also told me that if we got to perform on TV to wear light blue shirts as they appeared whiter on B&W TV than white ones did. Helpful suggestions to 'rookies' in the business.

Another 'good guy' was the late Joe Dolan. We had just put down several tracks for a single and had met Joe and his band in a cafe on our way home from a gig. Naturally the talk got around to the music business and, on learning that we had just been in the studio, Joe suggested that before we settled on a final sound mix we should play a copy of our tracks on as many different outlets as possible - a home hi-fi, a car radio, a portable record player - as many diverse players as we could get our hands on, and note the different sounds so that we could produce a mix that sounded good on most of these outlets - another helpful suggestion.

Now For The 'Travelling' Stories

I remember one night on the way home from a dance, Pete Coburn's double bass instrument fell off the roof rack on top of the van and ended up on the side of the road. Needless to say, it was damaged in the process - Pete was mortified, but luckily it was repairable.

On another occasion on the way to a gig, as an object was seen falling past one of the side windows from the roof-rack, a comment was heard - "its O.K. - its only Jimmy's guitar" [Jimmy McManus].

You have heard the phrase *"Anything that can go wrong will go wrong"*. The following report will prove that there is a certain truth in this saying. We were on our way to a gig, I think it may have been Rosnowlagh. Anyway, the weather turned nasty, developing into a full-blown storm. This slowed us down considerably, and then to add to our trouble, we rounded a bend only to be faced with a tree down across the road. A car coming from the other direction stopped and the occupants got out to survey the scene. We discussed our predicament and, hearing that we were in a hurry to get to a function, they gave us directions how to go back a short distance, take a few turns and we would be back on the main road again on the other side of the tree. We turned the bus and headed off, following the directions we'd been given. Either the directions were wrong or we were not very good at navigating, but we returned to the fallen tree again.

At this stage, several other cars had arrived on both sides of the scene, so we reckoned we had enough manpower to haul the tree to one side and get on our way. As we were planning which way to handle this operation, an old guy, in an even older Ford Anglia with no brakes, came puttering around the corner and straight into the middle of the branches of the tree. For some strange reason he had his window open, and one of the branches went straight through his side window and wedged firmly. This made reversing the car out of the 'greenery' impossible, and therefore moving the tree was out of the question. Eventually, one of the guys, who lived nearby, went off and came back with a chain saw and quickly made short work of our impediment. Hurray - we were on our way again.

On our way alright, but at least one and a half hours behind schedule. This called for a little 'wellie to the metal' by our driver. This was not a problem to us as our pilot was very competent. Well, to heap trouble upon trouble, after fifteen minutes or so of driving, we came to a major flood. Several cars were stopped in the middle of the water, due to travelling too fast through it and splashing water up on the electrics. Not so with our man - two miles per hour through the torrent carefully navigating around the abandoned vehicles and, I'm sorry to say, not stopping to help anyone - "if we stop now we may never get started again", said our driver. This was a reasonable enough summary of the situation. Out onto dry land (or should I say a wet road), and on our not-so-merry way again.

Not-so-merry because we were now nearly two hours late. By the way, I forgot to mention that Larry, our driver, who would only wear a cap as head-gear, was resplendent in a little tartan number bought in Scotland the previous month while we were on tour. This was its first outing, especially worn for this prestigious "gig". (Don't forget this!). Anyway, two hours to make up. The only remedy was to put the hammer down in a big way. We had just hit top gear and passing the 70 mph mark when we came to a sign for dangerous bends. Foot slammed down hard on brakes, but no reduction in speed. The brake linings were totally saturated after their voyage through the mini-lake half a mile back. Fortunately, or unfortunately, the sign was misplaced, because instead of dangerous bends, we were confronted with one of those nasty little humped-back bridges, with a gradient of about one in three. We were still travelling at around 60 mph when we hit it. Thankfully the road was straight, because we took off from the peak of that bridge and travelled through the air for what seemed like half a minute before landing. Now, to add to our lateness problems, we had the possibility of having a boot full of 'broken parts' instead of a full set of band equipment. There was nothing we could do about it till we got there, so we bashed on regardless.

We duly arrived at the venue to a tirade of abuse from the management of the hall, on account of our being at least two hours late. On reflection, it said a lot for the band that the fans turned out in their hundreds in the middle of a near blizzard. However, we eventually got started, and the equipment didn't seem to be any worse for wear after its 'crash landing' earlier.

We had played just about three or four numbers when all the power in the hall failed. We were left in darkness and silence. It appeared that the main fuse tripped, because rain was being forced through the cracks in the building by the strength of the wind and some of this rain found its way onto the main fuse board. The caretaker of the hall appeared with his flashlight and reset the switch. Off we went again only to be cut short in our prime by the same tripping fuse. For the rest of the night, the caretaker stood by the fuse board resetting the fuse each time it tripped, and we performed at a rate of about two and a half songs per reset. Not the most enjoyable of experiences. During the performance it snowed. It seemed that someone had put a curse on us ...!

The arrangement at the end of the night would go as follows: after playing the national anthem, the guys in the band would dismantle the equipment, and have it packed ready for loading. The driver would bring the van to the entrance of the hall and load the gear while the band changed from their stage gear to their civilian clobber. Unfortunately, due to the rain and snow, the van got bogged down, so we had to go out and push it until it got to firmer terrain. We had not changed our clothes at this time, but were very careful! All, that is, except Mac, our vocalist. He had positioned himself immediately behind one of the back wheels, so when we got the van moving and the driver put his foot down, the back wheels spun and Mac was transformed into what looked like a reject from the *Black & White Minstrel Show.*

Eventually, everything was loaded, including ourselves, and we headed off into the night, glad to have this episode of disasters over. Or so we thought. Fate had not finished with us yet! Half an hour into the journey home, the ignition light on the dashboard came on. This is usually the sign of a broken fan belt. On inspection of the engine, this was confirmed. Disbelief. Then, unbelievably, Lar, our driver, said; "Don't worry lads, we have a spare". At last, we had broken the curse. The middle seat of the front row lifted up to reveal the engine, so the replacement of the fan belt could take place without anyone having to get out in the snow. Another winner. Work started, the bolt was removed from the alternator, new belt fitted, bolt inserted.

"WHERE'S THE NUT?" - shouted an irate Lar! Now, for those not acquainted with the higher points of engineering - a bolt is usually accompanied by a nut.

"Oh crap!" The nut was nowhere to be seen. It must have fallen through the engine compartment and into the snow beneath the van. The only answer was to push the van forward a few yards, (we couldn't start the engine as it was), and then search through the snow with our bare hands. Half an hour and eight sets of blue fingers and thumbs later, it was agreed that we were not going to find this accursed nut. As we stood up having abandoned our search, the wind decided to increase the pressure. This managed to lift Lar's precious cap off his head and it was last seen, (the cap, that is), heading south in a force ten blizzard, totally beyond rescue and never to be seen again.

After many suggestions and ideas for a way out of our predicament, it was decided to wedge a drumstick down between the alternator and the side of the engine. This was done and, when the engine was started, the alternator behaved perfectly, we were ready to head off again. Only one problem, though! We could not close down the seat over the engine while the drumstick was in place. We had no option but to travel the rest of the journey, over one hundred miles, with the engine cover open. This subjected us to a constant supply of engine and exhaust fumes, coupled with a freezing gale, for the final two and a half hours of our journey - not at all nice. The next day, as the van was in the garage to have the fan belt problem sorted, it was discovered that the elusive "nut" never existed - the bolt screwed into the side of the alternator. Our final discomfort of the previous night had been quite unnecessary! Ah yes...the joys and tribulations of a travelling showband! Another event that could have had a very serious outcome happened when, having completed a successful tour of England, travelling the length of the country, we were just driving back home into Arklow, crossing the bridge, when our driver, Jimmy, thought he heard a strange sound coming from the back of the van. On investigation, it was found that on one of the wheels, three of the four wheel nuts had become unscrewed and were rattling around inside the hub cap.

A Close Encounter

We were travelling from some town in County Sligo, I think it could have been Enniscrone on the main road to Dublin, at about 3.30 a.m. We had played to a full house and had just left the limits of the town and some of us were just about to settle down for forty winks in the rear seats of the van. It was a really miserable night, strong winds and sheets of rain blowing across the road. I reckoned we wouldn't get much sleep in these conditions. Just then, the driver noticed a girl standing at the side of the road, hitching a lift. He pulled the van in and we opened the door. The van was a Commer minibus, the type with three rows of seats. When we had bought the van we reversed the centre row of seats to face the back, to facilitate the constant card games that took place to pass the time travelling. As we opened the door that accessed this section of the van, to let the girl in, the five of us in these two rows of seats could clearly see someone seemingly lying or crouching at the side of the hedge. The girl pulled the door closed behind her and sat down, rain dripping off her all over the seats. One of the guys asked her about her friend outside, but she said to drive on.

I noticed a slight chill, but put it down to the fact that we had had the door open for a while and that the weather outside was bitter. However, as we proceeded on our journey, I felt that instead of getting back to normal, the air was getting colder, (I found out later that the rest of the guys had the same experience).

As we travelled on towards Dublin, she gave directions in order to bring her to her home. Our next turn was a left off the main road up a narrow side road. We took this turn, and as we travelled, I noticed that everyone had gone very quiet, very unusual for 'our boys'. Keep in mind that we were all in our early twenties, been around a lot, no drink taken as the ballrooms were not licensed at that time, and we had been relatively hardened by the ups and downs of life as fulltime musicians. 'Cynics' would have been an appropriate a description for us, as well as musicians.

Anyway, the road was getting narrower by the minute, but then she said; "Stop here, this is where I live, come in and meet my mother and have some tea before you travel on". She slid the door open to get out, and looking out we saw, not a house, but a derelict ruins. Immediately (and unanimously) we declined the offer, and with some difficulty convinced her that we should be going, as we had a long distance to travel. Reluctantly, she agreed, but before she closed the door she told us that if we carried on up the road we were on, it would lead us back down onto the main road, turn left and on for Dublin. This sounded fine to us, and with a certain relief we started up this narrow road, which was fast becoming a laneway.

For some reason, everyone still seemed reluctant to speak, and the van didn't appear to be getting rid of the chill factor. However, our relief at "getting away" was short lived as the lane had now become a dirt track, so narrow that the briers at the sides were starting to scrape along the windows, and grass was growing between two tracks. Eventually, the driver stopped and said that he thought we had better turn back, and asked one of the gang to walk behind to direct him as he reversed the van back to where we might be able to turn. Again, strangely, no one would get out of the van, but reluctantly we slid the side door open and peered out to watch our direction. After what seemed like ages, we reached a spot where we knew that we would be able to turn the van around.

At this everyone started talking together and, naturally, we tried to rationalise the situation. The logical decision was that what we stopped at was where a bungalow must have been built just behind the ruins, and these ruins probably would be knocked down in the near future to give open road frontage. We decided to confirm this as we passed on our way back, but strangely no sign of a bungalow, and stranger still, no sign of any ruins appeared, only open fields. We were still searching for some signs of life, with no success, when we arrived at the junction where we first turned off the main road. We turned left, heading for Dublin in a state of bewilderment and, feeling a certain 'psychological' chill, we headed for home. The van was beginning to win the battle with the inside temperature, and things were beginning to get back to normal when we approached a sign on the side of the road that said 'Enniscrone'.

Impossible as it may seem, we were going in the opposite direction than the way we should. The "feeling" that we were dealing with conditions outside the norm once more came over us, but still, not to be defeated, we did a U-turn and headed back, watching out on both sides of the road for the junction where we turned off just after picking up the girl. We drove on and came to the next town without finding any turn off. At this stage, none of us could give any logical reason for what had happened, and peculiarly, no one seemed to want to talk about it. Several months later, we were playing in the same town, same ballroom, and one of us mentioned to the doorman about the incident on the way home. "Oh", he said, "that has happened a few times. A girl was killed about a mile outside the town around a year ago. Her body was found lying on the side of the road beside her boyfriend, who was severely injured. It appears they had been hitching and were struck by a hit-and-run driver ..."

A Future Taoiseach

On Friday 1st of January, 1965 the Columbia played in the Fairyland ballroom, Roscommon. Also on the bill was Houston Wells (a.k.a. Andy Smith). The Fairyland, as were all the other '... lands', was owned by Albert Reynolds, a future taoiseach and a great country music advocate.

1965 - A 'Record' Year

On Thursday 25th of February, 1965 Eddie Mac and Jim Tyrrell attended a meeting with Irish Record Factors in Dublin and through them signed, on behalf of the band, a one year contract with Decca Records. Decca's label for Ireland at that time was Rex Records. We were contracted to produce four tracks in the year, so the following Monday we recorded our tracks, one of which was 'Before This Day Ends'.

Other recordings followed and eventually, towards the end of the year, George and Audrey Meredith wrote 'Way Out Of Reach' for us. This we recorded, together with 'The Spinning Wheel' and two country songs. 'Way Out Of Reach' and 'The Spinning Wheel' were to be two 'A' sides, each backed by one of the country numbers. 'Way Out Of Reach' was to be released first, to be followed quickly by 'The Spinning Wheel', but when the release date came round the management of the record company lost their bottle and put the two 'A' sides on the one disc and called it a double 'A' side. Although our double 'A' side met with reasonable success, reaching number six in Ireland's Top Ten, we were left without a follow-up in the can, as at that time country music had not achieved the following it has today.

'Concrete and Clay'

On Sunday 2nd of January, 1966 the Columbia played in the Crystal Ballroom, Dublin. We were told by our then manager, the late Hugh Hardy, that we could be doing an Irish tour with the group Unit 4 plus 2, who had a chart success at that time titled 'Concrete And Clay'. This had made No.1 in the UK charts the previous year. We had great hopes that OUR new release would appear in the Irish charts the next evening.

'Way Out of Reach'

At 6.45 p.m. on Monday 3rd of January, 1966, 'Way Out Of Reach' entered Ireland's Top Ten at number ten. During the following weeks it worked its way up to number six before exiting again through number ten. Unfortunately, due to the record company's lack of confidence in the song, we didn't have a follow-up to piggy-back on our chart success.

'Baby Come Back'

Later on Jim found a great song for our repertoire - 'Baby Come Back'. This was a huge success for us in the dance halls, so much so that we decided to record it, together with some other tracks. The original was recorded by The Equals but, unfortunately, when their record company heard that we were releasing our version, they rushed-released The Equals' track as a single, which went to No.1 in Ireland and the U.K. How unlucky can you get?

Funny Incidents – Depending Upon Who You Are!

An incident that happened early in the band's career took place one night when we were setting up our equipment to play in the Tara Ballroom, Courtown. At the time, we used small speakers, which we tied up to the top of the pillars at each side of the stage. To reach them, in the absence of a ladder, Joe Weadick put a chair on top of a table and stood up on it to place the speaker on the pillar. The speaker was heavier than Joe anticipated and he overbalanced and the inevitable happened. Down came Joe, speaker and chair in a heap. Larry Kenny, standing close by, went running over to the site of the accident shouting; "I hope the bloody speaker isn't damaged"? Fortunately, Joe was only a little dazed!

The staple menu for the band at break time, when playing in Barry's Ballroom, Rathdrum on Sunday nights, was stale black pudding sandwiches, probably left over from the previous Friday night. Having arrived to play in the Edel Quinn Memorial Hall in Kanturk, County Cork, we were directed to the local cafe where a meal was available for us at the committee's expense. We went in and gave our order. We were the only customers at that time of the evening. While sitting waiting for the food to be prepared, George noticed that the sauce bottles had fallen over on each of the nine tables in the room. Being the 'Good Samaritan' that he was, he decided to stand them all up properly, just in time for the waitress to arrive from the kitchen to give him a 'lecture' - the bottles had been laid down on purpose to ensure that the sauce was at the top of the bottle for easy dispensing!

We arrived in Glasgow on a Thursday evening to play a weekend gig, only to find it was the wrong weekend - we were to be there either the previous week or the following week. We had to borrow money to pay our ticket home on the ferry! Another (Columbia) 'Highlands' occasion. We played a long weekend in Aviemore, a ski resort about ninety miles north of Glasgow. At that time, the Highland Games were being held there and it was a great occasion. We were free during the day, with plenty of time to go site-seeing and mountain climbing.

One day we decided to stay around and watch the games. Eddie bought a raffle ticket, and when the draw took place his ticket was drawn. Being on the opposite side of the field, Mac thought he had better get himself over to the stage to claim his prize. To this end, he decided to take a short cut across the field. Just at that time a whistle blew, signalling the start of the semi-finals of the caber tossing. Mac found himself running across the field with small branchless trees falling on either side of him. Ironically, the prize was a bottle of whisky and he was a teetotaler!

We arrived in Dungannon, County Tyrone on a Friday night to play a gig. As we arrived, Sonny Knowles and the Pacific Showband arrived at the same time. One of us should not have been there - guess who? One phone call later and it was discovered that we should have been in Duncannon, County Wexford - not in Dungannon, County Tyrone!

A Not So Funny Incident

It was to be our BIG BREAK! We were going on tour to the 'States'! As the time drew near everything was in order. We played a 'going away' gig in Arklow, taking requests from some of the punters for their friends and relations living in the US, and who would be coming to see us during our trip. In those days, there was a reciprocal arrangement with the American music industry, in so far as that for every American band that travelled to Ireland, an Irish band got to go to the States. We were on this deal. Having made all the necessary arrangements, we were all ready to go, except that two days before our departure, the American band was involved in a serious traffic accident, which put them off the road. We were not allowed to travel as there was no band to exchange with us. We were told this ONE day before we were due to travel.

The Big 'O' and the Everlys

One of the highlights for me, and I'm sure for the rest of the band, was that for a time we got to travel Ireland and share the stage with some top American bands. One artist that will always stay in my mind was Roy Orbison. A thorough gentleman who would sit in the dressing room with the band and discuss life on the road in Ireland. In the same bracket I would place the Everly Brothers. They always had time to chat to you and showed a genuine interest in what you had to say. I'm sure the rest of the band will be mentioning other artists, some good experiences but, unfortunately, some not so good.

What Was I Thinking?

Before I finish I had better mention my worst experience with the band, before some of the other members mention it for me. We were in a recording studio in Dublin. We had just put down some tracks for our next single release. The session went very well. In those days, you didn't take months to produce a single track - one or two takes and you had to accept the outcome - the record company didn't believe in spending a lot of money on studio time.

However, on this occasion we had a little time left and the studio engineer suggested we try something different, just to fill in the balance of the four hours. At that time, one of my instrumentals with the band was 'The Sailor's Hornpipe', which went down well with the audiences around the country. I had just found a similar track called 'Happy Heindrick's Polka', which I had been working on, so the guys suggested I put this down on tape. Naively I tried it, but when it was finished I looked at the people in the control room, to see them laughing their heads off. I knew that I hadn't really cracked it, but didn't think it was that bad!!! Later on, I did get it right on stage and the 'Polka', like the 'Hornpipe', was relatively successful with the fans!

The 'Hi-tech' Sixties

When I think of those recording sessions I realise how primitive the facilities were. Usually the full band, plus vocals, were all recorded at the same time. I remember on one occasion, when setting up for recording, the engineer came to connect my amplifier. I expected at least a direct inject box, but he had a long cable with two 'crocodile clips' on the end. These he clipped on to the terminals of one of the speakers in the cabinet and that was it. Not the most hi-fidelity technique. Another experience I had was in Eamon Andrews Studios (which used to be the Television Club in Harcourt Street). This had been converted into a recording studio. I was playing an acoustic guitar on one of the tracks and was put into a cubicle. 'Cubicle' was the operative word - it was one of the cubicles in the gents' toilet. It had a mike and a set of headphones. It was so small I had to reverse into it and take the guitar in after me. I had no visual contact with the band and had to take my cue from George's count-in. When I hear the criticisms of the showbands by some of our current 'top bands', I often wonder what they would have produced under the same circumstances.

Appreciation

At this stage I would like to pay tribute to Mark Canavan from Avoca, who supplied the musical foundation to so many of us musicians whose memoirs appear in this book. He was the consummate musician and gentleman.

In Retrospect

Towards the end of the band's days, Eddie, Pat, Pat's wife Breda and myself continued with the Family, a cabaret group we had been experimenting with for a little while. With the addition of that great musical talent, Matt Sharpe, the Family went on to considerable success, the high point being an appearance at the Royal Albert Hall, London.

The Columbia ceased performing during September 1969, the year Teresa and I were married. Since then I have played guitar with many different line-ups: The Family; Misty; Sheelagig; Homers Knods; a two-piece with Liam Garret; Kynochs; Black Velvet and the eleven piece Arklow based Nashville Experience; meeting new musicians and renewing old friendships with the remaining band members.

I have nothing but great memories of the Red Seven and Columbia, among which are Pat Tyrrell's version of 'Jake The Peg'; George's contribution to 'Speedy Gonzales'; the marquee dances with their five pole tents and who can discuss the Irish showband scene without the name Dermot Hurley and his 'crazy boxes' cropping up. Finally, of course, there's our several appearances on Irish television. Such a pity that RTÉ recorded over the tapes.

The Circle Is Complete!

In the list of bands I played with since the Columbia, I mentioned my last performance (for the time being), playing with the Nashville Experience, a great Arklow eleven piece country band. It was in the Arklow Bay Hotel and, much to my great joy, two guys came to see me that night - they were Larry Kenny and Des Mulhall, the same Larry and Des who, way back then, gave me my first break with the Red Seven.

I joined the Red Seven with a cheap guitar, three chords and great expectations, but left with a slightly more expensive guitar, a head full of chords (thanks Jim) and a flight case packed with great memories.

Larry Kenny, Freddy and Des Mulhall
at the Nashville Experience Show in the Arklow Bay 2004

Columbia Showband in 1963

Red Seven Showband at the Arklow Entertainment Centre in 1962

Arklow's Homers Knods
Michael Kennedy (r.i.p.) John Kenny and Tom Grogan

Chapter 9 *George Byrne*

Whenever I am asked why I decided to be a drummer in a showband I always have to think for a while before answering. You see I was not particularly musical nor were any of my immediate family. However, from the early age of seven I did have a habit of tapping my knife and fork or indeed a spoon, to the sound of any music playing on the radio while sitting at the family table - waiting for my dinner or tea - much to the annoyance of my mother and father. Little did I think then that fifty years on I would still be tapping - but now to put the dinner or tea on the table! You see I have never worked at anything else – keeping the beat has been my life professionally since I was sixteen years of age. And in 2010 I am still loving it.

Looking back on it now I realise I must have had a natural ability for rhythmic sounds. Perhaps a musical gene which manifested itself in the beat and rhythm of music. Come to think of it I did have an uncle – my mother's brother George, who was very musical. He went to America around 1920 when he was very young. At that time one had to go to Liverpool from Ireland to get the boat to America. On the boat over to Liverpool he was feeling a bit sad having to leave Ireland and to cheer himself up he wrote (on the back of a Sweet Afton cigarette packet I was told) his version of the lyrics for the famous evergreen song of the time 'Step It Out Mary My Fine Daughter'. I only became aware of this in 1985 from my Aunt Ethel, shortly before she died at the age of 88, when I visited her in America with some of my family to celebrate her birthday. It was the first time I heard that little gem and moving story in the context of the period.

When the suggestion came up from some of my school friends in my early teens to start a little musical group I was all on for it – "yes" I said, "I will be the drummer". Apart from myself the group consisted of Seoirse O'Toole who played an accordian, John Kavanagh guitar and Terry Cummins who played the shakers and tambourine. We used to practise every Saturday in the late George O'Toole's garage beside his house at the Coast Guard Station, Seabank. My priceless (!!!) set of drums consisted of three poppy tins and two saucepan lids. I remember we held a band concert for our parents and neighbours one Saturday when we had a few tunes learned off. Two of the tunes were 'When the Saints Go Marching In' and 'Whistling Rufus'.

That group fell apart for some reason but I continued practising with other friends. Pat Mc Carthy, who had a piano accordion(eight years later Pat played with me again professionally in the Columbia Showband), Billy Lee who could play a tune on a harmonica, Jimmy McManus sang (Jimmy also played for a while in the Red Seven Showband) and Margaret Greene played piano. I upgraded my drum kit with an old snare drum which the mother of my friend, Michael Kennedy (printer) gave me. Also, my own mother, probably realising that possibly here was a future genius drummer! brought me to Dublin and bought me a small 18 inch base drum and a foot peddle in Goodwins of Capel Street. I was chuffed with myself and home I thought I would never get to try them out - nothing was going to stop me now.

Somehow the late Dennis Garvey, Templerainey School principal heard that I could play drums and one day during P.E. he handed me a drum and made me lead the class marching up and down the school yard keeping time. I felt I was in the Artane Boys Band !

I was so fascinated with drumming that I went to great lengths to further my chosen career! When the Arklow Entertainment Centre opened in 1958 I used to climb up to the high windows on the outside wall during dances to watch and listen to the drummers of visiting bands playing there. Unfortunately, or fortunately as it turned out, one night I was caught by the Centre Manager the late Paddy Lynch who was none-too-pleased. However when I explained that I wanted to be a drummer he took pity on me and let me in on occasion to listen to the bands.

I vividly remember the first real showband I saw and heard there, The Johnny Quigley Showband. I was enthralled by their drummer Tommy McMenniman. I particularly remember them playing two numbers 'Run Samson Run' and 'Yakadi Yac'. They were from Derry and they had a really great sound. Whatever doubts I had about my future career, after that experience my mind was completely made up - at the age of fourteen, in the year 1959, I was hooked on drums.

For those of you who may not know, I had a serious heart condition from birth which affected my growth. In 1959 I had to undergo a major operation in the Mater Hospital Dublin to re-arrange my heart mechanics - to put it simply. The operation included the first heart valve replacement in Ireland and thank God it was a major success, but I was out of action for up to six months. It was national news at the time and even to this day, a half century on, I am called on by the heart medical experts to prove that I am still alive?

I will never forget Des Mullhall for his humanity and concern during my re-cuperation period at that low point in my life. Des used to pal around with my brother Reg and another friend Roy Dempsey. He knew I was interested in playing drums and he brought me a set of drumsticks to the hospital. He wrote out on a card the way to play the single and double roll on the drums ... "left, left, right right, left left " and so on ... I eventually progressed to the paradiddle!

You know life can be very funny at times. Many years later one of the dedicated nurses who minded me so very well in the Mater Hospital had reason to hear socially about a very good young professional drummer. When she realised that this young drummer was in fact me she let it be known very vocally how I used to break her heart tapping the sticks on everything in the hospital, disrupting the whole place ... aaahhh but she was a saint and I was very fond of her. I think her name was Nurse Grey.

Shortly after I came home Des arrived at my house with, and gave me as a present, a big old set of drums, which he had got from somebody in Waterford. I can only say that I looked at them in disbelief and wonderment. I was over the moon with joy. He was an inspiration to me and there is no adequate words to describe his generous gesture. Not only did he give me the drums but he continued to teach me all the basic drumming skills which have stood to me to this day.

I quickly got back to practising with Pat, Margaret and Jimmy McManus. When we built up a sort of dance programme we looked for bookings and managed to get one playing for Marie Boyle's 21st birthday party. It was held in the K.B. Hall on Ferrybank and our fee was five shillings. We just about managed to get through the night, and I can't remember if I ever got paid! For some reason, I can't remember why, our group faded out after that. However Pat and I got a booking to play at the wedding reception of the late Billy Forde. It was held in O'Toole's Restaurant on Main Street in August 1960.

I continued to improve my drumming and before long was asked to play with two other friends I knew - David Orr and David Purcell who were starting a small group. I agreed and started practising with them. I do remember we played a gig in Dunganstown and believe it or not Freddy Cutland, who I was to join with later in the Red Seven Showband, played on that occasion with us. In October 1960 I was lucky to be asked by the late Noel Maguire to play with his new Arklow band, The Harbour Lights. This gave me an opportunity for regular playing and I was able to brush up on all the different dance timings. But I do remember that when I first played with them I was very tired due to the length of time we had to play - I was not used to playing five hours!

In December 1960 I had my first experience at playing with a big professional orchestra. You see my father worked in Brennans Bakery and they held their annual staff dance every New Year's Eve. It was one of the biggest social events of the year in the town at that time. My parents went and brought me along. My father happened to mention to the late Jack Quirke, who was manager of Brennans and chairman of the dance committee, that I could play the drums. Mr. Quirke persuaded the orchestra leader, the nationally known Jack Hanly, to let me play a few numbers with them. Which I did and if I may say so myself it sounded very good - the dancers responded with great applause and I was naturally delighted as were my parents. I was fifteen years old at the time (1960) .

In July 1961 Des Mulhall announced that he was leaving the Red Seven Showband to go professional with the Jack Ruane Orchestra from Ballina. He had left his job in the Arklow Pottery. The man who was to take over from Des in the Red Seven was the late Paddy Lee from Rathdrum. Paddy had been auditioned and was practising with the band and had played once in the Ormonde Ballroom during the tea break. By the way it was normal in those days to play up to five hours at a dance. The band always split up for a tea break half way through the night. Did you cop that I said "tea break" - there was very little alcoholic drink available in ballrooms in 1960. Enough of that for now. When Des finally left, Paddy, for personal reasons, backed out when asked to join fulltime. I believe it may have been due to transport difficulties from Rathdrum where he lived. Very few young people could afford cars then.

It's ironic that the next time I saw Paddy Lee after his brief sojourn with the Red Seven was many years later when I was driving through the junction at Deans -grange, Dublin. A young child suddenly ran out in front of my car and I stopped suddenly - but he continued on and made contact with the side of the car and fell down. However he only received superficial injuries. As a precaution an ambulance was called - and who was driving it - Paddy Lee. I often wondered was there a particular lesson in that experience! To this day I have not been involved in another car accident while driving.

So, at the tender age of sixteen years I got the opportunity of a lifetime when I was asked to try out with the Red Seven Showband. I remember my first night with the band was in the Tara Ballroom Courtown in July 1961 where they were in the middle of their second summer season residency there. For some reason I did not travel down that night in the famous passion wagon - Martin Byrne's minibus. Maybe the boys felt I was not yet grown up enough! I was picked up at home by Joe Weadick in his Austin Somerset.

Needless to say I was petrified during the performance in case I would make a mistake. But I need not have worried as I surpassed myself and never looked back… I was on cloud nine. Remember I was only sixteen then and was in fact the youngest drummer to play in a showband in Ireland at the time. And because I was small in stature I only looked fourteen and this fact alone made me very special in the eyes of the patrons and indeed made the band unique.

After I was accepted in the Red Seven as a permanent member I went all out and bought my first kit of Premier Drums from Pigott's Dublin. I remember the salesman was Tim Wren. Because we did not have a car (my mother was with me) he was good enough to drive us to Arklow with the set of drums. He was actually going to Tinahely for the weekend. I remember he was driving a black Morris Minor.

After the summer season residency in the Tara Ballroom ended in August 1961 the band continued to go from strength to strength and I was enjoying every minute of it. I was satisfied that I had proved my worth. Indeed the drum solos that I played became more technical and entertaining as time went on and always drew a large crowd around the stage. Two of the solos were 'Let There Be Drums' and 'Wipe Out'. To this day I am still asked to play 'Wipe Out'.

Because of the band's continuing success the possibility of going pro was discussed seriously. While most members liked the idea, some gave it very deep thought weighing up their future in terms of their day job and possibly their on-going financial security. Of course this did not apply to me as I was not working at the time. However the result was that there were a number of personnel changes in a short space of time.

Before I joined, Freddy Cutland, who I have previously mentioned, had been added to the band and was a great addition on lead guitar. Paud O'Brien, an original member had already left and was replaced by Leo McHugh who played trumpet - a good jazzman, but had his own unusual individual style of playing. Pete Coburn, our lead singer left in September 1961 and was a huge loss. Paddy Merrigan of Kilahurler, who was known as a good singer, was recommended, auditioned and taken on but only stayed a few months. I believe he went on to university.

Jimmy McManus was recommended by Larry Kenny to replace Paddy and taken on for a trial period of three months, was quite good but unfortunately did not get the permanent job. Heads were put together again to look for a good local (if possible) solo singer and a number of people were auditioned. Eventually we were successful in taking on Eddie McElheron, recommended by Freddy Cutland as an excellent ballad and country &western singer. At the time Eddie was working in Avoca Mines, was a very agreeable person and fitted in very well with all the lads.

Apart from the problem of getting some good lead (front) singer to replace Pete Coburn, which was now hopefully solved, there was the concern that we needed someone to manage the band (Pete had up to now been the manager, even though he got no extra money for this job!).

I remember one winter's night in the practice room we had a very serious meeting about electing one among us to take over the band manager's job. Even though I had only recently joined I was included in the discussion. We all agreed that we could not afford to hire an independent manager. There was a lot of heated discussion and several times during the night the band was on the verge of disbanding because nobody was prepared to take on the responsibility. Remember there was a lot of work attached to running a band which included taking bookings, looking after the finances, i.e. paying travelling expenses, members wages and paying income tax on an annual basis for the group.

Looking back on it now one can see the humorous side of it all. On the night in question we had lost the key to the main door to the practice room and someone managed to open the back window, which we all got in through on arrival. So we had to leave the same way. Many times during the aggravated discussion someone would lose their patience, mumble a few expletives and decide to leave ... through the window ... and half way out would be persuaded with some comforting words by a budding negotiator, to come back in again and resume discussion. This happened to a few of the lads before the final resolution was reached. Can you imagine the scene, - one stepped out and then stepped in again - another stepped out and then stepped in again!

Yes, there was the funny side to it but the problem was regarded as very serious at the time. The person who eventually took on the responsibility was Joe Weadick. Shortly after that Jim Tyrrell, who hadn't yet joined the band but very involved behind the scene, came on board and agreed to act as booking manager from January 1962. He played guitar and sang and took over playing trumpet in May 1962 when Leo McHugh finished with the band. Leo left the Avoca Mines then to take up work in Dublin.

I remember another very heated and vocal meeting taking place - in our minibus, at no less a place than the Arklow pier head, to decide on the person to replace Eamon Lee, who bowed out of the band in 1962. We chose that area so that nobody would be able to hear us shouting etc. A number of musicians had been mentioned, including Mick Tyrrell and James Kenny (Larry's brother) who was in fact being tried out with us. Like in all walks of life there was a certain amount of politics involved. However Mick Tyrrell won out in the end because he was regarded as the most suitable for the position at the time and was recruited on bass/vocals. Joe Weadick got the unenviable task of telling the unsuccessful candidates.

I could go on forever telling stories about the Red Seven/Columbia Showband from the time I joined in 1961 to 1969 when it terminated. But I will settle for a sample of my most embarrassing, interesting, sad and funniest experiences.

Since the dreaded word 'Income Tax' was mentioned above I will start with a very embarrassing story about tax difficulties on my band earnings. A lot of people reading this would, I'm sure, never have heard of the "Town Crier". Well this was a man employed on a casual basis by the town council, government or indeed by some other institution/business to announce to the townspeople some urgent or interesting event about to happen in the town. For instance the town council would hire him to alert the townspeople about drinking water problems (e.g. that the water will be turned off for some period for repairs etc.). The local auctioneer might hire him to announce an upcoming auction. He would walk all the streets of the town suitably dressed, ringing a bell continuously. At the same time shouting repeatedly "Hear Yee, Hear Yee" - followed by the agreed message.

In my case the Income tax sherrif, a Mr O'Leary if I recollect correctly, arrived at my house with an official notice which he said he was going to erect at the front gate to advertise an auction of items in my house to recoup £170 for unpaid income tax which was owed by me to the revenue commissioner. He threatened to hire the 'Town Crier' to walk by my house ringing the bell to announce the auction. The Town Crier at the time was a local man known affectionately as Jim Skerries.

Needlesss to say my mother was mortified when she heard this and immediately made arrangments to pay the bill the next day to stop this public disgrace on the family. I don't ever remember anyone else subjected to this humiliation before or since. It happened around 1967 at a time when each member of the band was responsible for sending in his own tax returns and paying any money due. Of course I had got notices and reminders but was a bit lazy about dealing with it - it was a good few bob in those days. If this system was in vogue today the Town Crier would be a very busy man! - maybe it should be resurrected again!

Back to more enjoyable memories. We would often play in conjunction with visiting artists from abroad. One such person we played a number of gigs with was Houston Wells. He was an English country & western singer who had hit records with, among others, 'Only the Heartaches', 'Wild Side of Life' and 'When My Blue Moon Turns to Gold'. His dress nearly always included a black leather jacket adorned with a yellow cravat around his neck (his trade mark).

One evening while we were having a meal in a restaurant before performing with him, Pat Tyrrell up to his usual showpiece tricks, tied a big yellow duster around Eddie Mac's neck much to the amusement of the other band members, and told the staff and diners in the restuarant that he, Eddie, was Houston Wells. Of course very quickly everyone present asked for his autograph. Eddie duly went along with the crack and signed autographs for everybody present. We all ate up quickly and left before Hueston Wells arrived. I don't think the skit went down too 'well' (excuse the pun) with Mr Wells. I believe he is still hail and harty and singing to this day in New Zealand where he eventually emigrated to.

We played a number of times in two band sessions with the English chart topping group Brian Poole and the Tremeloes. I will never forget the evening we played with them in Thurles. Their drummer, Dave Munlin, helped me set up my new set of Ludwig Drums which I had just bought (for £170) and about to play for the first time. It was one of only three sets of Ludwig in Ireland at the time. The Tremeloes and Brian were a very friendly bunch of lads.

Other groups touring Ireland that we played warm-up to, or on a double bill with were, Roy Orbison (a brilliant artist and a gentleman), Rolf Harris, The Brook Brothers, The Everly Brothers, Dusty Springfield, Sandy Shaw, The Rockaberries, Big Dee Erwin, Unit 4 plus 2, Marty Wild and the Wild Cats, Bridie Gallagher, Maisie McDaniels, Georgie Fame and the Blue Flames, Cliff Bennet and the Rebel Rousers, and The Magnificent Seven.

The Red Seven/Columbia were well known for doing showpieces/sketches. Effectively taking a leaf out of the Clipper Carlton Showband's book, who were famous for their 'Juke Box Saturday Night' shows. Two very popular sketches we did were 'Doctor I'm in Trouble' and 'Theres a Hole in the Bucket', featuring Pete Coburn and Pat Tyrrell. I also did one with Jim Tyrrell who sang the hit song 'Speedy Gonzales' recorded by Pat Boone. I donned a very wide mexican hat and sang in a high pitched dramatic mexican twang '... laa..... lala lal a lal a la....' during the solo breaks! Being so small you could hardly see me under the large hat. The number went down great with the dancers. Most of the sketches/showpieces we did were show stoppers - where a large crowd would stop dancing and stand around the bandstand watching and enjoying the sketch.

Pat Tyrrell did a few other sketches. One, during a Rolf Harris number 'Jake the Peg With My Extra Leg' which Jim sang. In the middle of the song Pat would go behind the stage curtain and come back out strutting around the bandstand wearing, between his legs, a big 'Third' (artificial) leg - with trouser and boot on and a big water tap attached to the top of it. It is hard to describe the spectacle here but believe me it looked extremely funny and Pat's antics were hilarious - it went down a treat with the crowd.

Another of Pat's sketches which had the crowd in stitches was performed when Jim sang the Ernest Tubb classic 'I'm Walking the Floor Over You'. During it Pat used tramp around the bandstand stamping his feet loudly in front of the audience, with the legs of his trousers pulled up above his knees and deliberately looking ridiculous, making faces in response to Jim's antics while singing - all part of the show...brilliant.

Over the years we performed many other special showpiece numbers, all of which were popular with the dancers. Like - 'Up Went Nelson', 'The Jolly Tinker', 'You're Sixteen', 'Let There Be Drums', to mention but a few.

The Hucklebuck song, made famous on the Irish circuit by Brendan Bowyer and recorded by him in 1965 was, I believe, first played in Irish ballrooms by us and in fact was one of our main showpiece songs from 1962. Jim Tyrrell, who sang it, had resurrected it from a record by Chubby Checker he heard some time previously.

One night after a dance in the Arklow Entertainment Centre where we played warm up for the visiting Royal Showband, Michael Coppinger, their sax player, asked us about the Hucklebuck, which we had finished our session with. It had, as usual, gone down great … The Royal, I believe, had not heard of it before or if they had they didn't realise its potential until they experienced the reaction we were getting from the dancers.

Michael Coppinger took up his sax and asked Pat Tyrrell to play it on his until he, Michael, worked out the beat and tune. I tapped the rhythm with my drumsticks. It was not long after that the Royal put it into their repertoire and finally, in 1965 Brendan Bowyer recorded it and it immediately became a hit for him. To this day it's one of the most performed dance songs in Ireland.

One of the most embarrassing moments I can remember during my nine years with the showband, was on the night of my 21st. Birthday. We were playing in Dungiven, Northern Ireland. In the middle of a dance set, Pat Tyrrell brought out onto the bandstand a big fancy parcel, announced to the audience that it was my birthday, handed me the parcel and insisted I open it. With a packed hall and all eyes staring at me I had to unwrap the many layers of paper to reveal a very small toy drum to all and sundry! - the place erupted in laughter. I, being a very shy type - in public - was wishing that the floor would open up and swallow me. And of course the boys sang 'Happy Birthday' and the dancers joined in.

Food and eating arrangements was a very important aspect of our lives in the band. Many interesting experiences come to mind. We used to grade the venues we played in by the way they treated us in the food/refreshments area. One particular hotel ballroom we played in regularly always produced the same type of sandwiches which were always ice cold, obviously served to us straight out of a fridge. We were convinced that the sandwiches were put back into the fridge freezer if not eaten to await our return when they would be served up again. We even put a mark on one of the sandwiches to see if it turned up the next time we played there - I don't believe it ever did.

The Longford Arms Hotel, owned by Albert Reynolds, who was later to become taoiseach, was a very busy place, catering for all the bands playing in any of the Reynolds ballrooms in the area. All stopped off there on their way to the venues as part of the booking arrangement, to enjoy a substantial meal - and I might say in fairness to Albert, the food and service were always excellent. You would often get three or four bands dining together on a Sunday evening and the craic would be mighty.

The Richmond restuarant near Portobello Bridge, Dublin was another popular place for bands dining - at 2 or 3 in the morning after gigs around Dublin. A lovely lady named Molly (from Tinahely, I believe) was the boss there, knew everybody in the band business and looked after us all with the best of steaks, onions, mushrooms, chips etc. Molly used to let a particular 'Man of the Street' (I think his name was Norman) in on occasion and give him a meal. He was a simple innocent fellow who used to sit out of the way in a corner making brass instrument sounds with his hands over his mouth, entertaining one and all.

By the way, those after hours meals had to be paid for by the band and could be costly. Our lot liked their food and never held back. If one of the boys decided to have steak everyone had steak. If one of the boys wanted chips, mushrooms and beans everyone had chips, mushrooms and beans. You see, when the bill had to be paid out of band expenses all made sure to get their worth! A brilliant food related story concerns us playing at a carnival in Pilltown, County Kilkenny. We were having some tea and sandwiches in the catering tent and beside us was a canvas screen shielding the kitchen area from us. There was a gap of about three feet between the bottom of the screen and the ground. Pat Tyrrell noticed a lovely pair of legs, obviously attached to a young lady working in the kitchen, and said to Eddie Mac; "how would you like those legs wrapped around you?" Suddenly, a mature woman came from behind the screen, slapped Pat on the face and said; "that's my daughter you are talking about". The moral of the story was; if you are going to say something controversial, make sure you are not heard by the wrong person!

We had many food experiences while on tour in England. One occasion stands out in London when we stayed in a bed & breakfast place owned and run by an Irish couple. We, of course, were very good living then, believe it or not, and always went to mass on Sunday, wherever we were. When we got up after playing on Saturday night, Eddie insisted we go to mass. Some of the lads wanted breakfast first, but the landlord said he would have it ready when we arrived back. When we did come back after mass, there was no sign of breakfast. We were ravished with the hunger and when we could wait no longer someone asked where is the breakfast. To which the landlord replied; 'sure the dinner will be ready shortly. No need for any breakfast now'. We learned very quickly that there were more problems than we needed in that hostelry - your own doesn't always look after you!

Writing about food reminds me of a very sad tragedy that stands out in my memory. It happened one night after we stopped on the way home from a dance, at Mick's Hamburger Stand in Blackrock, to get something to eat. The lads from the Mexican Showband were there and pulled out just ahead of us. Shortly after we left, we came on an accident and stopped. The manager of the Mexicans, Tom Cranny, who we had just been talking to at the hamburger stand, had also stopped and had gone across the road to see if he could help the person in the crashed car, but was knocked down by another oncoming car and killed.

Travelling was a risk that was part of life for all showbands, particularly when traversing long distances to and from gigs through the night in all weathers. In the early days of the band, we used to hire a minibus from the late Martin Byrne, who I'm sure has been mentioned many times with affection by other lads.

When funds allowed in 1962, we bought our own minibus. Much to Martin's disappointment, not so much because he was losing business but because he really enjoyed being with, and almost part of, the band for almost two years. He loved it all. Our first minibus was a secondhand red and yellow coloured Volkswagen. It looked well and for a year or so was reasonably reliable. I remember we bought it from Glenbrook Motors, Bray for £145, and I think the number was ZP 347. We all took turns driving it and this in itself increased the risk driving home from gigs when we were tired.

In 1963 we went big time and bought a new state of the art powder blue coloured Commer minibus. It looked very well and give us a perceived higher status in the showband world. Although not yet fully professional, we were travelling much longer distances and this put an extra strain on us driving. To ease the situation, we used to change drivers every sixty or so miles.

When we turned professional in 1964, with elevated status and better funds, we mostly employed drivers. The late Jimmy Cullen was our main driver and he was invaluable to us in that he was also a mechanic and could carry out most of our repairs. Not only that, but his dry wit was priceless - you could always rely on him to cheer us up when the need arose during long journeys. I must also mention here his three brothers who also drove us from time to time when Jimmy was not available, and all were mechanics too. They were the late Larry, the late Frank and Mick, who is himself an accomplished piano accordian player still busy on the local circuit today. Also, on occasion, Anthony Maguire drove. We eventually sold the Commer minibus and did a hire deal with Percival Motors in Gorey. The colour of this new minibus was beige. Ned Harney, Tom and Jim Mulhall were our main drivers thereafter, until the winding up of the showband.

One incident with the Commer minibus I remember well happened when Jimmy was driving us to play in Bandon, County Cork. Someone looked out the side window and saw, through a reflection in a shop window across the street, the back wheel of our minibus on fire and shouted Jimmy. He quickly stopped and Eddie was quick to run into a nearby church looking for a fire extinguisher to put it out. There was a women in the church cleaning and she refused at first to give Eddie an extinguiser because she said; "I need it in case the church goes on fire!" Eddie's quick persuasion convinced her to give it to him and the bus was saved. Jimmy nursed the bus along to the venue, but it eventually broke down there.

Getting away from travelling and transport stories and back to the showband highlights. Without doubt, the most memorable occasions I had the good fortune to be involved in with the band included the making of the records listed below. Of course, the real highlight was when we appeared on the RTÉ *Showband Show* in 1966. We played our new record at that time, 'Way Out of Reach', sung by Eddie Mac. It went to No 6 in the Irish hit parade. It was one of six singles we made during the lifetime of the showband, listed here:

1964 … Before This day Ends/In Your Arms	(Eddie McElheron)
1965 … Way Out Of Reach/The Spinning Wheel	(Eddie McElheron)
1967 … Back To The Hills/Song Of The Sea	(Eddie McElheron)
1967 … She Thinks I Still Care/That's My Pa	(Eddie Mc/PatTyrrell)
1968 … Someday You'll Call My Name Devoted To You	(Eddie McElheron)
1968 … Baby Come Back/Born to Lose	(Jim Tyrrell)

Other great shows we were involved in at RTÉ were *The Life of Reilly* and *The Go 2 Show.*

During the sixties, which was essentially known as the Showband Era in Ireland, many came and went and most were very professional. I have to say that my favourite showbands were (1) The Plattermen -great brass, (2) The Freshmen - Billy Browne and Derek Deane were excellent performers, especially doing Beach Boys numbers and (3) The Dixies - Joe McCarthy was out on his own for showmanship, and he is still performing.

We must have played in hundreds of ballrooms in the eight years I was with the Red Seven/Columbia and I can honestly say we were received very well everywhere we performed. Some great venues and very hard to pick favourites, but the ones I particularly thought had that little extra atmosphere, and looked forward to playing in, were the Tara Ballroom, the Arcadia (Cork), the Arcadia (Waterford), the Brandon, Tralee and the Four Provinces/TV Club, Dublin.

Incidently, mentioning Waterford reminds me of the only time my health let me down when playing to a packed hall one night in the Arcadia. For some reason, I got very weak at the drums. Pat Tyrrell noticed me about to fall over and grabbed me. I was helped off the bandstand discreetly and Pat took over until I recovered about fifteen minutes later. 'The Show Must Go On', was our motto, and I wasn't about to break that principle. The crowd hardly noticed the disruption and it never happened me since, almost fifty years on, on the professional stage. I have been very fortunate and hope it continues for a long time yet.

After the demise of the Columbia Showband in 1969, Jim, Michael, Timmy and I got involved in a new country & western band called the Ranchers until 1973 when Jim, Michael and I started the very successful Jim Tyrrell Trio, which continued until the late eighties.

Because I am still at the music entertainment game and reasonably busy with the 'Groove', I have not, until writing my experiences contained herein, given much thought to the past and my time with the showband - now nearly fifty years ago. But I must say I have enjoyed thinking and looking back with nostalgia at what was a most fullfilling part of my life. All the boys I worked with were a tonic to be with. There was never a dull moment, plenty of fun and jokes and pranks. Yes, from time to time differences of opinions did arise about many aspects of the business, but never a serious confrontation about anything. I feel privilged to have worked for such a long time with a great bunch of talented musicians. It is so sad that we have lost two of our brothers along the way. Eamon Lee, who as a young man in the Red Seven, I always thought was a true professional, and Jim Tyrrell who in my mind was a true musical genius and who, I believe, never achieved his full potential.

In conclusion, I want to mention one very special part of my life with the Red Seven/Columbia Showband. Most of us met our partners during our time in the band and each has his own particular story. I vividly remember the circumstances I met Oonagh, my beloved wife of twenty-five years. I was travelling to Ballybunion from Cork on my own to see Tommy Horan, who owned a ballroom there, when my Triumph convertable broke down in Macroom. We had played in the Arcadia, Cork the night before, stayed in the Victoria Hotel, and the boys had gone home to Arklow in the bandwagon.

As my sister Gladys and brother-in-law Jim lived in Castleisland, I rang them and Jim came to the rescue. He gave me a loan of his car while mine was being fixed. That night outside the ballroom in Ballybunion after the dance, three young girls who recognised my brother-in-law's car, came over and asked for a lift home to Castleisland. Having explained the car situation, I agreed. When we arrived at their destination, the girls asked me in for a cup of tea as a 'thank you' for the lift.

I could not take my eyes off one of the girls who introduced herself as Oonagh and whose home it turned out to be. For me, it was definitely love at first sight and the rest, as they say, is history.

George and Joe - taken in Trafalgar Square, London in 1964 while on Tour in Britain

Practising with my first band in 1959 with the set of drums Des gave me. Terry Cummins, Seoirse O'Toole and John Kavanagh. Fans! looking on were: right to left – Jim, Gerard and Francis Kavanagh, Lorcan O'Toole, Anthony Dermody and John Dermody (standing)

Nightshade
George Byrne, Thomas Power, Maureen Smith, James Kinsella

Vintage in Woodenbridge Hotel 1981.
L to R: Liam Garrett, Jim Tyrrell, Pat McCarthy, George Byrne, Joe Weadick, Michael Tyrrell
(not in picture, Bobby Byrne).

The Groove

Martin Byrne, James Bannon, George Byrne.

Chapter 10 *Leo McHugh*

I was born in Sligo town into a musical family. My mother, my two sisters, Monica and Cepta, my brother Gus and myself were all musical. In our teens, Gus and myself started the Connelly Pipe Band of Sligo - Gus became pipe major and I leading side drummer. I enjoyed every minute of it. The band is still strong today over sixty years on.

Incidently, the pipe band performed at the famous writer and poet William Butler Yeats' re-interment in Drumcliffe, County Sligo in 1948. He had died in France and was buried there. His wishes were that he be buried in County Sligo. After fifteen years, his wishes were carried out.

After hearing Dixieland jazz music played by the Coliando Orchestra in the Ritz Ballroom in Sligo, I decided that was the music I would like to play. Every Saturday, I would listen to the band rehearsing. I got to know Louis Henry, the lead trumpet player and he sold me an old silver slide trumpet for five pounds. Louis' father taught music and, after six months learning from him, I was ready to play in a band. Louis let me sit in with the band at times to get used to playing with a group.

Around that time – the early fifties – a local man, Tom Reynolds, had a small group in Sligo and he asked me to join them. We played in all the local halls around the county. It was good experience. The pay was five shillings a night.

At the time, I was working in the construction industry as a junior surveyor. To qualify as a quantity surveyor, I had to go to Dublin. About 1952, I arrived in Dublin where I attended Bolton Street College. In my spare time, I played in various groups around the southside of the city. The Pat Jones Band played all the tennis club halls and Jim Phillips played in the National Ballroom, Parnell Street. At the time, we only played on Sunday nights.

In 1955, I joined a company as their quantity surveyor and had to go around the country on various contracts, so I could no longer play in bands. I married Ann Costello from Sligo in 1956 and had two sons, Nigel and Ken. Ken played a great piano. I wanted him to play in a band - he never did.

As a matter of interest, I got to know Joe Lynch the actor and singer - well known in the RTÉ series *'Living with Lynch'*, *'The O'Riordans'* and *'Glenrow'*.

He asked me once to loan him the old silver trumpet for a prop in one of his series. I never got it back. Joe has since passed away.

In 1957, at the age of 27, I came to work in St. Patricks Copper Mines, Avoca, as a quantity surveyor and mining surveyor. I was involved in the construction of the mines houses, canteens, workshops, main milling plant and finally the underground mine shafts and tunnels. My assistant surveyor at that time was Terrance McNamara, the bank manager's son from Arklow. Sadly, during my annual holidays in 1960, I got word from the mine survey department that Terrance was killed in an accident underground. Roy Dempsey from Arklow then became my assistant surveyor. Roy was, and still is, a great lover of jazz music.

One day, shortly after coming to the mines, I mentioned to the late Des Kinsella of Glenealy, who ran a local dance band, that I played the trumpet. He invited me to join the band. However, I told him that I did not have a trumpet. He soon arrived into work with a coronet, which he got a loan for me from a friend of his – I believe his name was Byrne.

While I was very grateful to Des for taking me into his band, I soon realised the the type of music the band played was more of the 'Ballroom of Romance' vein and little or no jazz, my favourite music.

While discussing this with my work colleague Roy Dempsey, he told me of the Red Seven Showband and mentioned that they may be looking for a trumpet player. I went to listen to them and liked what I heard. I then expressed an interest in joining them and was accepted. At that time Larry Kenny, the trumpet player, decided to change onto a clarinet. Joe Weadick played the trombone, Pat Tyrrell played saxophone and Freddy Cutland played guitar – this was the making of a good jazz band.

The Red Seven Showband had a great sound and were a great pleasure to play with. As well as all the hit tunes of the day, they were very competent at playing jazz which was right up my alley. We all played pretty tightly together, even though we had no written arrangements in front of us. We did a lot of practice to get it right.

I had the pleasure of playing with Des Mulhall, a great drummer, in Courtown Harbour, just before he left to join the well known Jack Ruane Orchestra. George Byrne took over from him and was the youngest and smallest drummer in Ireland at the time, however he quickly made a name for himself. I distinctly remember him drumming during my jazz solos. It was not long before he mastered the timing that I liked to play to. I believe he is still playing professional after all these fifty or so years. He really enjoyed drumming and I felt then that he was in it for the long haul.

I joined the Red Seven Showband mid-1961 and had to leave around May 1962 as I left the mines to work in Dublin where I joined the South City Jazz Band. We played every Sunday night in the Green Lounge on St. Stephen's Green. However, after some months my work took me outside Dublin and I had to leave that band as well.

I must say that of all the bands I played with, the Red Seven Showband was to me the best. We played well together. The sound was very good, a good band plays to each other and the Red Seven Showband did exactly that.

Joe, Des, Leo and Pat taken in Leo's house, Glenageary in 2007.

Chapter 11

Paddy Merrigan

One day, in the summer of 1961, I got a visit from two of the members of the Red Seven Showband – I am not sure who they were, but one may have been their lead guitar player, Freddy Cutland. At the time, I worked in the Avoca Mines with Leo McHugh, who was in the band, and I understand he recommended me for the position of vocalist/rhythm guitar, because they were looking for a replacement for Pete Coburn who was leaving.

I had been interested in music from an early age. So much so that I purchased a guitar and taught myself to play it – I still have that guitar today. I also play classical guitar. I had a reasonably good voice and could accompany myself on the guitar, so the idea of joining the Red Seven appealed to me, as the band was very good and very popular throughout County Wicklow and County Wexford at the time.

I agreed to be auditioned and remember singing 'Living Doll' at it. The boys in the band listened, were satisfied and offered me the position. I started practising with them right away and, in September, started performing at dances. I remember three of my favourite numbers were Cliff Richard's 'Living Doll', as mentioned above, and 'The Young Ones' and Johnny Tillotson's 'Poetry In Motion' – all of which were in the hit parade around that time.

I received an excellent response at the dances and was really enjoying the experience. I'd have to say playing with the Red Seven was the highlight of my life during that period. Particularly playing in the Arklow Entertainment Centre and in the Tara Ballroom. Unfortunately, I had to leave that November, because I had started my education in UCD and it was not practical to remain in the band. While I often sang a few songs at family events throughout my life, I never got involved in the music entertainment scene since those happy Red Seven days, which I still treasure and feel privileged to have been part of.

Chapter 12

Jim Tyrrell (r.i.p) written by Joe Weadick.

Jim Tyrrell was born at 54 Lower Main Street, Arklow, on November 5th, 1938. His talents were first recognised while he was still at primary school in Templerainey, where he was very good at drama and recitations. He was entered every year in the local *feis* and won many trophies and medals.

At the age of six, Jim started learning to play the piano with his aunt Kathleen Tyrrell, who was a renowned piano teacher for over half a century in Arklow. It was not long after starting piano tuition that Jim was able to name any note on the piano while undergoing aural tests. In later years, Seán Bonner, musical genius, who is mentioned many times in this book, said of Jim that he had perfect pitch– a rare talent.

Jim's mother kept holiday-makers during the summer, like many houses in Arklow during the forties, fifties and sixties. One of her guests was the piano player from the resident band playing for the season in the Ormonde Ballroom called Billy Driver. He introduced Jim to jazz by teaching him 'In the Mood'. Even though he was only nine years of age at the time, he became so interested in jazz that he used to listen to all the big American and British orchestras on A.F.N radio. Another tune he couldn't help but learn around that time was 'I'll Take You Home Again Kathleen'. It was sung by some man in 'Failey' Rafferty's pub across the road every Saturday night after consuming copious pints of Guinness.

When Jim was fourteen years of age, yet another guest in his home, Eddie Harrison, a trumpet player in the Ormonde Ballroom resident band, used to practise in the back garden and Jim became so fascinated with the sound of it that he persuaded his mother and father to buy him one. And where was it bought ... by mail order in Cotts of Kilcock.

After attending St Patrick's Academy on Gregg's Hill, (affectionately known as Mac's Shack), Jim continued his education in Gorey CBS, and passed his Leaving Cert there. He taught English in McCarthy's School for a year before getting a good secure job as a clerk in CIE, Bachelor's Walk, Dublin. Most young men would give their right hand at that time for such a job with great potential for a life long career. But he continued to have a great love of music and obviously had other ideas.

It was not long before Jim, staying in a bed-sit in Harold's Cross, bought a guitar, mastered it sufficiently to get a position playing it, the trumpet and piano in the Dublin band of Johnny Gavin. When the opportunity arose towards the end of 1961 he joined the up-and-coming Red Seven Showband on trumpet and vocals. Jim was, of course, the older brother of Pat who played sax in the band, his younger brother Michael joined shortly after Jim in 1962.

While working in Dublin, Jim found it difficult to play gigs with the band and get back to work on time, so to solve this problem he bought himself a new Austin Mini, the extra money he was making in the band helped pay for it. The mini was his pride and joy. Once at practice, there was a discussion on how many people could fit into an Austin mini and Jim, reluctantly, allowed eight of the lads pack into it to prove a point and he carried them from the practice room on Ferrybank to Bumpta's Snooker Hall for a game. Can you imagine the nine guys piling out of the mini in front of the garda barracks which was situated nearby at the time!

In January 1963, the success of the Red Seven was such that it was decided to change the name to the Columbia and aim for professionalism. Jim, who had already been the booking manager, took over full responsibility for running the band from yours truly. It was not long after that that Jim decided his work in CIE was getting in the way of his music career and it had to go ... the job that is. A major lifetime decision for most people, but as I recall Jim took it in his stride. Like most of us at the time, he saw a future of fame and fortune. It's fair to say that he and the showband achieved some fame, but unfortunately no fortune.

Early in 1964, those who still held down a full time job gave it up to pursue a professional career in the Columbia. At this time also, Jim, with approval of all band members, worked out a managerial deal with Arklow man Dan Bolger who promised greater opportunities. Dan, who was studying in University College Dublin at the time, was involved in booking bands for student dances and had important contacts in the showband world, promoters, ballroom managers etc.

Everything went well for nearly a year, but bookings were slacking off and in early 1965 Jim suggested to us that he could do better himself, so we came to an amicable termination agreement with Dan. Dan went on to manage a new band starting out called the Express Showband, but gave that up a year later after graduating as an engineer from UCD and emigrating to Canada, where he still resides today. Dan's own interesting recollections of the Columbia are contained in this book.

From 1965 to its demise in 1969 Jim saw a number of changes in the line-up of the band. I left in 1965 and was replaced by Pat McCarthy. Pat was head-hunted by the Miami Showband in 1967 and was replaced by Oliver Merrigan. Oliver left in 1968 and Timmy Weadick was recruited.

Over the same period (1965 – '69) various deals were done with three more managers namely; the late Hugh Hardy, Mike Nolan, and finally the

Jim Tyrrell Trio
Michael, Jim, George. 1970's

Coolgreaney Jazz Band in the 1970's
George Byrne, Jim O'Callaghan, Michael Tyrrell, Jim Tyrrell, Pat McCarthy and Andy Cusack (sitting)

late Jim Hand. It seemed that nothing was going to stop the downhill slide, brought about mainly by the natural end of the showband era. Only a few top showbands survived on the national scene into the seventies and beyond.

Forecasting the end of the line for the Columbia Showband, Jim started, with George, Michael, Timmy and others, The Ranchers, a country & western band, which ran for four years. During that time he also formed, with George and Michael, the Jim Tyrrell Trio. It was hugely successful throughout the east coast and went on until 1986. As an extension to the trio, Jim started the Coolgreaney Jazz Band, which included three additional members, Pat McCarthy, Andy Cusack and the late Jim O'Callaghan. It too ran successfully well into the nineties. In the early eighties Jim, Michael and

George were also part of the band Vintage. The other members of that band were Liam Garrett, Pat McCarthy, Bobby Byrne and myself.

Throughout all his years in the Red Seven/Columbia, Jim gave his full energy to promoting the band, but more importantly to ensuring its musical success. He was a prolific music arranger - nothing less than perfection was his motto. He was brilliant at arranging and performing harmony numbers, in particular Beatles and Rolling Stones songs with Eddie, Pat and Michael. His singing/recording of 'Baby Come Back'/'Born to Lose' in 1968, the last disc made by the Columbia, was excellent even though it did not get anywhere in the charts. Jim arranged all six of the records the band made, five of which were sung by Eddie Mac (Pat sang 'That's My Pa' on one of them). All very good quality numbers, but unfortunately only one made it to the Irish Top Ten at No.6, that was 'Way Out of Reach'.

As mentioned many times in this book, the Red Seven/Columbia accompanied many visiting artists to Ireland. One of these Jim was particularly proud to have been involved with was the iconic singer Roy Orbison who, during a chat after the show, encouraged Jim to write songs. This he did after the Columbia days and wrote 'The Well Runs Dry', 'The Light Of Day' and 'Tommy Tin'.

Jim was also very proud of one other musical part of his life. It was the teaching of his neice, Roisin Murphy - the now famous 'Moloko' - the finer points of singing. Roisin made a special visit to Arklow to perform at Jim's 'This Is Your Life' tribute in the Arklow Bay Hotel in 2003.

You will remember the story I related earlier about Jim's Austin Mini and his sojourn to Bumpta's Snooker Hall with nine lads in the car. Well, on another occasion attending that snooker hall he did something that was perhaps the most important act of his life, although he did not appreciate it at the time. You see when he arrived in the hall he saw the girl of his dreams - the late Willie Kavanagh's daughter Linda playing snooker - stretching across the table with cue in hand sizing up a shot as he passed by. He couldn't resist giving her a gentle tap on her buttocks.

The reaction was not quite what Jim was expecting. It was swift and direct - Linda quickly turned and gave him a stinging slap in the face. Jim, despite the pain, forced a smile and immediately thought of Linda's father (known as Bumpta among the snooker players – but dare anyone call him that) and the possibility of being banned from the hall for life. One of Bumpta's strict rules was; "You can look but you can't touch". However, Jim managed to charm Linda into forgiving him. Needless to say, it was not love at first sight, but love did blossom in time and they got married four years later in 1967. In 1969, their son and heir Ronan was born.

Throughout the showband era of the sixties and the succeeding years of his professional career Linda was Jim's rock - and soul mate - surviving all the ups and downs, especially the financial business associated with the Columbia. One thing she was particularly proud of was when Jim, who was forever looking for new material to sing in the band, came across the 'Hucklebuck' on a Chubby Checker record he heard in 1962. He sang it, made it his own and turned it into a crowd stopper for the band. The Royal Showband heard him perform it as they waited to go on stage at a two band session in the Entertainment Centre one night, expressed interest in it and soon after they had it in their repertoire, eventually recording it in 1965.

An emotional farewell

Linda looked after Jim's every need when he fell into bad health until his untimely death in 2007. Her abiding memory of him is that he lived, slept and consumed music to the end and he would not have been happy any other way.

Jim had a fitting and emotional farewell from his colleagues of the Red Seven/Columbia who performed a guard of honour at his funeral. And a selection of his fellow musicians led the funeral cortege into the cemetery playing 'Just a Closer Walk With Thee' - a New Orleans Negro Spiritual funeral march. At the graveside after Jim's burial, the boys played 'When the Saints go Marching In', and finally 'The Party's Over'.

I'm certain Jim would have been really chuffed with this moving musical tribute on his final journey. He was so particular in organising band activities one might think he organised it too. He all but did plan it, you know. Six weeks before Jim died, Pat McCarthy happened to mention to him that he, Pat, could not attend a relative's funeral in Dublin because he had been booked to play at another funeral that day. When Jim heard this, he said to Pat; "Well I am booking you now to play at my funeral".

May he rest in peace.

Jim with Roy Orbison in 1966 when he appeared with the Columbia Showband in the Las Vegas Ballroom in Tuam, County Galway.

Jim's 'This is your Life' celebration in the Arklow Bay in 2003 with Joe, Eddie, Pat, George, Oliver, Michael and Des.

Chapter 13 *Jimmy McManus*

My introduction to music began when I was in Arklow Boys National School. The late Seán Bonner was my teacher and he started up a school 'Harmonica Band' which I joined. I, and all the boys in the band, got to love the music - perhaps it was partly because of the diversion from the reading, writing and arithmatic lessons which could be trying at times. Looking back now, we did not really appreciate how lucky we were to have such a musical genius among us. I'm sure Seán was responsible for hundreds of young lads taking an interest in some form or other of music during their lifetime. Due to the musical gene aroused in me, thanks to Seán Bonner, I started taking part in the Arklow Youth Club Boys' Choir and Christmas pantomimes under the direction of Michael Byrne, who eventually went on to form the Arklow Silver Band. I played Fagan in *Oliver*. Another show I took part in was *Rosemarie* and remember singing 'Three Lovely Lassies' in a trio with Michael Molloy and Vincent Walsh.

I palled around with Pat McCarthy during my technical school years, and I got involved for a while with him in a small band which included George Byrne, who was to become the professional drummer in the Red Seven/Columbia Showband. Pat, who also later joined the Columbia for a while, played the piano-accordian and I sang. Margaret Greene was in the band too, as was Billy Lee.

When George got the drummer slot in the Red Seven Showband in the summer of 1961, we were delighted for him. Pat and I often listened outside when the band was practising in Sweeney's building beside the Arklow Memorial Hospital - now the Arklow Bay Hotel. On a few occasions, we saw George walk out in bad form and go straight home. He was probably under pressure trying to keep up with the programme – remember he was only about sixteen and the band was, you could say, semi-professional at the time. Such was our interest in the band that we used to make a point of listening outside the Ormonde Ballroom and the Entertainment Centre when they performed there.

Seeing George enjoying the Red Seven Showband made me itch to get involved seriously in the music business, even though I was only sixteen years old. That same summer, I too got lucky. I was asked by the late Noel Maguire (a true gentleman) to sing with the new Harbour Lights Showband he was starting. I was delighted and cut my teeth, so to speak, with them.

Towards the end of 1961, I heard through Larry Kenny that the Red Seven were looking for a singer. I expressed an interest even though I was only just coming up to seventeen years of age and, at the time, could not play a guitar. However, I was auditioned along with Eamon McDonald and the late Larry Mythen and, surprise surprise, I was the one who succeeded in getting a trial run with the band. Needless to say, I was over the moon.

Unfortunately, the trial period only lasted for three months, to March 1962. Joe Weadick, on behalf of the band, thanked me for my great efforts and wished me the best for the future. Shortly after that Eddie McElheron was taken on as lead vocalist and rhythm guitar player and he remained in that slot until the Columbia Showband broke up in 1969.

Avonaires Showband 1963
Mark Canavan, Paud O'Brien, Frank Harper, Matt Sharpe, Kevin Harper.
Sitting: Jimmy McManus and Eamon Lee

During my time with the band I played in a number of ballrooms and enjoyed every minute of it. The most memorable night for me was the Mayfair Ballroom in Kilkenny city. Among the numbers I sang that night were two very popular hit songs from the charts, 'When my Little Girl is Smiling' and 'The Night Has a Thousand Eyes'. Even if I do say so myself, they went down very well with the crowd.

Apart from enjoying the actual performances in the Red Seven, I also loved the craic travelling to and from the dances. One of the drivers who I remember very well was the late Tom Farrell. Like most of the drivers the

Kynochs - in the Eighties
Pat Tyrrell, Jimmy McManus, Anna Kennedy, Freddy Cutland, and John Joe Brauders

Red Seven/Columbia had in their time, Tom had his own unique character. It wouldn't be long after arriving at a venue that he would check out the refreshments and where appropriate he would announce; "there's a crate of beer laid on tonight lads". Every town and village we passed through on the way, Tom would give a running commentary on them and finish each time with his famed witticism; "SALLY BANANA".

Aahhhh ... I would have to be honest and say I did miss the buzz when my time was up with the band. But life went on and it was not long before I was on the road again spending some time in a number of bands including the late Jay Byrne's, The Echos and The Avonairs, led by two stalwarts in the music business of the time, Mark Canavan and Kevin Harper. All this time I matured as a vocalist/rhythm guitar player. I finally joined yet another new Arklow Group, the Avonsiders, run by the late Paddy Coleman. Out of the Avonsiders was born Kynochs, which became very popular along the east coast and which I eventually ran for many years after.

In conclusion, I must say that I still have happy memories of my time with the Red Seven Showband and the experience gained in it has stood to me throughout my musical career.

Chapter 14 *Eddie McElheron*

I joined the Red Seven Showband in the spring of 1962. A friend of mine, lead guitarist with the band, Freddy Cutland, told me that they were looking for a good singer since Pete Coburn left and he asked me if I would be interested. Even though I had no experience what-so-ever in singing with a band, I was keen to give it a go. I was invited to a practice session, sang a few songs and was immediately offered the lead vocalist job, much to my surprise, and I accepted.

I have to say, I had no real musical background nor did any of my family that I am aware of except perhaps my brother Vincent, who could sing a decent song. I do believe Freddy thought of me because he remembered me singing well in McCarthy's Secondary School. My initiation into singing was in fact in Arklow National Primary School where I was picked to sing in the School Boys' Choir, which was started there by a new young and enthusiastic teacher called Seán Bonner - who was to become immersed in everything musical in Arklow throughout his career, until his untimely death at the age of 58. Indeed Seán, I believe, helped the Red Seven get started by arranging some of their material.

I remember the first night I played with the showband. It was on Whit Sunday Night 1962, in Barry's Hotel Ballroom, Rathdrum and my divi was £2 - not bad considering that the average weekly wage at the time was about £9. I can't remember much about that first night, except that it was a very late dance to 2 or 3 a.m. - and that during our break we got hot soup and freezing cold sandwiches (a feature of Barry's late night cuisine).

When I joined, Jim Tyrrell was the musical director and booking manager, while Joe Weadick managed the financial end. It was a co-operative arrangement - everyone got an equal cut after expenses. Joe handed over control of the finances to Jim in January 1963 after Jim bought a new binson echo chamber for the band in Hurley's, Cross Guns Bridge, Dublin, and produced it at Brennans staff dance, where we were playing on 31st December. Even though Jim's intention was good, and the echo chamber was a great addition to the band, Joe was concerned that, in keeping with band policy, any money spent should be agreed by all members beforehand.

Due to our continued success throughout 1962 we decided, in January 1963, to work seriously towards making the showband a full time career. At the time the Avoca Mines, where I worked, was nearing closure so taking the gamble of a new career in the music business was worth a try. Particularly since the showband phenomenon was in full swing throughout the country, including Northern Ireland. The opportunity for bookings across the water in Britain was also very real. We believed that we had the ability and enthusiasm to do well.

To raise the profile of the band we decided to change the name from the Red Seven to a more sophisticated sounding title and after many names were bandied about we settled on Columbia Showband. We also traded in our old Volkswagen minibus for a new upmarket light blue coloured Commer minibus, which looked the part ... we were on our way!

Liam O'Reilly, who was the eighth member of the band at the time, decided not to pursue a professional career so he left in the summer of 1963. This left the line up as follows, Jim Tyrrell on trumpet/vocals, Pat Tyrrell on sax/vocals, Freddy Cutland on lead guitar, Joe Weadick on trombone/keyboard, Michael Tyrrell on bass guitar/vocals, George Byrne on drums and myself lead singer/rhythm guitar.

One of the necessities when going pro was that we had to join the Irish Federation of Musicians in order to be allowed perform in Dublin. I remember we all had to sit a music exam. The late Jack Flahive was the examiner on the appointed day and he sat down at a piano and asked me to sing two verses of a song. I passed with flying colours, and so did the rest of the boys!

The first night we played as a full-time professional band was in May 1963 in Moynalty, County Meath. The reason I remember it so well is I had just got a few months care and maintenance work in the Avoca Mines, which had closed down some months previously. I was to start at 8 o'clock the next morning and was not at all looking forward to it after getting home in the early hours, but could not afford not to go as our band receipts, even though we were doing fairly well, still needed a bit of a boost. I got very little sleep that night.

As we got better known around the country, our good reputation reached Northern Ireland. Towards the end of 1963 we were getting regular bookings there. Remember this was long before the so called 'Troubles', which effectively began in 1969. It was the time of the 'B Specials' police. While we never had any real problems when playing in the North, we always felt a certain amount of tension in the air. Some examples of our experiences are given in the following paragraphs.

It was always necessary when arriving at a venue to ask which national anthem we were to play at the end of the night. If it was a Catholic area it would be the Irish national anthem and in a Protestant area it would be the English national anthem. In the cities, where there would be a number of halls with a mixture of patrons, we would be instructed to play no anthem.

We once made the mistake, in the Astor Ballroom, Belfast, of unwittingly playing 'Fine Girl You Are', a famous Makem and Clancy song in the hit parade at the time. It created a tense reaction among the dancers and we were wrapped over the knuckles by the hall management. We never got another booking there.

One night preparing to depart after playing a gig in Dungannon, a young man came running to us in some distress and asked for a lift away from the area. We obliged, but never got to the bottom of his predicament.

While playing in a packed ballroom in Lurgan one night, a violent row erupted among dancers in the middle of the floor while we were playing a number (can't remember the song). Chairs were flying over heads and very quickly a group of bouncers arrived at the fracas. From the bandstand, we had a full view of everything and, needless to say, we were frightened that the row would envelope us and perhaps damage us or our equipment, so we made a quick decision to continue playing until things returned to normal, which they did after the bouncers unceremoniously hauled the offenders away. Boy, were we relieved!

One night when playing and staying in Armagh, the late Lar Cullen, one of our minibus drivers, who was known to play a few tricks from time to time, took Ritchie Hall's hot water bottle from his bed, loosened the cap and put it back under the blankets. When Ritchie went to bed it was wringing wet. He had to go from room to room until he found a dry bed to sleep in. Incidently, Ritchie Hall was one of our faithful followers and regular roadie. He travelled with us many times.

On the same night when I was getting ready for bed, I could not find the bottom of my pajamas. I asked all the lads if they knew where it was, but to no avail. The next morning when leaving, I saw it hanging from a flag pole outside the house. Eventually Lar owned up to it!

To give Lar some of his own medicine, one night when staying over in Smith's Bed & Breakfast House, Portadown, I placed, with Mrs Smith's approval, two of her bed sheets in a brown paper bag and planted them under the driver's seat. Before driving off the next morning, Mrs Smith came out to the wagon in a huff and said that two of her good bed sheets were missing and wanted to know if anyone knew anything about them. She acted the part very well, sounding very annoyed and insisted we check everywhere on the bus. Someone put their hand under Lar's seat and brought out the brown bag with the sheets in it. Needless to say, Lar was mortified and denied any knowledge of them. Mrs Smith carried on the skit by accusing him of taking the sheets. Eventually we all started laughing and owned up before Lar had a fit. When he realised he was the butt of the joke, he was furious and what he said is not fit (excuse the pun) for repeating here. By the way, Mrs Smith's Bed & Breakfast House was well known for keeping showbands from the south and she was a lady - now long gone to her rest.

We used to play regularly in Damian Scanlon's (Dana's husband) Ardmore Hotel outside Newry. One evening, when we were checking in at the border security post on our way to play at the hotel, we met the Dubliners who were also going north. That day, the last match of the Triple Crown was being played between Ireland and England and the Dubliners asked us if we knew anywhere they could look at the match. We suggested the Ardmore Hotel where we were headed. They followed us and we all looked at the match together. When the anthems were being played Ronnie Drew, Luke Kelly and Barney McKenna stood up and sang Amhrán na bhFíann, much to the uneasiness of some people in the room. We were worried that we might be thrown out or lose bookings there, but we managed to survive.

Mentioning the border post reminds me of the tedious procedure we had to go through every time we crossed it. The bus was always checked, together with all our instruments, which we would have listed on a declaration form. They would be interested in any type of illegal materials. I must say that my experience was that the northern security men were always courteous and helpful. In contrast, the southern security officers at the time tended to be very ignorant, unhelpful and in fact seemed to abuse their position.

Our first tour of England was during Lent in 1964, thanks to a well known Arklow man, the late Joe New of Abbeyville, who organised it when he was working and living in London. Joe had good connections within the Irish community there and got us booked into several of the Irish clubs. One was Kilburn, where he lived at the time. I remember that on the night we played in Kilburn, the late famous Fr. Cleary was also on the programme. He sang and told yarns and jokes to the dancers.

It was during the period of the outbreak of Foot & Mouth disease and because of that we flew to London, rather than take the minibus on the ferry. We had problems in Dublin airport on the way back with the Irish customs men who, for some reason, had no record of our musical instruments leaving the country. They were very unhelpful with our plight, indeed I would go as far as to say they were abusive. They maintained we had bought them in Britain and wanted payment of tax before releasing them. I got a brainwave. I pleaded with them to ring the customs in Northern Ireland who, because of our regular visits there, had the serial numbers of all our instruments on file. Confirmation was quickly given and it allowed the release of the equipment. With absolutely no thanks to own customs public servants!

In April 1964, we again toured Britain. This time for three weeks, with great success may I add, taking in Irish clubs in London (Tottenham Court Road, Harlesdon, Ballam, Slough, Kilburn, The Gresham (Holloway Road), Birmingham, Coventry and Manchester. This tour was organised by our first outside manager Dan Bolger of Arklow. Dan was a great friend of mine during our school days. Those who may not remember Dan, he is a son of the late Mrs Bolger who was principal in the Arklow Infant Boys School from the fifties through to the seventies when she retired. His brother Paddy helped with some of the band management duties during his sojourn with the band. Dan eventually emigrated to Calgary, Canada, where he has now retired.

Dan was our manager for fifteen months, from September 1963 to the end of 1964. He was studying engineering in UCD at the time and very involved in organising dances in the Four Provinces and elsewhere in Dublin for the 'Sivilkems' students union. He had gained a lot of experience dealing with showband managers and promoters and had made many contacts. He admired the Columbia and figured we had a great future. He came out one night to the Palm Beach Ballroom, Portmarnock, where we were playing and made us a proposition. It seemed reasonable and we decided to do a deal with him. Dan lost no time in getting us into the best ballrooms throughtout the country. One of the first such bookings was in the Four Provinces, in Harcourt Street, Dublin, subsequently called the Television Club.

Through his contacts he succeeded in getting us double bill performances with a number of British and American artists touring Ireland. Many of them great people to work with, but as always there were some who were not so friendly. The following is a sample of some of our experiences with these visiting performers.

We toured a lot with the British country & western singer Houston Wells. He was a humorsome guy, who once asked me out to fight after a dance because I sang a few of his songs during our performance.

We played one night in the Jetland Ballroom, Limerick, with the Bachelors (one of their hit numbers was 'Ramona') when they were on tour in Ireland. They were totally unfriendly, not just to ourselves on the night, but also to fans looking for autographs. I distinctly remember one of them throwing away an autograph book handed to him by a young fan seeking their autographs.

Marty Wilde and the Wild Cats performed in Coalisland, County Tyrone, one night and we were on the double bill with them. Before the dance, Marty was trouncing up and down in the dressing room chain smoking. Each time asking his manager for a cigarette. I made a remark to his manager at some point about the amount of cigarettes Marty was smoking and he said; 'Yeah ... when someone else gives them to him'. During their performance, some dancers threw pennies up on the bandstand, because their performance was so poor!

On the subject of throwing pennies, I also remember an incident in the Olympic in Waterford when Georgie Fame performed. Such was the annoyance of dancers that they too threw pennies onto the bandstand. The ballroom manager went looking for us in a panic to go back on stage quickly to rescue the situation.

Roy Orbison, who we played with in Tuam, County Galway, was the nicest person I ever met. I will never forget the ballroom manager coming to Roy after the dance while he was talking to us and asked him to come and have his meal. Roy asked if we were coming too and the manager replied that we would get it later. Roy said he would wait until we can all dine together! I could see the manager was completely deflated by Roy's response and agreed to include the Columbia as well as Roy's entourage at the meal.

Towards the end of 1964, Dan was finding it very hard to win sufficient return bookings to maintain a reasonable income for us. Money got so tight that I remember one week we got no pay and Jim had to go to Dan's mother to see if he had left any money for us. We knew he was doing his best, but it was the consensus among the members at a crucial band meeting that the situation was deteriorating and that we might do better ourselves or with another manager. So, we reluctantly terminated our contract with him. It was a very difficult decision, as he was one of our own Arklow colleagues and a close friend of mine, but he took the whole situation very well. The financial affairs of our contract were worked out and agreed and we parted on good terms. Dan went on to manage the new Express Showband from Dublin for about a year (with the help of his brother Paddy) while still studying in UCD, before moving to Canada in 1966.

Joe Weadick, regretfully, decided to leave the band in March 1965, because he was not long married and was worried about the future of the band and his financial security. Joe persuaded another Arklow colleague, Pat McCarthy, to take his place and we were very happy to take him on. Pat, who was a good piano-accordian player, trombonist and a decent singer proved to be an excellent choice. Pat was very dedicated. He proved to be a talented performer and boosted the band's performance tremendously. Unfortunately for us, Pat was head hunted by the Miami Showband two years later and he joined them. Needless to say, he was a great loss, but we understood and were delighted for him as he was progressing to one of the top bands in the country.

In keeping with our policy to stick with local artists, when Pat left we recruited another Arklow vocalist, Oliver Merrigan. Oliver was an excellent singer with a wide vocal range and worked hard during performances to entertain the dancers. Two of his crowd stopping solos were 'Boolavogue' and an Elvis Presley number 'This Time You Gave Me a Mountain'. By the way, there was one experience I'm sure Oliver will never forget. It was on arrival home to Ireland after playing one weekend in Scotland during the time of the Foot & Mouth disease there. He was not allowed to go home to his family farm for a number of weeks over the Christmas period because of the danger of contaminating the cattle!

Arklow man Timmy Weadick was taken on when Oliver decided to quit the showband scene in 1968. Timmy, a young up-and-coming singer, had tremendous talent and was a great performer. He stayed with the band until September 1969, when we decided to call it a day, due mainly to the general demise of the showband business. Small groups were enticing the younger people into lounge bars where they could sit, drink and listen to music in comfort without bothering to dance. Only the very top showbands were getting enough income on the road to stay the course.

The last three years of our showband period were a roller coaster ride in terms of surviving in the business. We got involved with three different managers, namely the late Hugh Hardy (who managed Larry Cunningham and the Mighty Avons), Mick Nolan who managed and later married Anna McGoldrick, and the late Jim Hand (a true gentleman), in an effort to boost our bookings and money. Our arrangement with Hugh Hardy was that he took a percentage of our fees and, as the value of bookings rose, so did his fees. Similar arrangements were made with the others. We also got involved with dance promoter Jim Fox who arranged a number of tours for us in England.

Through these arrangements we got, for a while, quite a number of bookings around Ireland, England and in Scotland. One particular place I always looked forward going to in Scotland was the Cairngorm Hills HolidayResort. We got well treated there with very comfortable accommodation and the best of food.

It was near Glasgow and we used to visit the famous 'Barrows' Market there. I remember once we all bought great bargains in special fashion nylon stockings to bring home to our spouses etc. However, when we later opened them they were all seconds – some the length of a bed! It was just another expensive lesson we learned along the way.

We had one very unfortunate experience in Glasgow. On arrival there for a weekend booking we discovered that the Cowboys Showband was advertised. We were quickly told we should have been there the previous week. I was the only band member with any amount of money. We ended up sleeping in the ballroom for two nights and Jim had to borrow money from the manager there to survive until we got home.

As they say, if you can't beat them, join them. So when we finally wound up the Columbia showband, Jim, Michael, George and Timmy got involved with a new Dublin country & western band being formed called The Ranchers, which lasted for four years. In parallel to that Jim, Michael and George started the Jim Tyrrell Trio, which was successful for many years. Timmy continued to sing and play with a number of local groups and is still performing to this day.

Pat, Freddy and I went on to form the Family Group along with Pat's wife Breda, and Arklow man and all round musician Matt Sharpe. We played very successfully during the seventies in cabarets, lounges, hotels, weddings and concerts.

The Family highlights included the All Ireland Scouts Mass in Enniscorthy Cathedral, and the annual St. Patrick's Day Festivities Concert in the Royal Albert Hall, London. On occasion, when Pat and Breda were unavailable, we invited John Kenny and Tom Grogan of Homers Knods to join us and they were always an excellent addition to the group.

In 1978, I retired from the music entertainment business and took the day job in the 'Fert'. I was very happy there and, in 1979, the Harper brothers of the Avoca Ceile Band approached me to go to America with them as vocalist for the St. Patrick's Day celebrations. After some deep, thought I agreed to go and ended up accompanying them for three years in a row.

We had a brilliant time each year, touring the New England states which included parades, concerts, dances and cabarets. I made lifelong friends with the Ernde family (members of the Knights of St. Patrick), the Leonard family (record producers), and the late Tom and Ethel Kelly (members of the Ancient Order of Hibernians) and formally of Arklow. Everywhere we went we were treated like royalty, they could not do enough for us. It certainly taught me that the Irish immigrants in America really cherished their Irish culture and heritage - something we tend to take for granted at home.

Back to the seven years I spent in the Red Seven/Columbia Showband –

I have to say, it was a very happy and fulfilling period of my life. However, it was not all plain sailing from the financial aspect. We never really reached the high earnings we had envisaged when we embarked on our professional journey. But we did have many good laughs and highlights along the way. Among the most memorable ones for me were:

- Appearing on the RTÉ *Showband Show*
- Appearing on the RTÉ *The Go 2 Show*
- Appearing on the RTÉ *The Life of Reilly* (with Brendan O'Reilly).

Sharing stage with such illustrious visiting acts as Roy Orbison, the Everly Brothers, Brian Poole and the Tremeloes, Unit 4 plus 2, Sounds Incorporated, Big Dee Erwin, the Brook Brothers, Dusty Springfield and Georgie Fame were also highlights.

The release of a total of six records listed below. The first five featured myself, except for the B side of 'She Thinks I still Care', which was 'Thats my Pa', a great comedy number sung by Pat Tyrrell. The last record featured the late Jim Tyrrell.

- 'Before this Day Ends'/'In Your Arms', 1965
- 'Way out of Reach'/'Spinning Wheel' (6th in Irish Charts), 1965
- 'Back to the Hills'/'Song of the Sea', 1967
- 'She Thinks I Still Care'/'That's My Pa', 1967
- 'Someday you'll call My Name'/'Devoted to You', 1968
- 'Baby come Back'/,Born to Lose', 1968

'Way Out of Reach' was the only original song recorded by the Columbia. It was written by George and Audrey Meredith who were well known composers on the Dublin scene .

'Back to the Hills' was a magnificently written song by our own Seán Bonner who gave us permission to record it. Seán had entered it in the Eurovision Song Contest in 1967. Performed beautifully by Patricia Cahill and came 2nd in the Irish final. Unfortunately, Patricia had been given two songs to sing that night and it resulted in her vote being split, which I believe stopped her from winning it. It would have been a great tribute to

Seán had it gone through to the Eurovision Final, but it was not to be. After we recorded it, we learned that Patricia Cahill had also recorded it and she was not at all happy, because it affected her own record's success.

It is ironic that some years later, when I was performing with the Family Group, along with a lot of other Irish performers for a special St Patrick's Irish Night Concert in the Royal Albert Hall in London, we got talking to Patricia Cahill, who was also on the programme. When she heard we were from Arklow, she made it known that she had one sour note about Arklow. She said some Arklow band, the name of which she could not remember, recorded 'Back To The Hills', and it affected the success of her record. I just replied; "Is that so?" She did not realise she was talking to some of the culprits!

A question that came up several times over the years was; "how much money did you or the showband make on the records? Well, the answer is - wait for it - "twelve shillings and six pence"! The market in Ireland at the time was very small and most showbands made very little.

While all the above experiences, when reminiscing about my involvement in the showband era, gives me great satisfaction and fulfillment, by far the episodes that I am really proud of, as I'm sure the rest of the lads are, were those Christmas Open Air Concerts we organised and performed in the Main Street Park in Arklow for a period. We used the proceeds from them to buy Christmas hampers and distributed them to the town's senior citizens. Some of the funds also went to the Arklow Youth Club and other worthy local charities.

Our organising of those open air concerts required a lot of preparation work. It included erecting a Christmas tree in the park, which we got free of charge from the Forestry Department at Shelton. Paddy and Tom Byrne of Byrne's Sawmills, Ferrybank (where the Bridgewater Shopping Centre now stands) brought it to the park free of charge. We, the band members, put it up in the middle of the night - this was long before the town council decided to erect one. We decorated it with the aid of Christmas lights loaned by the late Paddy Lynch, who was manager of the Entertainment Centre. The late Jack Fitzgerald was good enough to connect up the electricity to ESB standards (free) and the town council paid for the electricity used.

Winding up the story of my showband life, I must tell a very personal funny story which I and my good wife Jean has laughed about many times since - and really characterises the way we, as a close knit happy group of musicians, were.

Almost everything in life has a financial side to it and my wedding night was no exception. You see, on the night before I married the love of my life, Jean Dempsey - after five years courting - Jim Tyrrell handed me my wages (after a gig in the Town & Country Club, Parnell Street, Dublin), in an unusually thick brown envelope, in the presence of the rest of the lads, and wished me, on behalf of himself and the boys, every happiness during our honeymoon and future married life. He said he and the boys would like to give me more, but bookings were slack, as was the money.

Needless to say, my eyes were popping out of my head at the size of the

On Tour in England, 1964
Joe and I Feeding the Pigeons in Trafalgar Square London.

envelope. I was itching to open it, but decided (after profusely thanking all concerned) not to until I got to the hotel in London on our honeymoon night. When Jean and I settled in, I produced the closed envelope and said to her; "this, my darling, is my first pay packet to you and hope that all the future ones will be at least as big". Jean lost no time opening it with excitement, only to see a lot of confetti falling out. Eventually she discovered a total of twelve pounds. We looked at each other speechless!!!

I said above that I had some great laughs along the way, but in this case the laugh was on me. Well you can't win 'em all. I started in the showband business with nothing and I left it with nothing, but I wouldn't have changed it for anything.

Pat Tyrrell, Paddy Lynch, George Byrne, Freddy Cutland, Bridie Colvin (Madam Lazonga), Eddie McElheron, and Jim Tyrrell

Chapter 15 *James Kenny*

I was born in Rory O'Connor Place, Arklow. My big brother Larry was ten years older than me and, as you can imagine, when growing up I loved listening to him playing the trumpet. When he got involved with dance bands, I followed his progress with great interest and dreamt that I too could follow the same path some day and enjoy the music. When I was about sixteen, I was very sick with jaundice and was laid up for two months. During that time my parents bought me an old second-hand guitar and I started to learn it - at least sufficiently enough to accompany myself singing, as I realised I had a reasonably good voice.

Incidently, the old guitar I bought happened to be a semi-solid Framus guitar, which suited me alright until I was able to get a more modern one. However, I kept that old guitar all my life in the attic and recently (2010) my son was interested in it so I brought it to a guitar shop to see if they could do it up for me, and the guy there nearly collapsed when he saw it. He said; "do you realise this guitar is a special antique and when done up could fetch up to five thousand euros?"

In 1962, without any previous experience in bands, Larry got me a trial with the Red Seven Showband because Eamon Lee had decided to leave. Of course, I was delighted, did a few gigs with them and was getting to like it. However, the lads in the band decided that they really needed a bass guitar player to replace Eamon, even though he played rhythm. Eddie McElheron, who was their lead vocalist, was also starting to play rhythm. The person who fitted the bill as bass player at the time was Michael Tyrrell, Pat and Jim's brother, so he replaced me. It would be untrue to say that I was not disappointed, but that disappeared shortly after, when I got a slot playing with the Echos showband, which I stayed with for some time and enjoyed immensely. Note the other ex-members of the Red Seven in this photo. My brother Larry, who left the Red Seven shortly after me, and Des Mulhall.

Noel Maguire, Des Mulhall, Helen Plummer, Pat O'Regan, Larry Kenny Sitting: Billy Kealy, Willie Lawlor, and James Kenny.

Chapter 16 *Michael Tyrrell*

I was born into a musical family in 1944. My dad's sister, my aunt Kathleen, was a piano teacher who taught all my siblings to play. I received piano lessons from her too when I was about ten years old, but did not pursue it in any serious way. My mother was very much into the Marian Arts Society and encouraged us all to join, which we did as each became of age. I was a young teenager in McCarthy's secondary school when I joined and remember taking part in musicals and other concerts and loving every minute of it. At the age of seventeen, I got a mechanical fitter apprenticeship in the Avoca Copper Mines and transferred to Roadstone to continue with it when the mines closed in 1962.

Because my two brothers, Pat and Jim, were in the Red Seven Showband, I used to listen to them practising and went to some of the dances they played at. It was not long before I too got a yearning to join the band. I decided to buy myself a bass guitar and learn how to play it, in anticipation of getting into the band when an opportunity arose. I felt I also had a decent singing voice for rock'n'roll songs and reckoned it would be an advantage.

When Eamon Lee decided to leave the band in 1962, primarily because he did not want to go full-time in the showband business, I expressed an interest in the position. James Kenny, Larry's brother, was also interested and played and sang with the band for a short while, but declined to stay and I, to my delight, was brought on board to try out.

In a very short time, I was playing and singing well, loving the buzz and the boys decided to give me the permanent slot. I really enjoyed singing the following popular rock numbers of the time: 'To Whom it Concerns', 'Yesterday Man', 'Long Tall Sally', 'Rock'n'Roll Music' and Manfred Mann's 'High Lily, High Lily, High Low'.

It is very difficult to pick out any one highlight during my seven years in the showband, but I reckon our appearance on the RTÉ *Showband Show* would certainly stand out, as would another RTÉ programme *The Life of Reilly*. I was also very proud to be a part of the making of six records, which were all great experiences.

Our many engagements in Aviemore in Scotland were always a pleasure.

The Columbia Showband, Arklow

Columbia Showband playing in Dublin 1966

Myself and Pat McCarthy on tour in London in 1966 with the Columbia

We were looked after very well and I still have some great memories of our time there. But one thing I remember which could have turned out bad was when Eddie won a bottle of whiskey in a raffle during a field day and nearly got himself killed crossing the path of the 'Kilt Wearing Pole Throwing Men' to collect his prize. Aviemore was a great place in winter to enjoy the ski-ing and cable cars.

My worst experience was in Cricklewood, London during a tour, when my favourite fender bass guitar was stolen after the dance. Someone walked away with it while we were busy packing the minibus. I'm sure this was not an unusual thing to happen to bands over the years. There is always someone watching – one can never be too careful.

While I totally enjoyed the five years as a professional player with the band and would not have changed it for anything, it was not a financial success. Coming near the end it was extremely difficult to secure enough dates and we realised it was time to call it a day.

I was delighted when asked by Ben Dolan to become a member of Joe Dolan and the Drifters Showband (and was urged to take the opportunity by my wife Betty! whom I met in the Tara Ballroom, Courtown in 1963 and married in 1967), but declined due to loyalty to the Columbia boys.

After the Columbia finished in 1969, I went along with Jim, George and Timmy to start the Ranchers country & western band, but it only lasted four years. Jim then started the Jim Tyrrell Trio and the Coolgreaney Jazz Band, with myself and George, both of which ran very successfully for almost twenty years, and we did at least manage to make a decent income.

After a severe stroke in 1988, it was touch-and-go for a long time, but thankfully I am still here and enjoy seeing our children and grand-children grow up. I can appreciate good music and have wonderful memories of the Red Seven/Columbia Showband.

Chapter 17 *Liam O'Reilly*

My first memory of any real interest in popular music was listening to Radio Luxembourg during my teenage years in the fifties - in particular the top twenty record programme. But the seeds of my love of music were no doubt sown much earlier than that through listening to my parents. My father played the button accordian and mouth organ and was pretty good at both. My mother was also very musical, she was a member of the Old Templerainey Church Choir in her youth. My brother Seán was also talented, played the guitar and sang in the Echos Showband. My adopted sister Mary and first cousin James, who was reared with us like a brother, were also interested in music.

My first attempt at playing any musical instrument was when I got hold of an old family instrument called the "Jew's harp". For those who may not know, it is a simple, small steel musical instrument, shaped a bit like a large key, held between the teeth and played by striking the free end of a flexible piece of metal with a finger while at the same time blowing on it to get different notes. It was difficult enough to master, but I managed to knock a tune out of it. Before long, I progressed to playing an easier instrument - the mouth organ, which I enjoyed.

After finishing primary school in Templerainey at the age of twelve, I spent three years in the Rosminian Order College in St. Michael's in Omeath, where I spent some time learning the violin and later learning the piano. It was while I was there that I got very interested in singing, I used to sing in the college choir. The highlight of my singing in that college was when I was picked with five others to perform at the consecration of three new altars in Carlingford church. The chief celebrant at the consecration was the Bishop of Neve, Bishop Conway, who later became Cardinal of all Ireland.

I remember one year when coming home for the summer holidays, I was given an old violin to practise on and all I did for the three months was play it as you would a guitar. Like most teenagers in the late fifties, Elvis Presley and Cliff Richard were our idols. Guitars were the in-thing. Playing a guitar and singing the songs from the hit parade was all I wanted.

In 1959, after three years in St Michael's, I had to make up my mind whether I wanted to enter religious life (by the way, the education there was free in the expectation that some pupils would join the order). I decided that the priesthood was not for me and left. I often wondered if it was my fascination with Elvis Presley (maybe Elvis was my God at the time ... only joking) and his music which had a major influence in my decision. However, I was very lucky, and thankful, to obtain a job at home helping on the Bloomfield Laundry, Rathfarnham, van (formerly the Kilmantin Loundry van) with the late Ralph Timmons. Of course, I did not have the money to buy a guitar, but my lucky day came when my older brother Seán, who had one and was playing and singing in the Echos Showband at the time, had to leave to take up a job in Dublin, gave me the guitar. Not only that, but he also got me into the Echos in his place. Needless to say, I was delighted and loved every minute of it. Some others in the Echos at the time were Billy Kealy, Pat O'Regan, the late Noel Maguire and Des Mulhall.

Then in Sepember 1962, I heard that the Red Seven showband, one of the most popular showbands on the east coast, were looking for a singer. Apparently, Eddie McElheron, their lead singer, was concerned that he might have to leave to work in Dublin because there was a danger of the Avoca Mines, where he was employed, closing. The band decided to recruit someone to take his place in the event that he had to leave. I was asked to audition for it and, to my great surprise, succeeded in getting the vocalist/rhythm guitar position. I vividly remember singing 'Wolverton Mountain' at the audition and was as nervous as hell. As I walked in to be auditioned, I met Tom Craine leaving and I thought he would get the job. I was really chuffed with myself to get a chance with such a formidable showband.

Thinking about my audition experience reminds me of the band practice room. It was part of John Sweeney's coffin storage building. One particular night I remember, we counted the number of coffins in the storage room and there were seven regular sized and one small coffin. At the time we numbered eight in the band - seven regular sized guys and the smallest drummer in Ireland. Maybe our choice of practice venue was instrumental (pardon the pun) in the name 'Dead Seven' being at times attributed to us by a few local wits.

The first night I played with the band was in Camolin. I was collected from my home at Templerainey and we stopped at Eamon Lee's house to pick up his band suit (blue) which I was getting. Eamon had left the band a short time previously and had been replaced by Michael Tyrrell. When I put on the slacks of the band suit at the hall, it was miles too big for me. Pat Tyrrell got me to tie a piece of heavy rope around it, which he took from a curtain at the back of the stage. I put on the coat and it hid the bulky pants and away I went thrilled to be a part of a big showband – I had made it. That night I sang, among other tunes, 'How Do You Do What You Do To Me' (Freddie & the Dreamers), 'This Song Is Just For You' and, of course, 'Wolverton Mountain'.

During the period I was with the Red Seven/Columbia showband, from September 1962 to August 1963, I had many special experiences – some good and some not so good. Here are a few examples:

My most embarrassing moment in the band was on St. Patrick's night 1963 in Courtown, when my mind went blank in the middle of singing ... would you believe ... 'Wolverton Mountain'. Eddie and Jim, realising what had happened came in quickly and helped me out until I regained my memory again. When the set ended, Joe came over and asked what happened and I told him my mind went blank for a minute and he replied; 'not good enough Liam – not professional'. I do believe it was the big occasion that got to me as the hall was full to the brim – there must have been two thousand people there. During the dances, the stage vibrated with the floor bouncing up and down.

As I lived two miles out of town and had no car, Freddy used to collect me if we were playing locally. One night, when we were playing a two band session in the Entertainment Centre, Freddy was late and I decided to walk into town carrying my guitar. A car came along carrying some of the members of the Magnificant Seven Showband from Derry who were playing the two band session with us. They recognised me and picked me up. This little episode was a small example of the camaraderie amongst bandsmen. They were a great bunch of lads and excellent musicians.

I remember another night in the Entertainment Centre when we played a two band session with Dusty Springfield, who was big in the hit parade at the time and was touring Ireland. After her group's delay in setting up on stage following our performance, and before she started singing, she said to the crowd; "Sorry for the delay, I am not used to playing in such a small hall". The remark went down like a lead balloon and did not do her reputation in Arklow any good.

One very important requirement for showbands to play in Dublin city in the early sixties was that they had to be members of the Federation of Irish Musicians. In order to be accepted into it, each person had to undergo a music examination. Before Michael Tyrrell and I joined the band, arrangements for tests for the existing members had been made for one evening in Dublin. Michael and I were not being tested on this occasion, but we went along for the ride, as did two friends Reggie Byrne (George's brother) and Billy Kinsella. However, somewhere around Bray the minibus started giving trouble – not pulling very well. It was looking like we might not make the test centre on time so it was decided to off-load some weight to help the pulling capacity of the minibus. Under the circumstances, the dispensible guys were Michael, Reggie, Billy and myself, so we were dropped off in Bray. It worked. The minibus engine picked up sufficiently and the rest of the band members finally made it to the test centre and, I'm glad to say, they all passed the examination with flying colours. In the meantime, we (the dead weight) made our way into Dublin and were picked by the boys at the Green Rooster, and all managed to get home safely.

One of the most memorable performing nights for me was when we went down a bomb playing in a two band session with Maisie McDaniels and the Fendermen in the Mayfair Ballroom in Kilkenny. There must have been between two and three thousand people there. We were advertised as the 'Red Seven Showband - those fabulous exponents of Swing'. There was an unfortunate hiccup when the Fendermen came on and started warming up for Maisie McDaniels. They were playing only a short time when suddenly all music stopped. The main plug had come loose in the socket. Pat Tyrrell, who was standing beside the bandstand, saw what happened and came to their rescue by jumping up on stage and reconnecting the plug.

We went down very well in all halls we played in, but two ballrooms stood out for me each time we played in them. They were the Tara Ballroom in Courtown and the Atheneum in Enniscorthy. There was always a great atmosphere and our fans always responded enthusiastically to our music.

One of the smallest crowds, I believe, we had during my time with the band was Christmas night in 1962 when we were booked to play in the Arklow Entertainment Centre. It was snowing that night and, to make things worse, Emile Forde and the Checkmates, who were touring Ireland at the time, were playing in the Ormonde Ballroom. Remember their famous hit number, 'What Do Ye Wanna Make Those Eyes At Me For'? Well, we got twenty-four people at our dance, which under the circumstances was understandable. Rather than cancelling it and going home, we decided to play the full four hours so that we would get paid, which we did in fairness to the manager of the hall, the late Paddy Lynch. We treated the few dancers that were there to a unique performance, which they enjoyed very much. We played our hearts out and even got down from the bandstand and played and danced around the floor, and at times played while lying on the floor.

We played a few times in two band sessions with the Royal Showband at Arklow Entertainment Centre. I remember one night they were very late arriving due to bad weather – snowing. Normally, we would use their amplification, but as the ballroom was already filling up we decided to use our own gear. Just as we completed setting it up they arrived. When the late Tom Dunphy noticed our equipment in place he said; "What's this"? We explained that we were concerned, due their lateness, that we would have to start playing. He replied that the gear will have to come down and theirs put up, which we complied with. During the discussion, Jim mentioned that we were going professional and asked Tom's opinion. Tom said that it can be a good life or not-so-good, but whatever happens you can look back and say "Dunphy told me".

Towards the end of 1962, a decision was finally made that the Red Seven was to work towards going professional as soon as the time was right. But it was also decided that the name Red Seven was not dynamic enough if we were to be successful in this new important venture. Before the name Columbia Showband was finally decided on, several names were mooted. One such name I remember was the Hanging Stones. I forget who suggested it, but it was an attempt to relate the name of the band with something historical in the Arklow area. For those who may not know, the Hanging Stone is a large rock that overhangs the sea at the south side of Arklow Rock, which itself – the Arklow Rock that is - is now nearly non-existant due to the Roadstone Quarry eating away at it over the last fifty years, however the Hanging Stone still survives. One of our first significant bookings in the greater Dublin area as the Columbia Showband was in the Palm Beach Ballroom in Portmarnock. And the man who booked us was the well known showband promoter and band manager at the time, Liam Ryan. I remember that before he decided to book us he came to hear us in the Entertainment Centre in Arklow. He was satisfied enough to engage us, but made a few comments on the presentation of the band, which he said he would like improved. I distinctly remember him saying that Freddie was to have his hair cut shorter. Naturally, we were delighted to get the chance to play in the Palm Beach, as it was a prestigious ballroom in the north Dublin area. And we were well received there, despite being new to the patrons.

It's ironic that just a few weeks before we were due to play in the Palm Beach our 'temperamental' minibus broke down as we passed through Abbeyleix on our way to a gig. We were all out pushing it along the street to try get it going when a voice from a passing car said can I help lads. Would you believe, it was the same Liam Ryan! Embarrassment wasn't the word for it. Do you remember Murphy's Law; "If it can happen, it will happen".

We had changed our name from The Red Seven to the Columbia Showband. We were getting busier by the month, so the next obvious step was the question of going professional. The decision was made, but I decided to pull out. At that time, I was anything but the best at making decisions or taking chances. I always needed someone to make up my mind for me. I discussed this "Going Professional" with my parents. They were against it - too risky. They strongly advised that I keep my good job in Arklow Pottery, where I was starting to climb the ladder. Little did I know that the rungs of that ladder were so weak. Anyway, I decided against going pro. The lads in the band urged me to stay on, but I didn't. I had enjoyed my sojourn with the Red Seven/Columbia and missed it a lot. It's true to say that, many times, I had a chip on my shoulder (more like a bag of chips on both shoulders) as a result of that decision. Especially when I'd see some of the lads in the new Commer, which didn't require pushing, and when I'd see some of them in their new suits. When the records started being released - more chips - I regretted missing the few years craic and touring, but I had decided, rightly or wrongly.As things turned out, after a year or so I was asked to join the Quartermasters, another popular Arklow group, and ever since have been involved in various bands and groups, even a later version of the Red Seven. There's no use crying over spilt milk but I did have regrets.

Freddy, Pat, Jim, Eddie, George, Joe, Liam and Michael.

Quarter Masters
Back Row:
Francis O'Brien,
John Mahon,
Liam O'Reilly (inset).
Front Row:
Willie Lawlor (r.i.p.)
and John Clancy.

Chapter 18 *Pat McCarthy*

When I was seven years old my weekly routine was a visit to my Aunt Lizzie and Uncle Jack Conroy who always had the radio on, listening to the Jimmy Shand Accordian Band, and the famous Dinjo's *Take the Floor* programmes. I got to love the music and used to tap out the beat with two sticks on a biscuit tin. One would have thought this would annoy my aunt and uncle, but the opposite was the case.

Noticing my interest, uncle Jack made me a set of drumsticks from two birdcage perches, the heads of which he carved beautifully. He also gave me an antique Regal melodeon. It was about one hundred years old, but still sounded very good. He showed me how it worked and, before long, I was able to play 'A Happy Wonderer' on it. If I am really honest with myself, because of their constant encouragement, I would have to credit them with my lifelong interest in playing music and singing. I still have, and cherish, that melodeon – it's in a prominent place in our sitting room to this day.

My father, listening to my melodeon playing, was very impressed and, realising I was really into it, went and bought me a new 45 key piano accordian on the never-never. He also paid for me to have lessons with the late Jimmy Hogan (father of John Hogan of Boru). Needless to say, I was very happy and dedicated myself to mastering this lovely new instrument. I remember the first tune Jimmy thought me was 'Lady of Spain'.

The late Seán Bonner started a school band in 1954 and I joined it. It was a great experience and gave me a sound start in performing as part of a large band. We played in the Marian Arts Variety Shows and in the Arklow Youth Club Shows. It was in one of these that I first started singing. I accompanied myself singing 'Kevin Barry'. Michael Byrne was the musical director for the club shows at the time.

During my time singing in the chorus line in the Youth Club shows, I often found myself automatically singing in perfect harmony to the solo line. I remember asking Seán Bonner about this, because I was worried I might be out of line and he assured me it was a great gift which few people have and said it will be a great asset if I ever want to pursue a singing career. This immediately made me think of my mother who used play the piano and had a habit of singing in beautiful harmony to songs she was listening to on the radio - and I realised for the first time it was from her my musical genes came from. My acting would have came from my father, who in his day was an amateur actor.

Every year the Youth Club went on camp and I brought my piano accordian and played it around the camp fire at night with some of the other boys who played guitars, etc. I remember one night in Graiguenamanagh, a local guy joined us at the camp fire and he played an old full size piano accordian. I was very interested in it, because it was much bigger than mine and he offered to swap with me. Foolishly, I did swap and when I got home my father went berserk and insisted that Fr. O'Reilly (who was over the club at the time) drive me back to Graignamanagh the next day to retreive my new instrument - which he did, much to Fr. O'Reilly's and my embarrassment!

In 1957, my friend Georgie Byrne, (who I was to play with in the Columbia Showband eight years later), invited me to join a little group he and a few friends were starting. I was delighted to get involved, even though both Georgie and I were only twelve years old at the time. The others were Margaret Greene, who played piano, Billy Lee, harmonica and Jimmy McManus sang. We called ourselves The Harmony Aces and enjoyed practising. We did a few gigs, but the group eventually petered out, for some reason I can't remember.

As time went by, I got pretty good at playing céile music. So much so that my late aunt Esther Cullen (wife of the late Billy Cullen - manager in the Ormonde Ballroom), who ran the Cullen School of Dancing, got me to accompany her dancers on a number of occasions for performances and competitions. It was great experience in playing different strict tempos, which is so important for Irish dancers.

In 1958, myself and some friends from our local street decided to start up a boy band and we called it the Connolly Street Band. Matt Sharpe, brothers John Joe and Tommy Brauders, and brothers John and Pat Shelton were the founding members. We were quite good for our age and played in many local events, including the Marian Arts and Ormonde Hall Variety Shows.

My secret aim around this time was to join a dance band, so I continued practising whatever dance tunes I could acquire, and eventually I built up a type of repertoire. I managed to get my first wedding reception booking (with Georgie Byrne) in August 1960. The venue was in O'Toole's Restaurant, Main Street and the wedding was that of the late Billy Forde and Doreen Mulligan.

In 1961, I played for a while with the local Quartermasters, which at the time included John Clancy, John Mahon, Francis O'Brien and Liam O'Reilly. We were quite good and played regularly for Sunday afternoon hops in the Entertainment Centre and as warm up for some of the visiting bands.

During all this time, I was trying out an old trombone which belonged to the long defunct Arklow Foresters Band. Their instruments were stored in the Union Hall in Bradshaw's Lane where my father's office was, he being the I.T.&G.W.U. representative for the town. I was there nearly every week with him, and over time got to work out a few numbers on the trombone. This instrument is another pride and joy of mine and is also in a prominent place in our sitting room today.

In 1964, I finally got my wish, when asked to join Arklow's Echos Showband, playing piano accordion, trombone and singing. Their members at the time were Des Mulhall (drums), Larry Kenny (sax and clarinet), James Kenny (guitar) - all three were ex Red Seven Showband - Billy Kealy (singer and rhythm guitar), Pat O' Regan (sax) and Noel Maguire (sax and piano accordian and band leader).

I was very interested in jazz and took every opportunity to play and sing it. In particular, I got great experience playing the trombone, which I became addicted to. I loved it, and still do to this day. I remember playing very effectively the mute on the trombone when Billy Kealy sang Frank Ifield's 'I Remember You' and similarly for 'Sweet Georgia Brown'. I must acknowledge that all the lads in that band were marvelous and were always very encouraging.

Then, in March 1965, my big break came when Joe Weadick of the Columbia Showband asked me to drop down to his house. He told me that, as he was now married with one child, he had decided to leave the showband business. He asked if I was in a position to take his place in the band, because he did not want to let the boys down. I remember thinking this is a great opportunity, but what would my parents (my dad, in particular) think. I had not long started in a good office job in the new Nitrigin Eireann Teoranta plant. I told Joe I would think about it and get back to him.

I knew immediately what I wanted, but had to convince my parents. My dad lost his head when I announced that I was leaving my good job in NET and joining the Columbia, and it took a while before he calmed down. Eventually I managed to convince him and my mother that everything would work out alright - that this was what I wanted in life. Finally, but very reluctantly, they gave their blessing.

Joining the Columbia Showband was not automatic as I had to undergo an audition. However, this was not a problem and I was offered the position immediately. I was so excited about my new career that I completely forgot to enquire what money/wages/salary I would be getting. I was aware that the band was a co-operative setup, where everyone got an equal share after expenses, but as a new member I could not take this for granted.

I discussed money with the band leader, Jim Tyrrell, on being accepted and his approach to me was that I would get £9 per week and I held out for £10 which was agreed. I was a bit put out at this arrangement, because I genuinely thought that I would be part of the co-operative set up, but who was I to argue at that point. However, this arrangement only lasted six months. I was brought into the co-operative and got the same money as everyone else, but the money was even less than I had been getting. So much for the misconception of big money in the showband business. I very quickly found that high earnings only applied to a small number of top showbands in the country.

I had a great time with the Columbia and gained immense confidence and competence on the professional stage. Every gig we played had its own special story. Not all for publication of course ... One almost tragic event I will never forget happened when I brought my beautiful young girlfriend, and future wife, Phyllis on a band trip. We had played and stayed in Lahinch as we were travelling on to play in Listowel the next night. We decided to take the opportunity to visit the Cliffs of Moher. At the time, there were no barriers to stop anyone going near the edge of the cliffs and as foolish young people would, we went a bit too close to look at the spectacular view. Near the edge, the grass bank sloped downwards and Phyllis slipped on the grass and started sliding down. Luckily, I caught her hand and, with the help of Jim Tyrrell holding on to me, we managed to pull her back up the bank. A near thing - and Phyllis has been very good to me ever since!

Did you ever pass by a showband minibus on the road very late at night in the sixties and could swear you saw someone's bum sticking out through a side window? Well, if you did it may not have been an illusion, because it was known to happen when showbands passed each other in the dead of night. I suppose it was done through boredom ... or maybe barebum?

The dance halls that we played in around the country varied very much in every respect. Some were aesthetically very pleasing and warm, others looked sparse and cold. And in the winter, some could be very cold indeed. I remember one night playing in Ballyhaunis, it was so cold in the hall that I had to put on my pyjamas under my band suit to keep warm while playing - I kid you not - and there was a good crowd at the dance!

Once on our way to play in a marquee in Piltown, County Kilkenny, Freddy and I, travelling in his car, stopped in the village to ask two old timers for directions to the the carnival marquee. They said go up the road a bit and you'll hear the band playing!

My abiding memory during the two years I was with the Columbia Showband was not associated with any venues we played in. It was those Charity Christmas Open Air Concerts we organised and performed at every year in the Arklow Main Street Park. We put up a Christmas tree and collected money for hampers to distribute to old folk around the town. It was our way of giving something back to the community for their support and good wishes.

In 1967, while playing with the Columbia in Castlepollard, I got a message to ring Top Line Promotions the next day. Needless to say, I was curious to know what this was all about. When I rang, Tom Doherty, manager of the Miami Showband, answered and offered me a place in the Maimi, which at the time was being revamped. While I was enjoying the Columbia Showband and the lads were all my very good friends, the fact was that the band was not making a lot of money. On the other hand, the Miami Showband were one of the top five bands in the country in 1967, so it was an offer I could not refuse. I reluctantly left the Columbia with the best wishes of all the boys.

And you know, the grass always looks greener on the other side of the hill. But all was not as I hoped it would be in the Miami and within two years, in 1969, I moved on again to the Dreams. I often think now how lucky

I was not to have been with the Miami when the massacre occurred in 1975. The three men killed, Fran O'Toole, Brian McCoy and Tony Geraghty were all extremely talented musicians and wonderful human beings. I was devastated when I heard the news, and to this day think of them regularly. One thing I am very happy about is that the Miami were immortalised on an Irish postage stamp, which was issued in September 2010. I am personally honoured to be in the particular photo used.

My involvement with the Dreams ended in 1971 and from there I joined the the Brown & O'Brien Band, with whom I toured Canada. My involvement with showbands was coming to an end at that time. Over the years since then, I have played with many bands and groups including, Johnny McEvoy (with whom I toured the U.K.), the Jazz Coasters, the Coolgreaney Jazz Band, the Gerry O'Connor Jazz Band and, in recent years, I have been playing with the Paddy Cole All Stars. With some of these, I appeared on many T.V. and radio shows.

Throughout all these years I have kept up my solo act on keyboards, accordian, trombone and vocals.

The *An Post* stamp depicting the Miami Showband with myself, 2nd from left in back row, was one of four issued on the 23rd September, 2010 in honour of the Showband Era of the Sixties. The three other showbands featured were the Royal, the Drifters and the Freshmen.

EDDIE MACK and the Columbia Showband

1966: Standing - Eddie, Jim & Pat (Tyrrell)
Sitting: Michael, Freddy, George, and Pat (McCarthy)

Chapter 19

Oliver Merrigan

One lovely autumn morning in 1967, at the age eighteen, while working on my family farm in Kilahurler – milking - and if I may say so, singing to our dairy cows, I noticed two gentlemen walking into the farmyard. When they got close enough, I realised they were Jim Tyrrell and Georgie Byrne of the Columbia Showband. Needless to say, I was a fan of the Columbia and it flashed across my mind that they might be interested in me, because I had been singing with a young local showband called the Spotlights.

I did not know at the time that Pat McCarthy was leaving the Columbia. The boys quickly told me that he was moving on to join one of the top five showbands in the country, the Miami Showband, and they asked if I would be interested in singing with the Columbia.

I was taken completely by surprise. Here I was, only just out of college, never having worked except on the family farm, and I was being asked to join a professional, well established and nationally acclaimed showband which had already made two records, including 'Out of Reach' by Eddie Mac, which had reached number six in the Irish hit parade. If my memory serves me right, I believe I was inwardly chuffed at the offer, but at the same time apprehensive. They assured me that I had a very good and suitable voice, would be well up to the task and would enjoy the experience. They quickly added, as a by-the-way, that I would have to start learning the trombone, but they didn't think it would be a problem for me.

Now I was really worried. I reckoned that singing was not a difficulty but playing a trombone - that was a tall order. However, after some thought, I replied that I would give it a try but would have to get permission from my family, particularly my father. At this point, I would like to say that music was always part of our family. My mother, in her young days, was an All-Ireland champion violin player and my grandmother played the organ in the Brittas Bay Catholic Church. And, of course, my brother Paddy, who also had a good voice, sang with the Red Seven Showband for about three months in 1961, as replacement for Pete Coburn.

The first time I sang in public, I did a duet with a school friend, Elizabeth Lambert, in the Woodenbridge Hotel in a play put on by the Johnstown primary school, which I was attending. I was about twelve years old at the time. When I went on to St. Peter's College in Wexford, I sang solos (soprano) in the annual comic operas they put on for each of the five years I was there. They included 'The Mikado', 'The Gondoliers' and 'The Pirates of Penzance'. I was the first lay person there to take a leading male part. I sang 'A Wond'ring Minstrel' in the Mikado. I once sang at a function - also in the Woodenbridge Hotel - where there happened to be an agent of the famous Acker Bilk present. He was so impressed with my singing that he asked if I was interested in making a career of it. I just politely passed it off, but I often wonder how things would have worked out if I had taken him up on the offer.

To continue - my father had no objection to me trying out this new venture, and my siblings were very encouraging. It was not too long before I

Columbia Showband in 1968
Oliver, Jim, George, Pat, Michael, Freddy and Eddie

performed at my first dance with the band. It was in the Television Club in Harcourt Street, Dublin. I'll never forget the press release our manager at the time, Mike Nolan, gave the papers announcing my addition to the band. It read "this man has been singing since he was knee high to a milking stool". Very original! On that first night I sang, among others, 'The Swallow', the reaction to which I was very pleased with and felt I was justifying my place in the showband. I had started learning the trombone but, I have to say, I did not stay in the band long enough to master it in any satisfactory way.

The positive start had given me tremendous satisfaction and I threw myself into my singing with great vigour. We were very popular throughout Ireland and in the Irish clubs in England and Scotland. I revelled in my moment of fame.

However, as time went on, I began to feel we were not making sufficient money to sustain us in the long term. The showband scene was beginning to wane and I began to get cold feet, and decided there was no real future in it for me. I was only nineteen and felt I should start some solid career. Being from a farm and, with encouragement from the family, I finally made up my mind to leave and train as a butcher with a view to starting my own business - which I eventually did.

I told our band leader Jim Tyrrell, who was very disappointed, but understood my position. He and the lads wished me the best luck in my future endeavours. I was very sorry to see the passing of Jim. I thought he was a true genius where music was concerned. The success of the band was, in my view, largely due to his leadership and the work he put into arranging the material. He was ever so particular and ensured that harmonies in the numbers were of the highest order. I would go as far as saying that the band played some of the material better than the original recording artists.

My last performance with the Columbia was in the Gresham Ballroom, Holloway Road in London. We had travelled down from Glasgow and Abbeymore in Scotland, where we did two gigs. The Gresham was packed that night, with up to four thousand people attending, including many from Arklow. Looking back now, it was a very nostalgic night and I can honestly say it was really the highlight of my short career with the showband.

I will always remember the unique feature of the revolving stage in the Gresham. The circular bandstand turned as we played on, while the resident orchestra was playing off. The site of the crowd of dancers coming into our vision as we rounded to face them was something else. It gave me a shiver up my spine. I remember very well three of my showpieces that night were Gene Pitney's number 'Somethings Gotten A Hold Of My Heart', Gary Plunkett and the Union Gap's 'Young Girl', and the Bee Gees' 'Massachusetts'.

It was not long after leaving the showband that I began to miss the lifestyle and great craic we had along the way. Many times over the years since, I have deeply regretted my decision to leave. However, one cannot turn the clock back.

Chapter 20

Timmy Weadick

In 1964, as a teenager of fourteen years, I lived in Abbey Street, Arklow. My best friend was Tommy Mythen and we enjoyed ourselves doing all the simple things in life - that did not involve money! Parents in those days could ill afford the luxuries that children today have. After school and during the summer holidays, we spent most of our leisure time playing in Condren's field and up the Gusset Lane in Ryder's Lough, where we sometimes put up makeshift tents, built camp fires, roasted potatoes, and ate them with gusto. We used to sit around the campfire, emulating our favourite cowboy heroes Roy Rogers and Gene Autry by singing their famous songs much to the joy of our pals who nearly always joined in the choruses.

Our harmonious rendering of the popular songs of the day earned us a lot of praise from our neighbours, who often listened with great interest and requested us to sing their favourite songs and, such was our enthusiasm, we always obliged. Indeed we were lucky enough to get plenty of goodies for our talents from workers in the area. We got poppy crisps from the late Billy Briggs at Johnny Sheehan's Crisp factory at Hudson's Square, got broken chocolate from the late Phil Byrne and other workers in Sheehan's Chocolate Factory, and got ice cream from a man whose name I can't remember, when we sang, and helped him fill his refrigerator van/store at Old Chapel Ground .

Whenever I am asked where my interest in music, and love of singing in particular, came from I always credit my father. In his younger years, he had been taught by the nuns to play the harmonica, violin and accordian and was quite good at them all. On the weekends, he would play the accordian in our home and many of our neighbours would gather around and enjoy listening to him. My mother did not sing or play any instrument, but she loved listening to all kinds of music on the radio and that influenced me greatly too.

Word got around among the local musicians that I had a good singing voice and it was not long before I got an opportunity to join Arklow's Spotlights Showband. I do believe it was John Joe Brauders who asked me.

They had lost their lead singer, Oliver Merrigan, to the Columbia, where he had replaced Pat McCarthy who left to join the Miami. This was early in 1967, and I was only just gone seventeen. I was delighted for the opportunity and gained great experience of the showband scene with them. The other members of the band were Robert Hickson, Dermot O'Connor, Tom Grogan, Ritchie Hall and Pat Kavanagh. The late Tommy Hickson was the manager.

So how did I get involved with the Columbia Showband? Well, it happened one evening in the spring of 1968. George Byrne and Michael Tyrrell called to see me and asked if I would like to join the Columbia. They explained that Oliver Merrigan had decided to retire and they needed a replacement. They told me that Jim and the rest of the band members were impressed with my singing in the Spotlights and felt that my voice and the type of music I sang would suit the Columbia's ethos.

Needless to say, I was over the moon and inwardly began to believe I must have more talent than I realised. I told them that I was very happy with the offer, but felt very bad about leaving the Spotlights, especially after the Columbia had effectively poached their previous lead singer. However, the opportunity was too good to turn down. Particularly since I was being offered £15 a week before tax! It also meant leaving my steady job in Globophan Industries, which paid me nineteen shillings a week after tax!! I had to think hard about it - for about two minutes!

The only down side was that they told me I would have to buy a trombone and learn to play it over time. This frightened me, but I threw caution to the wind and said "no problem". I purchased a trombone (on the never-never) in Walton's Dublin, and went weekly to the Royal College of Music for about six weeks to learn the basics. Jim Tyrrell also helped me a lot. I did eventually play it in the band, but only very minimally.

My first pay packet was handed to me by Jim. Eddie Mac, who was beside me at the time, said to me; "I'm going to tell you one thing Timmy - you've got £12 more than me today". You see, I was the only employee; all the rest of the boys were directors and got what was left after expenses! I laughed off the remark, but I wasn't sure if it was a good or a bad omen for the future of the band.

Aviemore in Scotland was where my inaugural performance with the Columbia took place. A long way to go for a first gig. When we were due to go on stage, I had a glimse of the packed ballroom and immediately felt nervous and got butterflies in my stomach. However, when my turn came to sing, the adrenalin started flowing and I ploughed into the Tom Jones hit 'Just Help Yourself' and was very pleased with the reaction. That was the end of my nervousness. I followed it up with a Beach Boys' number 'Do It Again' and a Beatles' number 'Let It Be'.

The Columbia only lasted just over a year after I joined, but the musical experience I gained was profound and the craic we had off-stage was mighty. I would not have missed it for the world. All venues were different and interesting, but I really loved playing in marquees and at festivals such as 'Mary From Dunloe' in Donegal and 'Puck Fair' in Kilorglin. There was always a great holiday atmosphere at them. My favourite ballrooms were the Arcadia, Cork and the Galtymore in Cricklewood, London. I met some great artists when we played support or two band sessions, such as the iconic Slim Whitman, The Dubliners, The Tremeloes, and The Love Affair.

I mentioned above the craic we had off-stage. Well, a lot of that happened in the middle of the night, travelling home from dances from all parts of the country. We got used to knowing what bands were playing in the vicinity of our gigs and almost knew which band we were going to meet on our way home. Through boredom or, as a means of keeping awake while driving, many pranks and devilments were got up to by bandsmen, which were hilarious - to us at any rate. Here are a few examples:-

Imagine driving home at 4 a.m. in the morning, passing a lake along the side of the road and seeing two lads in shorts (underwear) standing by the water's edge, each holding a branch of a tree as fishing rods, pretending to fish!

Imagine passing two men at 4 a.m. jogging along the side of the road in their shorts!

Imagine driving through Borris-in-Ossory at 4 a.m. in the morning and seeing a stark naked man standing outside the church, on one leg with an arm stretched up towards heaven like a statue! I did not personally see this one, but it did happen before my time with the band.

Imagine passing a bandwagon at 4 a.m. in the morning and seeing two or three bare bums sticking out of the side windows. This was a regular between bands passing in the night!

Imagine seeing a bandsman pull down his pants and briefs and hang his glasses on his testicles ... it looked like the face of an old man with a long nose and plenty of hair.

I'm sure there were plenty more funny and innocent incidents that took place between showbands to brighten up our long journeys home, but it's hard to remember everything that took place over forty years ago that would be fit to relate here!

Michael Tyrrell was the person I related to most in the Columbia, possibly because he was more my age and we both had, shall I say, a devil-may-care attitude. He shone on stage with many of his rock beat numbers like 'Tutti Fruiti' and 'Travelling Band', and was extremely popular with the ladies. He was, and is, a very caring and generous person. Michael helped me out many times with a lift home from Wicklow when I was courting my

Columbia in 1968:
Back: Eddie, Jim, Timmy, and Freddy.
Front: Michael, George, and Pat.

future and beloved wife Chrissie, who I met at a dance in the Ormonde Ballroom, Arklow in 1968.

Winding up my Columbia story, I must admit that when the end came I was not too surprised, as the writing had been on the wall for some months. Bookings were diminishing. Crowds in ballrooms were getting less and less for most bands. The main reason being that music in lounges and discos were slowly taking over. Also, dedicated dancers were starting to follow the 'up and coming' country & western bands.

That is why, when the Columbia finished I got involved in a new country & western band starting out called The Ranchers. Again with Jim and Michael Tyrrell and George Byrne. That band ran for four years. After that I joined a new local group called Misty along with my great ex-Columbia colleague, Freddy Cutland. Also in it were Pat Kinsella, Robert Hickson and Pat Kavanagh. Over the years, with some of the boys leaving, I had the pleasure of playing with new members John Cullen, Pascal Moran and Brendan Brady. I am now semi-retired from the entertainment business, but am still enjoying the buzz in a duo with my old friend Pat Kavanagh, called Timbuck 2.

The Ranchers
L to R:
Frankie Carroll,
Michael Tyrrell,
Declan Curneen,
Jim Tyrrell,
Francie Lennihan,
George Byrne and
Timmy Weadick.

Chapter 21 *Michael Gilmore*

My interest in music started when I got a harmonica for my Christmas Box in 1949, at the age of twelve. I remember very well my father giving me the money (two shillings and sixpence) on Christmas Eve and I rushed down with excitement and bought it in a small shop on King's Hill (probably Paddy Power's who eventually moved to Main Street). I learned some simple tunes and the more I learned the more interested I got in music generally.

My first public performance took place about a year later. One Sunday night, there was a variey concert in the Marian Arts (McGowan's hall on South Quay). I was outside with a couple of pals as we didn't have the 6*d*. entrance fee. Paddy Lynch came out and asked me if I would do a couple of numbers. He offered me free admission. I said O.K. but my pals had to come too. Paddy, good hearted fellow that he was, agreed. I went on stage to play 'Kelly the Boy from Killane', 'The Minstrel Boy', etc, and got a great response.

In the mid fifties, there was a revival of interest in Trad/Dixieland/Jazz and I was enthralled by the music, and in particular the role played by the trombone. The slide trombone was the instrument I really wanted to learn and play. But, alas, as I was a sailor there was no way I could start to learn that instrument on board a ship. There were always chaps on watch below trying to sleep. One day, I mentioned this to my friend Ulty McCabe and he suggested I try the guitar (acoustic, of course). Next trip to New Zealand I bought one in Wellington. It was a great suggestion, because it was not long before I got the hang of it and, with plenty of free time on board ship, I soon could play most of the popular guitar tunes of the day.

By the time I was back home from the sea in the summer of 1960, I had bought my second guitar, another acoustic but had a pick-up fitted. I also bought a 10 watt amp. Any guitar player will know you are not going to 'blow'em away' with that amount of power!

The Red Seven Showband had been formed and my friend, the late Eamon Lee, was playing bass in the band. I knew all the band members. They had been engaged to play the summer season in the Tara Ballroom in

Courtown and they asked me if I would like to gig a bit with them. All the band members had day jobs and it was tough going for them as they played six nights a week and had to get up for work in the mornings. The band hired a minibus, and the driver-owner was Martin Byrne. Martin was known to appreciate the value of money and did a bit of farming on the side. I recall that everytime we passed a herd of cattle in a field Martin would always say; "there's money on the hoof, boys".

I was by far the least accomplished musician, but the lads were always ready with a friendly word of advice to help me along. I learned a lot about what it means to play in a group of musicians from the Red Seven.

When I think back now I realise what good musicians they were. They played such a wide variety of music and some really difficult numbers. I even sang a number with them titled, 'Someday'. I remember it was in Bb.

Every Sunday night in Courtown, there was always a top visiting showband and the Red Seven, being the resident band, would play support. Of course, on those nights the resident band would always use the visiting band's gear for convenience. One night the Royal Showband played and I was using their guitar player's amp. I had started to play a few basic solo numbers like '40 Miles of Bad Road' by Duane Eddy. It was a very simple number. I launched into it with sheer gusto and was getting a magnificent sound out of the big amp when suddenly the amp went dead.

Des kept up the beat on the drums and I could hear him imploring me, in somewhat colourful language, to "do something"! The ballroom was packed that night and I can still see all the dancers shuffling to a stop and turning to gaze at us. The Royal Showband's guitarist jumped on the stage and he re-plugged the amp as it had came loose from the socket. All was restored and we restarted the tune... phew... saved!

Another night we were playing when a guy appeared in front of the stage while I was playing a solo and he was doing "a solo dance". He had an overcoat and a tweed cap on and appeared to have drink taken. He was surrounded by a large group of young dancers, who made a circle around him and egged him on to greater efforts. Responding to the encouragement of the crowd around him he unbuttoned his overcoat and then started to unbuckle the belt of his trousers. We feared he was about to expose himself "to the vulgar gaze of the multitude". I recall Pete Coburn shouting to us to stop the music, which we did abruptly. The guy then ceased his antics and faded away into the crowd.

With the invaluable experience I gained playing with the Red Seven during my holidays in 1960, I very much looked forward to my 1961 holidays. I started a small group, with myself playing lead guitar, my late brother Colin on rhythm guitar, and George Kinch on drums. As the three of us were sailors, we called the group The Swinging Sailors. Eamon used to play bass with us when he was free. The Red Seven Showband sometimes asked us to play with them as support band. We played with them a number of times in Courtown and also in Kilkenny.

In the life of a musician there will always be times when something goes wrong on the night and it can be very embarrassing. I'm sure it happens to the best of groups. One such occasion happened when I was invited to play with the Red Seven at a private dance in the Marlborough Hall in Arklow. Before the band started, the boys discussed whether they would play the latest No.1 song in the hit parade at the time, 'Walk Right Back' by the Everly Brothers, which the band had been rehearsing. They decided not to play it,

Swinging Sailors in 1960
George Kinch, Michael Gilmore, Colin Gilmore

because it was not quite ready and we went on and started the gig. Somewhere along the line, there must have been bad communication because, in the middle of a dance set, Pete suddenly announced; "we are now going to play the No.1 in the hit parade 'Walk Right Back'". There was consternation on the stage. I asked Eamon what key was it in. He replied, "C" ... then started in F. Some other instruments started in Bb or Eb. Needless to say, the resulting discordant blare was frightful, but what happy memories they are.

Now, almost fifty years on, I live in France with my lovely wife Genevieve, where I still play guitar - an Ibanez electric guitar as well as a Gibson Acoustic - with the latest fender amp. I try to get about an hour's practice in every day. Sometimes I play around the village with a few friends, only for pleasure of course, no cash involved. Very often people ask me to play that famous Shadows' hit of the sixties 'Apache'.

At the risk of sounding a bit big headed, I have made considerable improvement in my playing since the sixties! "And so you should after fifty years, I hear you say"... And by the way I also sing in the local choir now ... time changes everyone and age plays a major part. Ahh yes ... they were great times.

Chapter 22

Dan Bolger
Stand-in and Manager

My stint with the Red Seven came about because of the band's name. Pat Tyrrell was unavailable for some dates that the band had and they needed to recruit a seventh member to complete the roster. I fitted the bill - filled the red jacket, well enough. It didn't matter that I wasn't a saxophone player like Pat, I could substitute as a piano player and fill in. We played an afternoon in the Arklow Entertainment Centre and a night in Newtownmountkennedy. I was fairly familiar with most of the tunes on the band's play list and really just had to vamp along. I should have paced my piano pounding a bit better because, with my enthusiasm to contribute to the occasion, I had sore fingers for my efforts.

Playing with the boys in the band was a comfortable experience for me. Growing up in Arklow, we all knew each other and largely shared a common experience. Live music in Arklow, outside the home, ranged from hearing traditional players like Lar Cullen on the fiddle, to the girls at St Mary's School putting on operettas. The Marion Arts Society put on concerts in McGowan's Hall and I remember Red Seven members Paud O'Brien and Pete Coburn with my brother Paddy on the chorus line of a 'Sinbad the Sailor' pantomime, belting out 'There's No Business Like Show Business'.

My introduction to show business came courtesy of Seán Bonner who organised a Mouth Organ Band when he came to teach at the Top School in Arklow. We performed in a concert at the convent that I'm guessing may have been for An Tostal – 'Ireland at Home' in 1953. I graduated from mouth organ to button key accordion and then took piano lessons from Seán, as did Joe Weadick at the same time.

Radio was a major influence on all of us although, oddly enough, I think my earliest memory of learning popular music resulted from the loudspeakers at the local carnivals blaring out such memorable Guy Mitchell hits as 'She wears Red Feathers and a Hula Hula Skirt' and 'There's a Pawnshop on a Corner in Pittsburgh, Pennsylvania'. I visited Pittsburgh many years later and was disappointed to be told that the pawnshop was long demolished, but the corner was still there. As we grew up, our listening broadened from

Radio Éireann to the BBC and eventually to Radio Luxemburg - 208 Medium Wave. Disc jockeys Pete Murray and Dave Gell pumped out the latest hits. This was reinforced by the juke box in the back room of Tracey's Bridge Café, where a lot of youthful social energy was expended to a background sound of Elvis Presley, Fats Domino, and others.

As for dancing, I was initiated in a roundabout way to 'Céili and Oldtime' through my passion for hurling. I played for the Arklow Geraldines GAA Club, and got to attend their fund raising dances to support the club. The Kevin Harpur Céili Band provided the music. Then there were ballroom dance lessons put on by a couple from Dublin from the Morrisoni - Whealan Dance School in the Ormonde Ballroom, and I signed up for those. There was a notice on the wall in the Ormonde Ballroom - "Rock 'n' Roll is PROHIBITED in this Ballroom" - and this would be enforced by a tap on the shoulder from Billy Cullen the ballroom manager. The Mick Delahunty and Maurice Mulcahy Orchestras, with twelve to fifteen man line-ups, were the big bands of the era. The first time I heard the Clipper Carlton Showband was in the Ormonde ballroom. Young people were embracing rock 'n' roll music, dance bands were getting off their chairs and abandoning their music stands, and the showband era was on its way.

My brother Paddy was secretary for the Arklow Cage Birds Society and they ran dances to raise funds. The society was the first to bring the Royal Showband to Arklow for a couple of dances in the Ormonde Ballroom. The Royal was on its way to becoming the premier showband at that time and was already drawing a big following.

I went to University College Dublin to study engineering. There was a vibrant dancing scene in Dublin, ranging from commercial ballroom dances to small club affairs. I remember going to the Clipper Carlton at the Mansion House, and the Paul Russell Trio at the Mount Pleasant Lawn Tennis Club. There were dances sponsored by various groups - gardaí, nurses, and university students. I got involved with the engineering students' dances as a foot soldier - pushing tickets into the civil service offices and so forth. Our dances were 'ticket only' affairs in the Four Provinces Ballroom in Harcourt Street. The 4P's had a bit of a rough reputation and the engineers 'ticket only' policy was an effort to control who got into the dances. The 4P's was owned by the Burke family who had plans to upgrade the place to the

Television Club and wanted a more up-market image for the venue. Being fairly tall and reasonably able-bodied, I got lots of experience on the front door checking tickets with the bouncers. We often accumulated a group outside that had been refused admission and sometimes things got a little tense. I learned quickly to be on guard for trouble and ready for a punch or head butt. If things were getting out of hand, we would have to call the gardaí. There was a garda in Dublin at that time, Sergeant Brannigan, whose reputation for dealing with crowd control was justifiably established by the way he could mill through a group of discontented young men.

Our dances were well attended and the showbands, including the Royal Showband, were keen to play for us. We used a small local house band for the earlier part of the evening and then put on the featured band for the rest of the night when the crowd had come in. One of the housebands we used, (I think it was the Echos) had a notable young Dublin singer - Dickie Rock, who had the performing charisma even then.

Our dances did quite well financially and at one time we were emboldened to bid on a troupe of performers that Phil Solomon, the London impresario, was bringing to Ireland. The main attraction in this troupe was country star Jim Reeves who had huge fan appeal in Ireland. Also part of the package was a new group with a creepy name - The Beatles - to get Jim Reeves you had to take them as well. We were unsuccessful in our bid and Jim Reeves went to the Crystal Ballroom in Dublin. As for the Beatles, well, they never came on that tour, their fortunes changed in the interim.

I got the responsibility of booking the bands for the engineers' dances. This put me in contact not only with showband managers, but with hall managers and media folks who would come to our dances to check out bands or do some business. Also, we sponsored a weekly radio programme on Radio Éireann to promote our dances and I arranged to have recordings of the showbands we used aired on this programme. I often visited other ballrooms to meet with showband managers and discuss bookings and was in the Palm Beach, Portmarnock when the Columbia were performing. The band was putting on an energetic performance and it was easy to see that they were enjoying the occasion. The dancers were lapping it up and there was a great atmosphere in the hall. That encounter led to some discussions with band leader Jim Tyrrell and the boys in the band, resulting in me taking on the role of manager. The goal we set ourselves was to enable the band to become fully professional and achieve its full potential. Becoming professional, or 'turning pro', meant raising the band's profile and generating enough revenue to sustain the band as full time musicians. This required more bookings and better fees, both of which meant getting the band into new venues while transitioning the band from part time to full time work status. The dancing demand was greatest on weekends, weeknight dancing was generally weak outside Dublin and Belfast. In any case, long travel to weekday dances could be a problem while some of the boys held jobs. Saturday nights were strong dancing nights in Northern Ireland and Friday nights were good also. Luckily for us, Saturday was a big dance night at the Arklow Entertainment Centre, where centre manager Paddy Lynch continued to support the band. My initial efforts then were directed at expanding our venues into the North, and extending into the bigger ballrooms throughout the country.

Through a contact I had, Bill Carvill from Portadown, we made headway into a variety of halls in Armagh and Down, and into Belfast. We played St Teresa's in Andersonstown and the Astor in Belfast city centre, quickly being sensitised to community culture in these areas. Our profile around the country was raised by a friend of mine, Michael Ryan, who wrote the 'Tempo' dance column in the *Evening Herald*. Michael also wrote or contributed to dance columns for various provincial papers and his pieces about the band helped us gain recognition. We did a full page spread in the *Irish Independent*. This promotional page was supported by advertisements from the halls we played in and from other showbands whose management we knew. I had copies of the page printed by the paper and used them as promotional material for the band.

My brother, Paddy, shared the travel and bookings workload with me. As well, in cahoots with Vincent McElheron, I developed an arrangement with Starlite Artists in London for booking its performers into venues in Ireland. This worked to get the Columbia some dates with the performers that came in and got the band exposure in some new halls. We played with Big Dee Irwin in the Arcadia in Cork, the Astor in Belfast and the Royal Ballroom in Castlebar. Big Dee's big hit 'Swinging on a Star' had gone to No.7 in the British Top Ten Charts. The Columbia did the backing for him at our dates and the band had some discomfort with this arrangement. We played with the Brook Brothers in places ranging from the Olympia in Waterford to the Orchid in Lifford. Their big hit had been 'Warpaint', that had gone to No.5 in the charts. The brothers, Geoff and Ricky, brought a back up guitarist with them and performed on stage independent of the Columbia and that seemed to work well. Houston Wells was another singer I got to know through this arrangement. Houston (Andy Smith), had 'Only the Heartaches' with the Marksmen in the Irish charts for ten weeks getting to the No.7 spot. Houston decided to stay in Ireland for a time and I did bookings for him with the Outlaws from Derry as the backing band.

During Lent the dance business in most of the rural ballrooms almost closed down, so we did a set of bookings in England - London, Manchester, and Birmingham. I caught up with the band at our digs in London, where Michael Tyrrell was laying traps for the unsuspecting with stink bombs. I had arranged for a talent scout from Starlite Artists to come and hear the band, but their big star at that time was Brian Poole and the Tremeloes and our act didn't fit into their plans.

Meanwhile, our market was expanding and fees were increasing. We got into the main venues around the country including the Reynolds' Ballroom Chain and Con Hynes' Associated Ballrooms. The Columbia got good responses from audiences and was building up its reputation. Like other showbands, we did a cocktail of rock, country, folk, and miscellaneous pop. A band's impression depended mainly on its vocalists and we had Eddie Mac (McElheron) as our featured vocalist with the romantic touch and Jim Tyrrell as our rocker. We had the punters gyrating energetically to Jim's 'Twist and Shout' and lurching romantically around the room to Eddie's soothing 'Spinning Wheel' lullaby, while a rotating crystal ball cast a magical starlit spell.

We put up lots of miles on poor Irish roads, but traffic was generally light when and where we travelled. Jimmy Cullen drove the bandwagon a lot of the time and helped with the gear. I travelled sometimes with the band, but mostly on my own. Even when I was connecting with the band at some dance I would take a route that gave me opportunities to meet with hall managers along the way. Luckily, we had few incidents on our travels. Michael Tyrrell and I did spend an uncomfortable night in my broken down car somewhere near Enniskillen, but we were none the worse for that. And I remember T.P. O'Connell, who had the Astoria Ballroom in Bundoran and also the Volkswagen Garage, kindly fixing my heating system for me after a cold trip across the Sperrin Mountains.

I don't remember ever getting too seriously lost, although I recall coming upon a red post box one night and realizing that I'd inadvertently crossed the border, but needing directions was a common occurrence. Once I was somewhere heading cross country on back roads for Kanturk and stopped at a crossroads to enquire from some locals where I was - one of them strolled over to the car and asked through my rolled down window; "Have you ever heard of the arse hole of nowhere"? When I acknowledged that I had, he said; "and now you're there boy"!

A more poignant incident occurred one time I was looking for the residence of Trevor Kane from Bangor. In the usual way, I pulled alongside someone on the road, rolled down the window, and made my enquiry. I got my directions and had a little small talk, including where I was from, when my guide enquired; "and what's it like living down there among all them"? I assured him that it wasn't too bad for me really and I went on my way feeling that I had done my bit for north/south relations that day.

We stayed in a variety of places, often influenced by who we played for. Some venues were in hotels like the Glen Eagles in Killarney, or Silver Slipper in Strandhill, and others had ballroom/hotel connections like the Reynolds' Longford Arms and Sammy Barr who ran the Flamingo in Ballymena and owned the Adair Arms there as well. On the other end of the scale were some dubious guesthouse accommodations frequented by the showband fraternity. Keeping in touch meant coin hungry telephone calls and always needing a supply of small change. Convenient telephone locations were kept in mind and the AA members' roadside boxes were always clean and reliable.

I enjoyed meeting the people that I encountered, marketing the band and negotiating fees. I dealt with lots of good businessmen (there were few women hall managers), and with a few sharp operators. It was a growth experience for me and it also involved me in various by-product activities, ranging from calling bingo numbers in Duncannon to a Beauty Contest Judge in Portstewart. One of the memorable characters, who perhaps unwittingly captured the spirit of the era, was Tommy Whelan who ran dances in some of the halls in County Wexford. Probably inspired by the Rose of Tralee Festival, or Mary from Dungloe in Donegal, Tommy had the audacity to organize a Fine Girl You Are competition for worthy Wexford contestants.

There was lots of hype in the business about how well bands were doing and how great the money was. A showband could do well if it got lots of good work. However, it was a competitive business with hundreds of bands vying for the available dates. As well, there was plenty of competition between the halls for the punters, and hall managers naturally wanted the bands that could attract the largest following on any given night. We played

Dan Bolger, Eddie McElheron and Joe Weadick in the Arklow Bay Hotel in August 2010

mostly for a negotiated fee and sometimes for a share of the door take. While we had made our way into the main venues, I think it would be fair to say that the boys in the band felt that we should be doing better for return bookings and fees. The arrangement we had was an obstacle to their ambitions and a parting of our ways became inevitable.

Shortly after, I was approached to manage a new band based in Dublin. Some well known musicians from the Jim Farley Showband, Tony Woods, Joe McIntyre, and Des Moore, had decided to form a new band and we launched the Express Showband together. Again, my brother Paddy took on a lot of the travel workload. Eventually the engineering side of my interests took precedence over my time. I emigrated to Canada leaving behind a thriving showband industry … without regret, and consider myself fortunate to have participated in that unique entertainment phenomenon at that stage of my life.

Chapter 23

Vincent McElheron The Correspondent

When Dan Bolger was contracted in 1964 to manage the Columbia Showband, we had a chat with a view to me assisting him getting new contacts in the business. He was aware that I was the Irish correspondent for the *New Musical Express* magazine which had not long come on stream in Ireland. One of the main aims of the magazine owners was to cater for the thriving showband industry which was sweeping Ireland at the time.

I, like most Arklow people, was proud of the achievements of the Red Seven/Columbia Showband, not least because my brother Eddie was the Columbia's lead vocalist, so I agreed to help Dan where I could to further the band's success in securing notable bookings ... no fee was involved other than normal expenses.

Because of my position, I had important contacts with Irish and English promoters whose main interest was getting bookings in Ireland and Great Britian for their acts, particularly singers who made it into the British or Irish charts. I was also on the books of RTÉ as a South East Correspondent, which was a great advantage. I helped arrange the Columbia's appearance on the RTÉ *Showband Show*, *The Life of Reilly Show* and the *Go 2 Show.*

I had a number of dealings with the well known London Promoter Peter Walsh, who was the managing director of Starlite Artists. He was interested in placing his major English and American musical acts into the major Irish ballrooms and theatres. Peter had asked me to get media coverage in Ireland for his touring acts.

I brought Dan to London to meet Peter and, as a result, we secured the contract for the Columbia to play support band with the American star Big Dee Erwin and a number of U.K. acts, including Brian Poole and the Tremeloes of 'Twist and Shout' fame. Incidently, I was instrumental in the Tremeloes recording the hit 'Silence is Golden'. I had heard the Four Seasons version of it on - would you believe - the Roma Cafe duke box and asked the late Mrs Aprile if it was possible to have it and she was very generous and gave it to me.

I gave the record to Peter Walsh and suggested to him that it would be very suitable for Brian Poole and the Tremeloes to record because of the unique harmony blend of Chip Hawks, Alan Blakeney, and Dave Mundon. Shortly after I gave it to Peter, Brian Poole left, but in 1967 the Tremeloes did record it, sung by their lead guitar and vocalist Rick West. It topped the English charts for three weeks, but alas there was no money in it for me!

During my dealings with Dan, we were able to get the Columbia Showband bookings in a number of top ballrooms around the country, namely, Con Hynes' Amalgamated & Associated ballrooms, Albert (former Taoiseach) and Jim Reynolds' ballrooms, D.O'Kane's ballroom in Dundalk, Bill Kenny's Olympia ballroom, Waterford, Peter Prendergast's Arcadia ballroom, Cork, Con Lucy's Redbarn ballroom in Youghal and his other ballroom in Crosshaven, O'Donoghue's Gleneagle ballroom, Killarney, Tom Finan's Seapoint ballroom, Galway, Jennings' Royal ballroom Castlebar and Byrne's ballroom Strandhill.

After Dan parted with the Columbia Showband I continued pursuing bookings with band leader Jim Tyrrell on and off until the band terminated in 1969. Their demise was more to do with the changing culture of the music entertainment business than any failure on the band's part. They saw the writing on the wall and agreed among themselves to form two small groups, The Jim Tyrrell Trio and The Family, to cater for the growing culture of entertainment in hotels and lounges. Among the first cabarets the new groups played at - with great success may I add - were in the Arklow Bay Hotel. I was entertainment manager there at the time and got the agreement to run the shows from Clive Culletin, the hotel owner.

One cherished memory that I will never forget about the Columbia was the night they played with Roy Orbison in the Las Vegas Ballroom in Tuam. It was the jam session they had after the dance with Roy in the primitive changing room off the stage that I refer to. In contrast to the lovely decorative ballroom, the changing room had bare block walls with nails stuck in them for hanging coats, no proper chairs, just an old mirror, a few old tables and drinks crates, cement floor and a substandard loo, to say the least. Typical of a lot of ballrooms around the country at that time.

When you walked into the room it was like stepping back in time fifty years. Of course, the boys were so caught up in their music they were oblivious to their surroundings - and I'm sure Roy Orbison was enjoying himself so much that the primitive changing room did not worry him. The session went on for over an hour. The ad-libbing between Roy, Jim and Eddie with the rest of the boys chiming in was a fantastic visual and musical experience to watch and listen to - priceless. These are the unplanned moments in music that make life worth living.

The Columbia Showband were ahead of their time, with Jim and Michael's modern trend, vis-a-vis the 'Top of the Pops' type popular and rock music, while Eddie was proficient in ballads, evergreens and country & western songs.

My involvment with Dan Bolger, Jim Tyrrell and the Columbia was a great pleasure for me. I look back on those times with fond memories of the very fine group of talented musicians that was the Columbia, and an honourable band manager and gentleman Dan Bolger.

Vincent McElheron, Joe Weadick and Brendan Bowyer August 2010

Chapter 24

Richie Hall
The Roadie

Back in the sixties during the Irish showband era, as a sixteen year old, I took every opportunity to listen to the music of the Columbia Showband when they played in the local dance halls and in their practice room. I could sing a little myself and had a secret ambition to eventually get involved in a showband. At the time, dancing was the main social outlet for young people and bands were cropping up everywhere. It seemed to be the thing to get into to really enjoy life if one was fortunate enough to have a singing voice or could play some instrument.

Eddie McElheron was a good friend of mine and, through him, I got to go to gigs with the Columbia. At first on the odd occasion and before long I was their regular roadie - helping to load and unload the equipment and set up and take down the gear in ballrooms and dancehalls. Of course, it was not a paying job, but I do remember that Jim Tyrrell - once!!! after about three years - handing me a fiver and saying; "there's a few bob Ritchie for all your hard work".

However, I did have the privilege of getting free accommodation and food with the boys, including the odd bottle of beer when I travelled with the band. I saw many ballrooms, towns, cities and scenic places around Ireland, including Northern Ireland, that I would never have had the opportunity to see at the time had I not been with them. Not to forget the great craic we always had.

I appreciated very much the friendship of all the lads and loved the Columbia so much that I used worry as much as any of them about the band's future when bookings were slow coming in. I thoroughly enjoyed the experience and have many great memories of that very happy period of my life - from 1963 to 1966.

During my time travelling with the showband, I observed a lot but said little, because it was not really my place. However, I don't mind saying here that in my opinion they made two big mistakes by not promoting themselves better nationally. The first was in not recording the 'Hucklebuck'. To my knowledge, they were the only band in Ireland playing it in 1963. Jim

Tyrrell sang it and it was one of the band's best numbers. I think it had been recorded by Chubby Checker a few years previously, and Jim liked it, started singing it and put it into the band's repertoire.

The 'Hucklebuck' always went down fantastically well with the dancers. So much so, that the Royal Showband picked up on it after hearing the Columbia performing it in the Arklow Entertainment Centre when the Columbia were doing a two band session with them. Indeed, I do believe (if my memory serves me right) that a few of the boys from the Royal showed up to listen to the band in other places ... I think the Arcadia in Cork and Clonakilty. Sometime after that, Brendan Bowyer recorded it and, of course, it became one of the best Irish recorded numbers of the sixties and still very popular today. I reckon that if the Columbia had recorded it before the Royal Showband they certainly would have taken off onto a higher plain on the Irish and English circuits.

The second big mistake I believe the Columbia made was that they did not put the 'Spinning Wheel' on the A side of their 1966 record instead of 'Out Of Reach', even though 'Out of Reach' went to No.6 in the Irish Hit Parade. At that time, Irish ballads were very popular and a lot of bands were successfully recording such songs. Had the 'Spinning Wheel' been well advertised and plugged on national radio, it too could have maintained the band in the Premier Division - to use a football analogy!

As I said earlier, I greatly admired all the boys in the Columbia and had a brilliant time as a roadie with them. It may be a strange thing to say, but there was never any real rows among them, which I believe was unique. They were always proper gentlemen. For me, the time came that I got a job and had to all but stop travelling with the band. I remember when I first started working - in a temporary job down at the dock - Jim came down and said; 'we need you tonight'. They had got so used to me working with the gear that they missed me. But of course I could not go.

I eventually realised my own ambition of singing with a band when I got involved with the Spotlights Showband in 1967. In the following paragraphs I relate a selection of my memories and reflections of the Columbia during the four years I journeyed with them.

I remember that in 1966, the band advertised in the national press for a singer to replace Eddie McElheron, who was contemplating leaving for personal reasons. I was present when they auditioned three people in the Television Club in Harcourt Street, Dublin. One of the young hopefuls, a handsome chap with blond hair was an excellent singer. I can't remember his name, but he probably would have been taken on except that Eddie changed his mind and decided to stay with the band.

We played on occasion in Falcarragh, at the tip of the Donegal. I will never forget that for our meal at the venue we were always served beans on toast – as much as you could eat – it must have been the tradition there.

Once, when the band played in the Romanos Ballroom in Belfast, Joe Weadick was in the process of taking down one of the speakers on the side of the bandstand. Beside the bandstand was a stairs up to the women's cloakroom and, just as Joe was stretching to extract the speaker from the hook, a girl came walking down the stairs and accidently tipped him on the elbow. Joe unbalanced and down he went with the speaker landing on top of him. Pat ran over and asked; "Is the speaker alright … !!! …". Joe survived to play another night!

One of the annoying episodes that the band had to go through when travelling up North was being checked by the border custom officers. On the way home, they would always ask to check the serial numbers of the sax and trumpet, a copy of which they would have got on our way up. These instruments were always packed in first, which meant we had to remove most of the equipment to get at them. We used to say they were doing it deliberately to make it awkward for us.

When we arrived to play a gig in Castlerea, County Roscommon, after travelling four hours, the first thing we saw was a poster advertising the Premier Aces ... the band was double booked. I don't remember what the problem was, but we ended up going home.

When Hugh Hardy took over as manager for a period in 1965, he succeeded in getting quite a lot of new bookings. He arranged an Irish tour for a British top group at the time, Brian Poole and the Tremeloes with the Columbia doubling which was very successful.

When I was helping to set up the gear one night in Belturbet, County Cavan for a gig, I accidently burst open the seat of my trousers when I bent down to pick up something. I was mortified as I had no way of repairing it and did not have a replacement. So I decided to hide my embarrassment by just sitting down near the bandstand and watch the show for the night. At that time - for those who might not know the tradition in the early sixties - all the women used to sit on one side of the hall and all the men sat on the other side, and when the dance set was announced there would be a rush of men across the floor to ask the girls they wished to dance with. However, because it was still early in the night women were arriving, but there were only a few men in, most were still at the pub as was also the tradition! Pat Tyrrell, knowing my predicament and up to his usual tricks, announced a 'Ladies' Choice'. I quickly realised what he was up to and, observing a number of beauties advancing in my direction, I quickly made a bee line for the band's cloakroom behind the stage and stayed there for the rest of the night!

One night when the Columbia was playing in a marquee in Coolgreaney, there was a crash involving the late Kevin Keogh's bus, which was on the way to collect a crowd from the dance, and a car driven by Vincent McElheron, who was on the way into Arklow. Vincent was badly hurt with internal injuries and some broken bones. He spent seven months in hospital as a result.

The Columbia's minibus once went on fire on the way to a dance in Newcastlewest and put out of action. Fortunately, we managed to put the fire out, but had to hire a bus to get to the dance and get the band home to Arklow. The Commer minibus had to be sent back to Arklow on the goods train about a week later where the driver, Jimmy Cullen, eventually repaired it.

Finally, I would like to pay tribute to the late Jim Tyrrell who I admired greatly. Musically, he was a genius. He was always very particular when doing music arrangments and ensured that they were done exactly as per the original record. In some cases, I felt the band actually played and sang them even better than the original record with excellent harmonies. One of my favourites by Jim was his trumpet solo playing of the 'Third Man Theme'.

Spotlights Showband in 1966
Top to bottom: Richie Hall, Robert Hickson, Paddy Kavanagh, Bobby Byrne, John Joe Brauders, Mark Byrne and Michael Broughan.

Chapter 25

Billy Lee
A Manufactured Musician

My great-aunt Maggie was in her late sixties when I was a young fellow. Her pastimes included listening to music, counting her pension and fainting at the drop of a hat. She possessed a wind-up gramophone, a number of ancient records and a beaten up leaky melodeon that nobody in the family, including herself, could play. As a small child, I developed a mild interest in the intricate workings of the instrument and managed, after several futile attempts, to squeeze a tune out of it – 'The Dawning Of The Day' as it happens. Maggie thought it was a wonderful achievement for one so young. Insignificant as it would prove to be in the long run, this would be the start of my musical odyssey.

This poor squeezebox was becoming increasingly decrepit through natural dissipation, coupled with my frequent assaults on it, so one day Pat Kavanagh, the milkman, suggested that a mouth organ might be a good buy for 'a promising young musician'. It was on his advice that a harmonica was purchased for me. This instrument was my constant pocket companion for many a day in my young life.

One year my aunt Eileen bought a violin for me and I was promptly dispatched to a music teacher for lessons. This was an intensely mortifying experience, as we lived about two miles from Seán Bonner's house. Once a week I had to run a gauntlet of jeering peers with my black beret and my fiddle under my arm, to learn 'Twinkle Twinkle Little Star'. However, it wasn't destined to last long.

Have you ever tried dragging an unwilling bow across unfortunate violin strings without being distressed by the excruciating sound emanating from it? If so, think of what it might sound like to other people. Now, my early, futile, attempts to master the violin were difficult enough for people in our house, but it magnified the oddness that was already apparent in our next-door neighbour. Her night-time amusement consisted of making loud banshee-like noises at the top of her voice, not unlike the noise I was making myself. Eventually, I'm afraid that the little star had to twinkle on without my help because, under intense pressure from anyone who was unfortunate enough to hear me practising, I gladly gave up the fiddle altogether. The melodeon, fiddle and mouth organ are sadly no more - and poor Maggie died in 1969. But all is not lost.

In spite of my abject failure with the fiddle, my mild successes with the melodeon and harmonica got me thinking about coming to grips with another instrument. I suppose I was getting on for fifteen when I got my first guitar for £6.10s in old money, and the Bert Weedon 'Teach Yourself The Guitar' book. This consumed my interest for the best part of my teens and indeed into adulthood, when I added a tenor banjo to my musical stable. The most complicated tune I mastered at the time was a guitar instrumental called 'Wheels' by the Stringalongs.

I have to admit that I was a very mediocre, no-flair player compared to some of my contemporaries, but I did manage to get into a teen band. Two of the four of us, Pat McCarthy and George Byrne, managed to make a life-long living out of music and Jimmy McManus was a great singer at the time. I was carried along in such good company. My contribution was minimal, strumming the guitar and occasionally playing a tune on the harmonica. The name of the band was The Harmony Aces.

The main outlet for our dubious talents was at the summer Sunday after-noon hop at the Entertainment Centre. We were contracted by the manager, Paddy Lynch, to 'warm the crowd up' before the main band (usually the Brigadoons) came on. Do you remember Clem Quinn and 'Guitar Polka'? Well, he was the lead guitarist in the band and, on occasion, he let me play his guitar.

We practiced in a room at the back of Sweeney's shop beside the Bay Hotel, the same room the famous Red Seven practiced in. Sometimes, our times overlapped and the professionals from the showband would take us in hand and offer expert advice. We made 'When The Saints Go Marching In' our signature tune and progressed from there to the Elvis songs and the national anthem. Jimmy McManus was great at singing 'It's Now or Never' and it became the big number of our repertoire.

I suppose I was about fifteen or sixteen when Joe Weadick called down to the house one evening with a totally unexpected proposition. "Would you be interested in auditioning for the Red Seven", he asked innocently. I was completely taken aback, here was an already accomplished musician, asking me, a person without a singing voice, who could barely play a note, if I'd like to join a band of semi-professional musicians. He seemed serious enough about it and he explained in detail why he was looking for an extra body in the band. "Thanks for the invitation Joe, but the answer has to be no. I'm not good enough," I politely declined.

I had heard the Red Seven performing in the Entertainment Centre from a vantage point outside of the hall. The fine tenor voice of Pete Coburn singing 'Rosemarie', the deep bass of Pat Tyrrell singing 'He'll have to go', the electrifying drum rolls of Dessie Mulhall, and the virtuoso guitar solos of Freddy Cutland all accompanied by an accomplished brass and bass section. During these and later times, Arklow produced hugely talented individuals and groups who made an impact, locally, nationally and internationally.

Nitrex in 1970
Billy Lee, Derek Gaddern and John Mahon

My misgivings about joining the Red Seven proved to be correct, because years later when I was more experienced and playing with another group, Pat Tyrrell approached me and during our subsequent conversation about music he observed in an matter-of-fact tone; "You're a manufactured musician, you know", then standing up to his full height, he added solemnly, "while I am a natural."

There's no answer to that... Anyway, my own children have taken to music like ducks to water, and now it's up to them, and people like them, to create the beautiful sounds that will rest on the breeze of future generations.

Chapter 26

Joe Weadick
The Final Chapter

We have now reached the end of the memoires of the Red Seven/Columbia Showband. If you have gotten even a fraction of the joy reading them as I had writing them I will be delighted. It was a true labour of love for me - particularly listening to and chronicling the many and varied stories told by the contributors. I can assure you the personal accounts are the true recollections of each individual and I have to admit that I did not think their memories would be so sharp fifty years on.

I would like to mention at this juncture that all but one member who played with the Red Seven/Columbia Showband over the ten years of its existence were Arklow men. The outsider was Leo McHugh, a gentleman and dedicated musician who worked in the Avoca Mines at the time and had, in his earlier life played a major part in fostering a great love of music and bands in his own native town of Sligo.

Other than references made to some of the top Irish showbands, most other bands referred to in these memoires were primarily Arklow based and the vast majority of their members were from Arklow – a great testament to the musical richness and talents of our young people of the sixties and after. This fact is sometimes not realised or appreciated.

Whatever might be said about Irish showbands and their music - and there have been criticisms, particularly of the lack of original music and songs of that era by some very renowned musicians and singers who established themselves in the pop and rock music entertainment world since – they, the Irish showbands that is, have entertained magnificently, hundreds of thousands of young, and not-so-young people in ballrooms throughout the country in a happy and prolific environment over a minimum ten year period, and gave a generation of Irish citizens wonderful lifetime memories, which can only be described as priceless. They have done Ireland proud and their recognition by our President Mary McAleese in 2001 was well justified, as was the immortalisation of a representative number of showbands on Irish postage stamps in September 2010.

The Red Seven/Columbia, together with many hundreds of other Irish showbands, played a major part in opening up, like the petals of a rose, a new horizon for social enjoyment which blossomed with the improving economic life and opportunities of the sixties. It is my firm belief that most of the very successful musicians and singers who reached dizzy heights on the Irish and international scene during the seventies and eighties were spawned in that golden era of Irish popular music.

Finally, it is fitting that I pause for a minute in remembrance of all those people mentioned in this book who have passed to their eternal reward, in particular our Red Seven/Columbia members Eamon Lee and Jim Tyrrell.

Ar dheis Dé go raibh a n-anam

Appendix 1

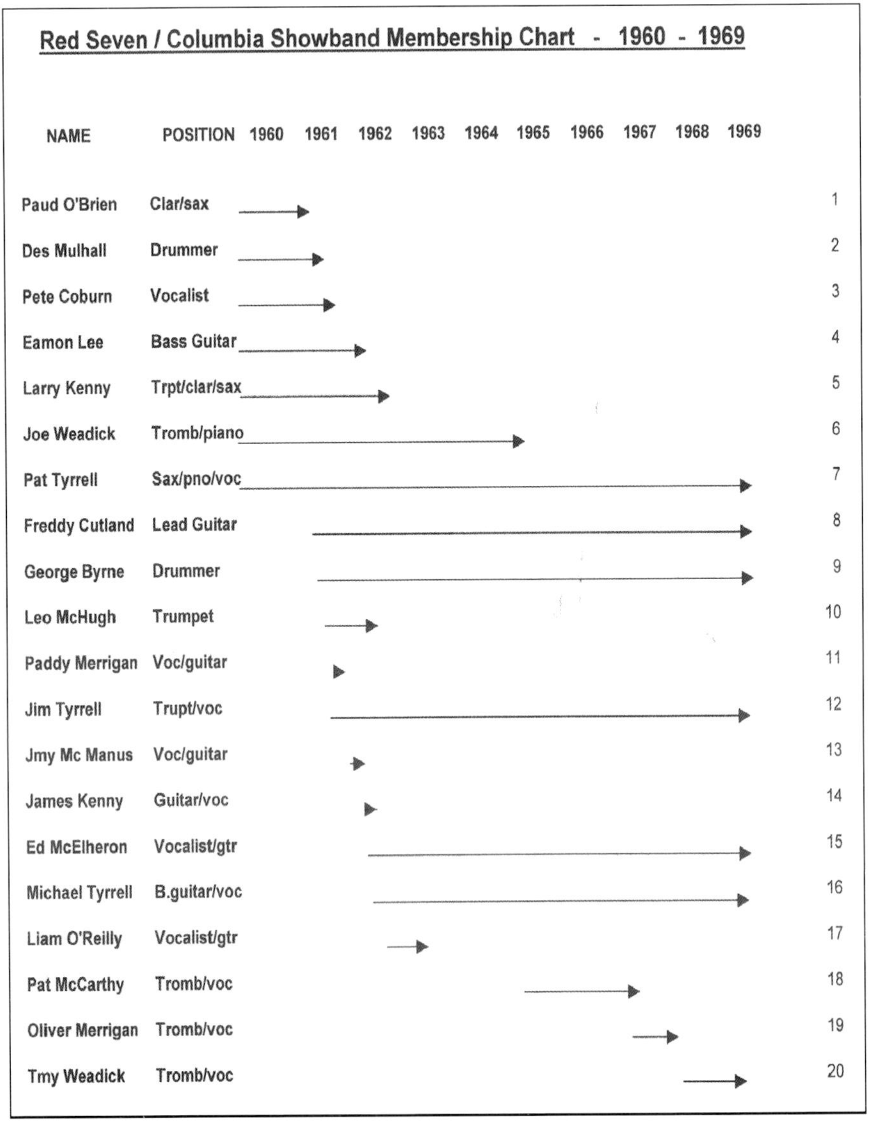

Red Seven / Columbia Showband Membership Chart - 1960 - 1969

NAME	POSITION	1960	1961	1962	1963	1964	1965	1966	1967	1968	1969	
Paud O'Brien	Clar/sax											1
Des Mulhall	Drummer											2
Pete Coburn	Vocalist											3
Eamon Lee	Bass Guitar											4
Larry Kenny	Trpt/clar/sax											5
Joe Weadick	Tromb/piano											6
Pat Tyrrell	Sax/pno/voc											7
Freddy Cutland	Lead Guitar											8
George Byrne	Drummer											9
Leo McHugh	Trumpet											10
Paddy Merrigan	Voc/guitar											11
Jim Tyrrell	Trupt/voc											12
Jmy Mc Manus	Voc/guitar											13
James Kenny	Guitar/voc											14
Ed McElheron	Vocalist/gtr											15
Michael Tyrrell	B.guitar/voc											16
Liam O'Reilly	Vocalist/gtr											17
Pat McCarthy	Tromb/voc											18
Oliver Merrigan	Tromb/voc											19
Tmy Weadick	Tromb/voc											20

Appendix 2

Sample of newspaper adverts for Red Seven/Columbia Showband

NORTHLAND BALLROOM - CASTLE HILL, DUNGANNO

Saturday, 14th December—

EDDIE MACK and the COLUMBIA

ST. MARY'S HALL PORTADOWN

TO-MORROW NIGHT

COLUMBIA

ARKLOW

The Showband You've Asked For !!!

BALLROOM CENTRAL NEWCASTLE

BEST PROVINCIAL DANCE HALL IN ULSTER

WEDNESDAY, 24th AUGUST

COLUMBIA

9—1 Admission 6/-

Popular Saturday Dancing

NORTHLAND BALLROOM - CASTLE HILL, DUNGANNON

Saturday, 14th December—

EDDIE MACK and the COLUMBIA

Sample of newspaper adverts for Red Seven/Columbia Showband

This Saturday Night

22nd AUGUST

THE COLOSSAL

COLUMBIA

ACCLAIMED ALL OVER IRELAND AS THE HIT BAND OF 1964

9—1.30. ADMISSION: 6/-.

No admittance after 11.30 p.m. Right of admission reserved.

(p2761-8)

ATTENTION! ATTENTION! ATTENTION!

WILL ALL DANCE PROMOTERS, BALLROOM PROPRIETORS, CLUBS, SOCIETIES, ETC., PLEASE NOTE—

ON AND FROM SEPTEMBER [illegible] 1960, ON COMPLETION OF THEIR SUMMER SEASON RESIDENCY IN THE TARA BALLROOM, COURTOWN, THE

RED SEVEN Showband

WILL BE AVAILABLE FOR ALL BOOKINGS

TO AVOID DISAPPOINTMENT, EARLY BOOKING IS ADVISED.

ALL ENQUIRIES TO:—THE MANAGER, ST. BRIGID'S TERRACE, ARKLOW

Sample of newspaper adverts for Red Seven/Columbia Showband

Appendix 3

Ballrooms in the 1940's, 50's & 60's
Arklow Entertainment Centre
with Royal Showband performing - early sixties.

Dancers in Kavanagh's Ormonde Ballroom (Marquee), Arklow, late fifties.

Ormonde Ballroom (Marquee) Arklow when it opened in the 1940's

Brennan's Mayfair Ballroom, Arklow in the 1940's

The Sicialians resident band in the Mayfair Ballroom 1946-1950.
L to r: Jack Quirke (trumpet), Mary Tracey (cello /vocalist), Alfie Duggan (sax), Noreen O'Brien (violin), Johnnie ??; John O'Reilly (drums), Lillie Mahon (piano accordian) and Miss McDonald (piano).

Wedding breakfast tables prepared for Jack and Mary Quirke in the Mayfir Ballroom, 1946

Peter Redmond's Tara Ballroom, Courtown in the 1950's or 1960's

Appendix 4

Music men from 1955...

Members of Sean Bonner's Arklow School Band taken in 1955. Oh, that the happy faces were still the same! Front row (l. to r.) – Michael Gannon, John Kearon, Noel Forde, Frank Cullen, D. O'Shaughnessy, Eamonn Byrne, Pat O'Reilly, Tommy Brauders. Second row – Pat Shelton, Michael Ward, Des De Courcy, Mick Cullen, Tommy Maloney, Pat McCarthy, Liam Doyle, Donnie O'Farrell. Third row – Owen Walshe, John Kenny, Peter Murphy, Murth Myler, Jim Bolger, Jimmy McManus, George Thewlis. Back row – Robert Murphy, Pat Fitzgerald (R.I.P.), Michael Redmond, James Kenny, P. J. Kinsella, and Willie O'Toole.

Seán Bonner, school teacher and musical genius, mentioned so many times in this book for his magnificient contribution to music over many years in Arklow.

Photo of Marian Arts Society members taken in the early fifties with Dublin's Lord Mayor and his wife at the Mansion House while on an outing.

Seán Bonner, their Musical Director, is at the back to the right.

Included in this photo with the Lord Mayor and Lady Mayoress of Dublin are, Joe, Pat, Eddie and Vincent McElheron, May-Ann Shelton, Olive Fortune, Pete Coburn, Oonagh Byrne, Kathleen Doyle, Paddy Lynch, Patricia Byrne, Mairead Doyle, Mary Crooke, Marie Clancy, May McElheron, John McElheron, Brendan Timmons, Annette O'Rielly, Bina McCrudden, Annette Horan, Gerry Fennell, Joe New, Eileen Tancred, Billy Kelly, Breda O'Connor, Ann Wadden, Abigail Brennan, Doreen McCarthy, Doreen Kavanagh, Eamon O'Brien, Philomena Doyle, Seamus Breen, Tom Jackman, Mary Birmingham, Joe Fitzgerald, Michael Morgan, Timmy Weadick, Paddy Hyland, Matt Myler, James O'Connor, Paddy Kelly, Kathleen Doyle, Myra O'Reilly, Sheila O'Connor, Joan McCrudden, Myles Rowan, Joe Hayes, Tim Weadick, Kathleen O'Neill, Eamon Byrne, Elizabeth Kavanagh, Anna Synnott, Gerry Stringer and Seán Bonner.